KU-481-510

THE GERMAN PEASANT WAR OF 1525 – NEW VIEWPOINTS

The German Peasant War of 1525 - New Viewpoints

Edited by

BOB SCRIBNER

Department of Historical and Literary Studies
Portsmouth Polytechnic

and

GERHARD BENECKE

Faculty of Humanities
University of Kent

943
- 03

London
GEORGE ALLEN & UNWIN
Boston   Sydney

First published in 1979

This book is copyright under the Berne Convention. All
rights are reserved. Apart from any fair dealing for the
purpose of private study, research, criticism or review, as
permitted under the Copyright Act, 1956, no part of this
publication may be reproduced, stored in a retrieval
system, or transmitted, in any form or by any means,
electronic, electrical, chemical, mechanical, optical, photo-
copying, recording or otherwise, without the prior permission of the copyright owner. Enquiries should be sent
to the publishers at the undermentioned address:

GEORGE ALLEN & UNWIN LTD
40 Museum Street, London WC1A 1LU

© George Allen & Unwin (Publishers) Ltd, 1979

British Library Cataloguing in Publication Data

The German Peasant War of 1525.
  1. Peasants' war, 1524–1525 – Addresses, essays,
lectures
  I. Scribner, Bob   II. Benecke, Gerhard
  943'.031'08   DD182   78–40624

  ISBN 0-04-900031-4
  ISBN 0-04-900032-2 Pbk.

Typeset in 10 on 11 point Plantin by Trade Linotype Ltd

Printed in Great Britain by offset lithography by
Billing & Sons Ltd, Guildford, London and Worcester

Acknowledgements

The essays of Professors Stalnaker and Sabean appear in their original language, and Professor Oberman has supplied us with an English version of a paper which was later rewritten and published in German. All other contributions have been translated first by the editors and then submitted to authors for approval before being published here. The essay of the late Dr Bücking has been checked by Dr Hans-Christoph Rublack. In some cases footnotes and/or text have been shortened. Readers who wish to follow up more detailed references or bibliographies are therefore referred to the original versions. *Umlaut* has usually not been included in the translation. Certain terms such as *Landschaft*, the meaning of which is by no means unambiguous in the original, have been translated as seems appropriate to the particular essay. 'Godly law' has been preferred to 'divine law' and 'old law' to 'ancient law'.

We should like to thank authors for permission to re-publish, and also to acknowledge the co-operation of their original publishers. The map and two figures have been produced by the Cartographic Unit, Department of Geography at Portsmouth Polytechnic, whom we thank for excellent draughtsmanship. The initial sub-editing was handled by Karin Benecke, and typing by the secretarial staff under Miss Revitt at Darwin College, University of Kent, and given the expert care of Mrs Sue Macdonald and her colleagues. For much-needed help with the problems of editing we are grateful to Keith Ashfield.

Portsmouth and Canterbury

BOB SCRIBNER
GERHARD BENECKE

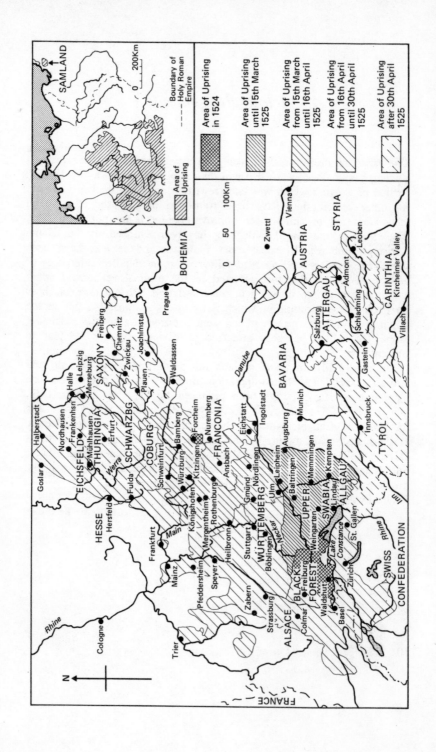

Area of Uprising in 1524

Area of Uprising until 15th March 1525

Area of Uprising from 15th March until 16th April 1525

Area of Uprising from 16th April until 30th April 1525

Area of Uprising after 30th April 1525

Boundary of Holy Roman Empire

Area of Uprising

SAMLAND

200 Km

100 Km

BOHEMIA

Prague

Waldsassen

Joachimstal

Plauen

Chemnitz

Zwickau

Freiberg

SAXONY

Leipzig

Merseburg

Halle

Nordhausen

Frankenhsn

Mühlhausen

Erfurt

THURINGIA

EICHSFELD

Halberstadt

Goslar

Fulda

HESSE

Hersfeld

Frankfurt

Mainz

Pfeddersheim

Speyer

Trier

Cologne

Zabern

Strassburg

ALSACE

Colmar

Basel

Waldshut

Freiburg

BLACK FOREST

Weingarten

Lake Constance

St. Gallen

Zürich

SWISS CONFEDERATION

FRANCE

Rhine

SCHWARZBG

COBURG

Bamberg

Würzburg

Schweinfurt

Königshofen

Mergentheim

Rothenburg

Heilbronn

Böblingen

Stuttgart

Neckar

WÜRTEMBERG

Gmünd

Nördlingen

Ulm

Leipheim

Baltringen

Weingarten

UPPER SWABIA

Kempten

Lindau

ALLGÄU

Memmingen

Kitzingen

Forcheim

Nuremberg

FRANCONIA

Ansbach

Eichstatt

Ingolstadt

Augsburg

BAVARIA

Munich

Danube

Werra

Main

Rhine

Salzburg

ATTERGAU

AUSTRIA

Vienna

Zwettl

STYRIA

Leoben

Admont

Schladming

Gastein

CARINTHIA

Kircheimer Valley

Villach

TYROL

Innsbruck

Inn

N

Contents

Chronology

1517: 30 Oct.	Luther's 95 Theses
1519:	Death of Maximilian I, election of Charles V
	Cortes's conquest of Mexico
1519–22:	Magellan's circumnavigation of the world
1521: Apr.	Luther in Worms
1521: June	War between Charles V and Francis I
1522:	Turkish conquest of Rhodes
1522–4:	Evangelical movements in numerous towns, including Wittenberg, Erfurt, Strassburg, Nuremberg
1523:	The Knights War in Germany
1523–4:	Refusal of tithes in the Rhine Palatinate and in the bishoprics of Bamberg and Speyer
1524: 26 May	First peasant risings in Forchheim, Franconia and in the Black Forest
19 Aug.	Rebellion in Mühlhausen/Thuringia
1525: 9 Feb.	Negotiations between the Baltringen Band and the Swabian League
14 Feb.	Formation of the Allgau Band
24 Feb.	Battle of Pavia, capture of Francis I
early Mar.	Formation of Lake Constance Band
6 Mar.	Peasant Assembly at Memmingen – Christian Union of the Allgau, Baltringen and Lake Constance Bands
19 Mar.	Printing of the Twelve Articles
1 Apr.	Rising in bishopric of Würzburg; formation of Tauber Valley Band in Franconia
2 Apr.	Rising in the Neckar Valley
14 Apr.	Rising in Alsace; formation of Bildhausen Band in Franconia
16 Apr.	Rising in Württemberg; peasant court at Weinsberg
17 Apr.	Treaty of Weingarten between Swabian League and Württemberg and Franconian peasants
18 Apr.	Rising in Fulda and formation of Werra Band
19 Apr.	Luther's 'Admonition to Peace, a Reply to the Twelve Articles of the Peasants'
23 Apr.	Risings in the Rhine Palatinate and Switzerland
26 Apr.	Occupation of Stuttgart; urban revolt in Mainz
27 Apr.	Urban disturbance in Cologne
28 Apr.	Peasant occupation of Erfurt

	2 May	Rising in Baden
	5 May	Luther's 'Against the Robbing and Murdering Hordes of Peasants'
	8 May	Peasants capture Würzburg
	9 May	Peasant rising in Tyrol
	12 May	Defeat of Württemberg peasants at Böblingen
	15 May	Battle of Frankenhausen
	17 May	Defeat of Alsace peasants at Zabern
	27 May	Execution of Muntzer
	2 Jun.	Battle of Königshofen, defeat of Odenwald peasants
	4 Jun.	Battle of Ingolstadt, end of rising in Franconia
	8 Jun.	Reconquest of Würzburg by the princes
	3 Jul.	Peasant victory at Schladming
	3 Sep.	Rising in Prussia
1526 :	Mar.	Fresh risings in bishopric of Salzburg
1527 :		Sack of Rome by German troops
1529 :		Turkish siege of Vienna
1530 :		Confession of Augsburg
1534 :		Anabaptist rising in Münster

Introduction

I

The German Peasant War of 1524–6 can be regarded both as the last great medieval peasant revolt and as the first modern revolution. It can also be seen as part of a broader movement of social unrest 'which extended across all of Europe, from Italy to the Low Countries, and from southern France to Bohemia' (Oberman). This alone should guarantee it a place among the major events of European history, yet it has been strangely neglected by English-speaking historians during the greater part of this century.

In 1903 A. F. Pollard devoted the bulk of a chapter to the Peasant War in vol. II of the *Cambridge Modern History* (ch. 6, pp. 174–95). This provided a succinct narrative and discussed crisply the major questions of interpretation. It still remains the best short introduction to the subject for the general reader (although readers may also wish to consult the brief narrative in Williams, 1962, ch. 4). Subsequent neglect of the Peasant War can be measured by the space accorded it in the equivalent volume of the *New Cambridge Modern History*, vol. II (1958), where it is passed over in four paragraphs. It has been kept alive for an English-reading audience largely by the socialist tradition of history. E. Belfort Bax published his *Peasant War in Germany* in 1899 (reprinted 1968), and the only other treatment in English has been the translation of Friedrich Engels's Marxist classic, *The Peasant War in Germany*, which has seen three editions since 1926 (Engels, 1926, 1956, 1967).

In 1968 the American scholar Kyle C. Sessions published an anthology of short readings under the title *Reformation and Authority. The Meaning of the Peasants' Revolt*. Here the Peasant war was presented not as an event of great importance in its own right, but within the context of what it meant for the course of Luther's Reformation and for sixteenth-century views on authority. The socialist tradition was also largely neglected by Sessions. Although he admitted in his bibliography that 'Marxist interest in the Reformation has had a distinguished career', the reader was offered a taste only of Engels's work, and nothing of the interpretation advanced by eastern European Marxist historians. However, Sessions did include an important work of revision by the Leipzig church historian Franz Lau (Sessions, 1968: 94–101).

Since 1968 there has been a gradual revival of interest in the Peasant War among English and American scholars. The lead was given by

David Sabean's 1969 thesis, *The Social Background to the Peasants' War of 1525 in Southern Upper Swabia*. Significantly, this received wider circulation only in German translation (Sabean, 1972). Other works, such as that from the American scholar Lawrence P. Buck, *The Containment of Civil Insurrection: Nuremberg and the Peasants' Revolt* (1971), have not been given the wider publicity they deserve. The same is true of the Cambridge thesis of Tom Scott, *Relations between Freiburg in Breisgau and the Surrounding Countryside, 1450–1520*, completed in 1973.

The 450th anniversary of the Peasant War contributed to this modest number of important works with a special issue of the *Journal of Peasant Studies* (vol. 3, no. 1, October 1975), now in book-form as *The German Peasant War of 1525*, ed. Janos Bak (1976). The socialist historians Frantisek Gaus and Adolf Laube discussed precursors of the Peasant War alongside articles from David Sabean and Peter Blickle. Heide Wunder examined two key concepts of the revolt, 'old law' and 'godly law', while H. J. Cohn and R. W. Scribner provided documentary material. The latter concentrated on visual evidence from the period, while Cohn presented an excellent short selection of documents, including the Twelve Articles of Memmingen, the most influential manifesto of the rebellious peasants. The remainder of the volume was devoted to discussion of the significance of Engels's contribution to the historiography of the Peasant War.

Another feature of the English literature is represented by A. Friesen, *Reformation and Utopia. The Marxist Interpretation of the Reformation and Its Antecedents* (1974). This dealt less with the Peasant War than with the origins and development of a specific historiographical tradition. However, it contains important chapters on sixteenth-century reactions to the revolt, especially on the clash between Luther and Thomas Muntzer. Apart from this handful of longer discussions, there have been several shorter articles in English on the Peasant War, which are to be found among the titles marked by an asterisk in the list of references (pages 190–9).

The paucity of English historical works is not surprising if one considers that the Peasant War has been almost as neglected in German historiography, although it has clearly remained a subject of interest to the local and regional historian, and has played a central role in the history writing of the German Democratic Republic. However, there is only one modern history of the war itself, by Gunther Franz, *Der Deutsche Bauernkrieg*, first published in 1933 and now in its tenth edition. There have been a number of substantial monographs (e.g. Waas, 1964; and Smirin, 1952, second edition, 1956), but nothing that has appeared since 1933 has caused Franz to alter the interpretation he laid down then (see his preface to the tenth edition, 1975). The 1975 anniversary produced an expected flood of articles and collections of essays, often the proceedings of conferences commemorating the event.

However, there were few larger works, despite the growing conviction of the need for a new general history.

In the absence of a modern general history of the Peasant War in English, this collection is designed to give the reader some idea of the variety and extent of the Peasant War, with articles on aspects of its development in Alsace, Swabia, Franconia, Saxony, the south German lands under direct Habsburg rule, and the remote north-east area of Samland. In particular, the articles by Endres, Rapp and Czok are models of the kind of close analysis of the Peasant War as a regional phenomenon on which a new general history can be built. The role of political ideas, of conceptions of justice, and of the right of rebellion can be seen in the contributions from Buszello, Hoyer and Oberman. The military organisation of the rebellion is discussed in a second article from Hoyer. Another important feature of the Peasant War, the close links between town and country, is discussed by Czok's highly original article on the role of suburbs. We have also attempted to give some impression of the variety of approaches to the Peasant War, choosing authors from the United States, France, the Federal Republic of Germany and the German Democratic Republic.

II

The German Peasant War has always been the subject of controversy. The most persistent point at issue has been that of its relation to the Reformation. This has been debated since the outbreak of the war itself, when it was claimed that the evangelical movement initiated by Luther's revolt against the Church encouraged the peasants to rebel against their lawful authorities. Protestant historians consistently denied this charge, and studies of the Reformation period from this viewpoint relegated the Peasant War to a subsidiary role in the history of sixteenth-century Germany. However, it still remains one of the major questions of interpretation, taken up afresh in the works of Sessions and Friesen mentioned above. In our collection it is discussed from various viewpoints by Blickle, Oberman, Hoyer and Steinmetz.

A more recent debate has been between Marxist and non-Marxist interpretations. The basic framework of a Marxist interpretation was laid down by Engels, and followed by other socialist writers such as Kautsky (1897) and Belfort Bax. This saw the Peasant War as an expression of socio-economic conflict, of which the Reformation was an ideological expression. Landmarks of Marxist interpretation in this century have been the 1921 monograph from the philosopher Ernst Bloch, *Thomas Müntzer als Theologe der Revolution*, reprinted several times since 1960, and the substantial work of the pre-eminent Russian historian, M. M. Smirin, which appeared in Russian in 1947 and in German in 1952 and 1956. However, since 1961 the Marxist tradition of interpretation has been identified with that advanced by the German

Democratic Republic. Building on Engels's basic framework, GDR historians advanced the thesis that the Reformation and the Peasant War formed an 'early bourgeois revolution'.

The debate between Marxist and non-Marxist interpretations has been until recently totally one-sided for western readers. Most non-Marxist historians refused to regard the Marxist viewpoint as worthy of consideration. This was changed in West Germany only in 1972, when R. Wohlfeil published a selection of GDR writings on the 'early bourgeois revolution'. The English reader has had no opportunity to judge the points at issue, being forced to rely only on anti-Marxist critiques such as that by Friesen. Replies of Marxist scholars to some of the charges against them are found only in the collection edited by Janos Bak. The most comprehensive short statement of the GDR interpretation was presented in 1961 by Max Steinmetz, and this outline, with minor variations, has remained much the same since then. We have thus decided to reproduce Steinmetz's 1961 theses here, in order to provide the English reader with the interpretive framework within which GDR historians such as Hoyer and Czok approach specific features of the Peasant War. The latter represent two pre-eminent examples of the careful scholarship devoted to the subject by Marxist historians which commands respect among non-Marxist colleagues.

Reaction against Marxist interpretations has perhaps led to a reluctance to examine socio-economic approaches to the Peasant War. Non-Marxist orthodoxy was embodied in Franz's argument that socio-economic grievance played little real role, and that the Peasant War was a political movement seeking to revive older principles of right and justice. Where Marxists saw it as a revolutionary movement, non-Marxists saw it as conservative, even reactionary. Recently there have been some stimulating attempts to bridge the gap between political and socio-economic interpretations. The most important has been the work of Peter Blickle, whose viewpoint is summarised in a set of theses, perhaps conceived by the author as a counterpart to those of Steinmetz. Certainly readers will find much to discuss about the Peasant War's relation to broader socio-economic issues by comparing the two sets of theses. Another important contribution in this direction comes from the American scholar John C. Stalnaker, who has been influenced by the émigré German social historian Hans Rosenberg. Of all the works to have appeared for the 1975 anniversary, Stalnaker's provides the best short introduction to the social dimensions of the Peasant War.

A third area of historical debate concerns the opposition between two figures long seen as the major protagonists of the Reformation period – Luther and Thomas Muntzer. The conflict between the two predated the Peasant War, but it became an integral part of their historiography. Even debates between Marxists and non-Marxists slipped into this older tradition of interpretation. The point at issue here was whether Muntzer was a revolutionary born out of his time, or merely a visionary fanatic with a chiliastic theology. On the whole, non-Marxist historians have opted for variations of the latter, seen at its best in Gordon Rupp's treatment of Muntzer in *Patterns of Reformation* (1969). Under pressure of criticism from their western colleagues, GDR historians have modified their Muntzer interpretation to give some credit to Muntzer the theologian as well as to Muntzer the revolutionary. However, western historiography has yet to come to terms with Muntzer the revolutionary. The most recent attempt on these lines stems from R. van Dülmen, *Reformation als Revolution* (1977), which appeared too late for us to include an extract in this collection. A more detailed discussion of Muntzer historiography can be found in Friesen (1965) and Stayer (1969).

The debate over Muntzer has distracted attention from the broader issues of the Peasant War. Much of it looks rather dated now, as historians have begun to investigate the wider social context of the sixteenth century. One could discern in it a struggle about the real hero of the Reformation, harking back to older notions about the decisive role of Great Men in history. Even Marxist interpretations fell into this trap, concentrating overmuch on the role of Muntzer to the neglect of wider issues such as the formation and development of classes, and their complex relations with the forces of production. Faced with a choice of what to omit from a wide range of material, we decided therefore to have no specific treatment of Muntzer, and to allow his importance to emerge from wider discussion of the Peasant War itself.

These issues have characterised discussion of the Peasant War and its importance, but we would like to set it in a broader historiographical context. By this we mean that it should be regarded not just as an episode in the age of the Reformation, or even as a convenient focus of some major issues in the social and political history of the sixteenth century. We see it rather as a subject which raises important theoretical issues for the historian. Nowadays the relation of history to the social sciences is continually under discussion, and the barriers which the historical muse has long erected against these impertinent younger sisters are beginning to crumble. We would like to justify the selection of many of our articles in the light of this discussion.

First, there is the historian's concern with the unique and the particular, and his notorious reluctance to generalise. This may be contrasted with the social scientist's search for broad general typologies and principles of interpretation. The Peasant War embodies this dilemma *par excellence*. Beginning with localised revolts, it occurs in the main in a number of clearly defined regions (exemplified by the pattern of dissemination shown in our map). It builds up only gradually to a supra-regional phenomenon, expressed more in peasant programmes than in any unified action. Awareness of regional variation and disparity has led many writers to question the unity of the war itself, to see it, at one extreme, as merely a number of disparate events, united only by the reaction to it of authority. Here the reader must consider what kind of historical explanation is best suited for such a phenomenon. Can we be content with empirical studies, however excellent, which look for no broader principles of interpretation? Or must we turn to analytical concepts such as class, long-term structural change, patterns of inheritance and family structure, peasant culture or peasant society? Such questions are posed by the contributions from Blickle, Bücking, Sabean, Stalnaker and Wunder, as well as by the Marxist contributions from Czok, Hoyer and Steinmetz.

In the long run, such questions must lead us to attempt to assess the Peasant War in comparative terms, as an example of peasant revolutions, or of peasant economy and society as a generic phenomenon. A good example of this approach, developing E. P. Thompson's 'moral economy of the crowd' (1971), is the recent work of James C. Scott on Burmese and Vietnamese peasantries (1976). Our contributors have little space here to take up this approach, but refer frequently to other attempts to set the Peasant War in wider contexts, such as that of Barrington Moore (1966). Suggestive thoughts along these lines are also found in contributions to Janos Bak's collection from Friedman, Geussing and Kippenberg (1975: 117–35).

Secondly, we must place the Peasant War in the context of long-term historical development, such as the change from feudal to capitalist society, so heavily stressed by Marxist interpretations. Marxists and economic historians in general see decisive historical change as dependent on long-term structural change, whether of modes and forces of production, or of other material factors such as demographic or climatic change. The more traditional historian is concerned to maintain the autonomy of ideas, religious values or other ideals, a case strongly put by Heiko Oberman's contribution. However, even if the autonomy of such areas is accepted (and many schools of social scientists make similar claims within their areas of interest), the historian must still face a crucial issue. What is the nature of the interrelationship between ideas and values on the one hand, and material factors on the other? As Marxist historians would put it, what is the nature of the dialectical relationship between superstructure and base. This, we believe, is a problem both for the Marxist and the non-Marxist historian, where neither can lay claim to definitive answers.

A third issue emerges here, that of 'monocausal' *versus* 'pluralistic' interpretations. It is often argued that Marxist interpretations are monocausal, tracing all historical events back to changes in the economic 'base'. To this is opposed the notion of 'pluralism' in interpretation, wherein differing interpretations compete, and none can lay claim to ultimate insights or completeness. This looks suspiciously like a 'free market economy' of interpretation, and may easily lead to an abdication of judgement by the historian, who may simply slide into an easy relativism in which any interpretation is as good as another and 'every man is his own historian'. Furthermore, Marxist historians may have good reason to feel aggrieved at being singled out as 'monocausalists'. They would argue that they, too, are aware of a plurality of factors in history. Moreover, they patently do not have a monopoly of mono-causal explanations. Franz's argument that the Peasant War was a political event is no less monocausal.

Another version in which the issue is raised concerns the nature of social interpretations. Here socio-economic interpretations are attacked as involving a 'debased' or shallow notion of the social, and a plea is entered for the importance of the family and community as the basis of society. Whether these represent any 'richer' or more profound concepts of society is highly questionable, and such approaches beg a number of important questions about the nature of society and community, and about the way in which the family mediates broader and more complex social and economic influences. Ultimately we believe that such formu-lations misconceive the question, and that the more important issue is that of holistic *versus* non-holistic interpretations. How far can the historian stress the randomness and arbitrariness of historical causation and change? How far can his own thought mirror this randomness, by turning to new interpretations in reaction to others with which he, for various reasons, feels dissatisfied? How far must he, on the other hand, turn to interpretations which search for structures and emphasise the interconnectedness of things? What, then, are the implications for his methods of investigation?

This leads us to the fourth and final question, the importance of interdisciplinary approaches. Historians are increasingly aware of the need to draw on findings from other disciplines such as sociology, anthropology, psychology, folklore and social law, a case succinctly put by Heide Wunder. This should be nothing new to the historian of the Reformation: it has been interpreted since the Reformation itself through use of the discipline of theology. However, there is an especial difficulty encountered by those historians, such as Bücking or Wunder, who have made such attempts. Frequently these sister disciplines of history operate through comparative analysis of differing types of society. The historian has rarely been interested in such comparative study, and often finds difficulty in applying new concepts and methods that have been worked out with such a broad brush to pre-industrial Europe. He is, after all, more at home with the traditional methods of more or less narrowly researched archive positivism. This difficulty is most pronounced in the application of social anthropology to history. On the other hand, some of these disciplines themselves rely on the empirical findings of the historian for construction of their range of comparative case studies, a fact very evident in the field of sociology of religion.

Working under these constraints, the historian is often forced just to take the concepts of other disciplines and to apply them to the particular case in question. If they do not fit, the concepts must be abandoned or the social scientist asked to modify his theory. At its best this procedure can open up new avenues of inquiry, seen in our collection by the application of the idea of legitimation to the relation of the Peasant War to the Reformation (see Blickle and Bücking). Frequently, however, the historian is too impatient and too suspicious of the sister discipline to engage in the arduous and careful dialogue this requires. It is important therefore to attempt to open up another line of inquiry, namely to apply the methods of other disciplines to historical questions. We have a highly original example of this approach in the essay by Sabean, who attempts to apply the method of social anthropology to an analysis of the causes of the Peasant War. It is a pioneering study, showing what the historian may hope to achieve along such interdisciplinary lines. It raises the question of how far the historian must turn to the social sciences not only for his analytical concepts, but also for his methodology.

Clearly, in presenting this collection of essays in such terms we do not wish it to be judged by the standard of whether it contributes any definitive judgements on the Peasant War in Germany. Rather, we wish it to stimulate discussion on its relation to wider problems of historiography. If it fulfils this purpose, it will be less a mere collection of recent articles on the Peasant War, but more the beginning of a wider debate about history itself.

MAX STEINMETZ

1   Theses on the Early Bourgeois Revolution in Germany, 1476–1535 *

I

1 'The first great action of the rising bourgeoisie' (Engels) in Germany reached its highpoint in the Reformation and Peasant War (1517–25), the most significant revolutionary mass movement of the German people until the November Revolution of 1918.

The Marxist conception of this highly significant event was first developed by Friedrich Engels in his treatise *The Great Peasant War* (1850). Here he proved that the years between the beginning of the Reformation (1517) and the end of the Peasant War formed the early bourgeois revolution in Germany. He showed further that in the course of these years the characteristic stages of development of a bourgeois revolution emerged with full clarity.

This 'magnificent attempt at revolution by the German people' cannot be understood, however, in isolation from the events of 1918/19. Engels was completely right to begin his account in 1476 and to end with the death of Gaismair, which he set incorrectly in 1527. The fact that Gaismair was not removed by his enemies until 1532, as well as the recognition that the revolutionary events extend beyond 1527 and up to 1535, force us to set the end of the early bourgeois revolution at this latter date.

2 In order to grasp correctly the whole process of preparation, maturation, culmination and decline of the events of the early bourgeois revolution in Germany, periodisation in three stages is proposed:

(1) A rising line of class conflict, stretching from the effects of the revolutionary Hussite movement, culminating in the *Reformation of the Emperor Sigismund* (first edition, 1476) and particularly in the rising of the Drummer of Niklashausen, through to the Bundschuh movement, Poor Conrad and the Dozsa rebellion in Hungary (1514), up to the beginning of Luther's Reformation (1517).

*Translated from Max Steinmetz, 1961, 'Thesen zur frühbürgerlichen Revolution', in *Die frühbürgerliche Revolution in Deutschland* (ed. G. Brendler), Berlin, part of 'Tagung der Sektion Mediävistik', Wernigerode, 1960 (eds E. Werner and Max Steinmetz).

(2) The Reformation and Peasant War as the kernel and highpoint of the early bourgeois revolution in Germany, from the posting of the Theses in Wittenberg to the defeat of most of the peasant armies in 1525/6.

(3) A falling line of class conflict, ending after the defeat of Zwingli (1531) and of Gaismair (1532) in 1535, the year in which Munster was conquered, the revolutionary anabaptist movement broken, and Wullenweber taken prisoner. The Wittenberg Concord of 1536 ended this development.

3 The years 1535–55 see the final victory of the Princes' Reformation. After threat of social revolution had declined, the most important conflict was that between princes and Emperor, though without abating the mutual rivalry between the princes. In this period a revolution from above succeeded as little as revolution from below had in the previous period. The so-called Revolution of the Princes is merely the final victory of the princely Reformation. This works itself out either in the setting up of territorial churches and the appropriation of clerical property, or else through conversion of ecclesiastical territories into hereditary princely territories, as for example with the Duchies of Prussia (1525) and of Courland (1561).

4 The long predominance and far from negligible effects of the Protestant legend about Luther has not only obscured our picture of Muntzer and the role of the anabaptists, but it has allowed important events to retreat into the background. Namely, that besides the field of activity of Luther, Muntzer and Carlstadt in Thuringia and Saxony there was also a second centre of the early bourgeois revolution in Germany: the alpine lands, especially present-day north Switzerland and Tyrol, the areas of activity of Zwingli, Gaismair, Niklaus Manuel and others. The influence of this alpine centre on the important upper German towns of Strassburg, Memmingen, Constance and Lindau lasted until the Wittenberg Concord of 1536.

5 Both centres did not link up, despite several attempts at mediation (the Marburg religious colloquy, 1529, the catastrophe of Zwingli's policy, 1531), for the princes did not trust the bourgeois-radical and republican tendencies of the Swiss, and rejected completely the revolutionary anti-Habsburg policies of Zwingli and Gaismair.

II

6 Germany's economic position is characterised by a significant upturn of commercial production. There were numerous technical inventions, particularly useful for development of new mineral resources, which were favoured by extended long-distance trade routes.

The decline of the feudal mode of production, and the incipient penetration of the economy by capitalistic elements and forms can be traced back to the mid-fourteenth century, but it accelerates after the middle of the fifteenth. Alongside the continued dominance of commercial and usurious capital, there appeared in west, south-west and central Germany an accumulation of capital through appropriation of surplus production.

The first impulses towards a capitalist mode of production arose from the penetration of capital into spheres of production. Capital began to accumulate in mining, smelting and textiles, where incomplete and rudimentary forms of the capitalist mode of production can be traced in the putting-out system. Here we find early forms of capitalist exploitation, leading to the formation of a stratum of plebeians, from which arose the pre-proletariat.

7 By contrast with industrial production, an ever broader and more comprehensive stagnation could be seen in agricultural and guild production. Increasing penetration of money–goods relationships led to a greater exploitation of the peasantry by commutation of natural dues into money dues. The peasantry, who were predominantly serfs and bondsmen and made up the great majority of the German people, bore the burden of 'the entire social structure: princes, officials, clergy, patricians and burghers' (Engels).

8 But primitive accumulation of capital was able to assert itself only moderately in Germany. The freeing of direct producers from the means of production occurred only to a limited extent. Transformation of the peasants into wage-earners was hindered by a second serfdom, which emerged from the mid fifteenth century onwards. It chained peasants and labourers to the soil, thus ensuring feudal landlords higher yields, enabling the transition to capitalist form of management to take place.

9 The basic details of Germany's economic and political position were worked out on the eve of the early bourgeois revolution, sharpening and increasing the inherent contradictions. The German empire was further splintered into ever more numerous, almost independent spiritual and secular territories. In the face of the growing power of the 'big Jacks' (*grosse Hansen*), central government sank into complete helplessness.

10 A divided and utterly helpless Germany became an easy prey for the papal Church whose growing financial demands stood in the sharpest contrast to the spiritual and moral decline of the whole ecclesiastical structure. This provoked an increasingly vehement ill-will among all classes and levels of society.

11 An increased sharpening of class conflict was the necessary outcome of this ever more apparent clash between the development of the material forces of production within society and the traditional relations of production, which had long since become shackles of productive forces, rather than forms of their development.

In the countryside, the chain of peasant revolts became tightly linked, and the influence of the revolutionary Hussite movement was of great significance in this development. In numerous revolts, social tensions emerged just as frequently in the towns.

There is no doubt that it was exactly the most economically progressive areas of mining, smelting and textiles, where primitive accumulation had its strongest effects and capitalist relations of production most established themselves. These became the centres of the early bourgeois revolution – such as in west, south-west and central Germany, the northern alpine lands and Slovakia. Yet the contradictions in these contemporary forms of production by no means sufficed to fuse all non-feudal strata into one battlefront. Commercial capital, which had always served feudalism, did not conflict with the strengthening power of the princes, but aided it.

12 The period of the maturing early bourgeois revolution was characterised by an incipient 'process of forming a nation' (Stalin), which expressed itself in a strong national consciousness, not only among the nobility and the burghers, but in growing measure among the popular masses. In the struggle against feudal fragmentation and being sucked dry by the Roman Curia, and against the collapse of central government, there arose a powerful national feeling which demanded with increasing vehemence an end to these abuses, culminating in the desire for a restored German unity.

One must regard in this light the strong impulse to consolidate central government which, even if undertaken by various groups and classes, was still directed against the anti-national forces, that is the princes, as exemplified in Nicholas of Cusa, *The Reformation of the Emperor Sigismund*, the plans for imperial reform of Berthold of Henneberg and the Heilbronn programme.

13 Heresy was an effective preparation for the early bourgeois revolution. As bourgeois heresy in the towns, it was directed against the economic and political position of the Church. As peasant-plebeian heresy, it demanded beyond that the restoration of early Christian relations of equality, that is, effective restoration of bourgeois equality, including equality of wealth.

14 On an ideological level, Renaissance humanism also prepared the way. Its advance after the middle of the fifteenth century brought about a great displacement of the medieval feudal world-picture, by furthering criticism of a worldly church, and by preparing the ground for bourgeois thought and inquiry. The adjustment of the Church's world-picture to the new needs of a bourgeoisie that was already part-capitalist first occurred at the Council of Trent.

German humanists sharply criticised the ecclesiastical and social relations of their time, and demanded unity of the Empire. In the fields of linguistics, historiography, geography, folklore, literature and the creation of bourgeois science, men like Reuchlin, Celtis, Pirckheimer, Hutten and Wimpfeling made a significant contribution to the formation of a German national consciousness. *The Epistles of Obscure Men* (1515/17) were a characteristic product of this specifically German form of humanism, written by Crotus Rubeanus and Ulrich von Hutten, and intended to support Reuchlin in his dispute with the Cologne Dominicans.

The popular masses, however, did not understand the humanists. The latter preferred to use a revived classical Latin rather than the mother tongue, thus depriving themselves of any broader influence and making humanism a purely academic matter. Several universities, for example Wittenberg, became centres of humanism, but did not succeed in entirely reforming the German universities in the humanist sense.

15 One must mention, if only briefly, the magnificent development of contemporary German art, through Grunewald, Durer, Cranach, the Beham brothers, Riemenschneider, the 'Petrarch Master', Rathgeb, Niklaus Manuel Deutsch and many others. The social life of the time, with its tensions and conflicts, was skilfully represented, especially in the graphic arts, through religious themes, which gave a vivid picture of popular life. It was certainly no mere chance that the great German artists and draftsmen fought with life and limb on the side of the people and the revolution.

III

16 'The revolution is impossible without a national crisis, affecting exploiter and exploited alike' (Lenin). Such a crisis had struck all classes of the German Empire at the beginning of the sixteenth century, and it became more acute with each year.

17 The supposed head of the Empire was the Roman King and Emperor, in fact invariably a Habsburg. The office had long since become nothing more than a national monarchy, pursuing political interests that had little to do with German national interests. The imperial election and the reign of Charles V laid bare the internal contradictions of Habsburg dominance. If Frederick of Saxony had been elected as Kalkoff claimed, there would still have been no solution to the crisis of central power, since Saxon territorial power had been weakened by the division of the Wettin dynastic lands in 1485.

All attempts at imperial reform foundered on the opposition of the Habsburgs, as demonstrated in the first and second imperial regencies of 1502 and 1524; or on that of the princes, such as opposition to Maximilian after the Bavarian War of Succession (1503–05) or to Charles V after the Schmalkaldic Wars.

18 The princes, the 'territorial authority' of the sixteenth century, had been able to assert themselves completely in struggles against the central government and against their own territorial estates of nobility, the towns and the Church. The sharpening of class struggle since the middle of the fifteenth century had necessitated the creation of firmer

forms of state organisation. It is characteristic and fateful that the building up of a state apparatus in Germany could be achieved only on the basis of small princely states, which thus gained a complete preponderance over the central power.

The striving of the territorial princes for complete internal and external independence included disposal of church property, and so the territorial churches of the princely Reformation were merely the outcome of a long development.

Yet it would be false to overestimate the stability of territorial states before the early bourgeois revolution. Often they had no capital to serve as a real economic and political centre. Following ancient custom, the princes moved from castle to castle, their possessions completely scattered and unconnected one with another. But exactly these circumstances made a transition to small-state absolutism unavoidable for their rulers.

19 The German situation was particularly complicated by numerous church states, that is, by territories subject to ecclesiastical corporations, and ruled by these on the basis of church law. This unique mixture of spiritual and secular affairs represented not only a double exploitation of their subjects, but also the temptation for secular princes to appropriate such possessions by any means whatsoever.

20 As well, the Catholic–conservative camp in Germany could no longer assert its domination as before. Its pressure to set aside the Grievances of the German Nation in 1524 provoked demands for a National Council, which, in turn, foundered on the vigorous opposition of the universalist Papacy and Empire. But in the years that followed, the Catholic-conservative camp was unable to dispose of the issue of the Grievances at the imperial assembly; that was only achieved by the Council of Trent.

21 The rise of the princes led necessarily to the decline of the knights, and to the loss of autonomy of numerous, formerly independent cities (Mainz, Halle, Erfurt and many others). The knights and the cities made vain attempts to resist this development.

22 The burghers of the early sixteenth century were still a long way from displaying the later class unity of the bourgeoisie. They stood at the beginning of their development as a capitalist class.

The patriciate in the cities had risen, through its leading members, to almost princely rank: the Fuggers and the Welsers attained high nobility. The middling and small burghers were still caught up in the prejudices of the guild system, which shackled their leading members to feudal conditions, leaving them without the will and power to free themselves for further development. The continuing division of Germany, the shifting of trade routes, and above all the poorly developed internal market hindered formation of a broad-based and self-conscious bourgeois capitalist class. Production for the court (luxury goods, military needs, fortifications, buildings) far outweighed production for the internal market, especially as the former offered only slight possibilities for expansion of production.

IV

23 The first stage of the early bourgeois revolution was a national movement precipitated by the Wittenberg professor, Martin Luther, posting his Theses against indulgences. For the first time in German history, this unified all classes and strata – with the exception of most spiritual princes and prelates, but including the mass of the lower clergy – under the leadership of the middling bourgeoisie in a battle against the papal Church (1517–21). The highpoints of this stage are Luther's writings of the year 1520, the burning of the books of canon law and the Bull of condemnation on 10 December 1520 and Luther's famous appearance at the Diet of Worms in 1521.

24 Luther began his translation of the Bible at the Wartburg castle with the New Testament (the September Bible). As a biblical translator, as the author of pamphlets and polemics, as the composer of hymns, Luther made a powerful contribution to the development, dissemination and implementation of a unified High German as a written and literary language.

25 The Lutheran Reformation created the 'cheap church' demanded by the bourgeoisie, led to the removal of church states and church law, to the dissolution of the monasteries and the release of their inhabitants into civic life. It removed the enforced celibacy of the clergy, did away with the whole system of devotion to the saints, feast days, the relic cult, pilgrimages and processions, and with church fines, indulgences, dispensations, remissions. The number of the sacraments was reduced, the church orders, confraternities, congregations, and foundations were removed, Latin was abolished as the church language and replaced by German, but not in the sphere of learning, where it survived until the eighteenth century. No one would disagree that 'the Reformation was a bourgeois movement' (Engels), which was extraordinarily enduring in its interventions not just in ecclesiastical life, but in social life as well.

26 But the second stage of the early bourgeois revolution began straight after the imperial assembly of Worms – from which point four religious-political camps formed (1521–4). This process of differentiation marked the end of a unified, national anti-Roman movement.

(1) *The conservative–Catholic camp* comprised all elements interested in maintaining existing relationships: the imperial power, the spiritual princes and prelates, including some of the secular princes and the richer nobility, and parts of the urban patriciate. At the head of this camp stood, among others, the Bavarian Chancellor Leonhard von Eck and Duke George of Saxony. It was first organised as a party at the Regensburg Convention of 1524.

(2) *The bourgeois-moderate Lutheran camp* comprised the propertied elements of the opposition, particularly of central and northern Germany: the bulk of the lower nobility, the bourgeoisie, and a not inconsiderable part of the secular princes, who had hopes of confiscating church property and attaining greater independence from the Empire. (The orthodox secular princes sought to extort these advantages as concessions from the Pope and the Emperor.) At the head of this camp stood the Elector of Ernestine Saxony.

(3) *The bourgeois-radical camp* under Zwingli, comprised the propertied element from Zurich and Berne, and merged humanist tendencies with the demands of the bourgeois-moderate Lutheran camp. It distinguished itself basically from the bourgeois-moderate camp, in which the princes were decisive from the beginning, by its civic-republican stand and by its will towards a practical, rational reshaping of public life in all its social, economic and moral aspects. In endeavours to reshape the Swiss Confederation, and in the resulting struggle against the Habsburgs, Zwingli found a superlative ally in Michael Gaismair.

(4) *The revolutionary movement* of peasants and plebeians alone encompassed all Germany. Its demands were most effectively expressed by Muntzer and Gaismair.

27 In all camps it was a matter of a process of development, not of an immediately apparent differentiation. Also, one should not regard the conservative-Catholic camp as too unified, nor was the bourgeois-Lutheran camp any freer from inner contradictions and opposition. But while the conservative-Catholic camp strengthened itself visibly after 1524/5, and was partly able to win back lost ground (Counter-Reformation, Trent, the Jesuits), the bourgeois-Lutheran camp increasingly collapsed through disunity and ineptitude (the bigamy of the Landgrave of Hesse, the discord between the two Saxonies, the Schmalkaldic War, the Wittenberg Capitulation). Indeed, the bourgeois-radical camp was forced into retreat, and the revolutionary camp was annihilated in the years 1525–35. This was only possible through a class alliance of all the threatened princes, who knew only too well how best to use the disunity of their opponents for their own purposes. This class-influenced community of interest also led to the defeat of Charles V and to the Religious Peace of Augsburg.

28 The collapse of the unified revolutionary front was manifest as early as the Wittenberg disturbances of 1521/22, but it first worked itself out fully in the separate revolt of the knights in 1523, in which the lower nobility sought to pursue their own interests in a struggle against the princes and the clergy. Their aim was to annihilate the spiritual and secular power of the princes, to split Germany from Rome, and to restore dominance of the nobility. All hopes of an alliance between the

nobility, peasants and towns were bound to fail, for domination of the nobility offered advantages only to the knights. The rebellion remained isolated and was crushingly defeated (Sickingen, Absberg and others).

29 Thomas Muntzer separated himself from Luther at an early stage, and in Zwickau, Prague, Allstedt, on the Upper Rhine and in Muhlhausen he developed a doctrine that was the most consistent expression of the People's Reformation (*Volksreformation*) in Germany. Muntzer's political programme demanded 'destruction of the princely state and, to liquidate the cause of the evil, transfer of power to the people' (Smirin). Muntzer 'expressed in theoretically complete form the popular conception of the Reformation' (Smirin). However, this People's Reformation was not only the affair of the peasant-plebeian camp, but represented a highpoint of national policy in our history. 'The People's Reformation, at the dawn of the epoch of the early bourgeois revolution, showed the truly democratic way to implement it' (Smirin).

30 Two wings, a moderate and a radical, formed during the course of the great German Peasant War. Characteristic of the moderate wing, whose notable representative was Wendel Hipler, were the famous Twelve Articles and the Heilbronn programme of Friedrich Weigandt. The radical wing stands predominantly under the influence of Muntzer and Gaismair. The influence of the latter extended throughout the alpine lands, while Muntzer attempted to combine revolutionary actions in west, south-west and central Germany. The main programmes of this wing were the Black Forest Peasants' Letter of Articles and the Tyrolean Constitution (*Landordnung*), both of which demanded destruction of the feudal system, handing over power to the people and setting up a democratic republic. The pamphlet 'To the Assembly of Common Peasantry of the German Nation' occupies an intermediate position between both wings.

31 The early bourgeois revolution, which culminated in the Peasant War, represented the first attempt of the popular masses to create a unified national state from below.

This aim could have been achieved had there been a unification of forces under a single purposeful leadership which would have been in a position to overcome the defective discipline, the narrow-minded localism and the weak connections of the peasants with the plebeian strata of the towns. Such leadership was certainly sought by the most prominent of the peasants' leaders, but they could not supply it alone.

The nobility and ecclesiastical princes were able to strike down the democratic peasant movement with bloody violence because the national force historically called to the task of revolution, the bourgeoisie of the towns, did not place itself at the head of the fight against feudalism. Left alone, and divided amongst themselves, the peasantry could not conquer its tormentors. [Documents of the Socialist Unity Party, GDR, 1956]

The peasants also lacked political experience. Before the conclusion of the Treaty of Weingarten they were in a position to destroy Truchsess, the commander of the Swabian League. Despite their favourable military situation, the peasantry deluded themselves that they could gain their rights without struggle by contractual agreements with the princes.

32 What the revolution could not create, namely a union of all opposition forces to ensure victory, was achieved by a counter-revolution of the princes. The class alliance of reaction conquered first the knights under Sickingen and Hutten, then the peasants and towns, anabaptists and finally the central government itself. All other conflicts took second place to maintaining the old social order and assuring feudal class domination.

33 In the violent defeat of the peasants, Luther played what might be thought a pitiful role. He had broken with the Wittenberg movement of the so-called 'fanatics', he had turned away Carlstadt and had Muntzer exiled. Now he summoned the princes to murder the peasants. And in the same year he finally broke with Erasmus and humanism, just as in 1529 he refused every accommodation with Zwingli. In this process the bourgeois Reformation was so cut to shape that it can be adequately labelled the ideological expression of the limited 'small state' outlook by the Lutheran princes.

34 Muntzer's doctrine influenced the revolutionary peasants and plebeians throughout the entire area of rebellion. His adherents, who stood for uncompromising action against the feudal lords and for 'the unity of the divided German homeland', were found in all peasant camps. With the execution of Muntzer, the early bourgeois revolution lost its most prominent leader. His adherents still attempted to work for the cause of the People's Reformation for more than a decade. Perhaps Gaismair is 'more bourgeois' than Muntzer, as are Zwingli and Calvin, but Muntzer cannot be measured by the standard of bourgeois progressiveness. His ideology – and this is decisive – is not at all bourgeois, but shows itself to be an early form of proletarian class ideology. Muntzer transcends his own time, as it were, and shows the way to a solution that was unattainable then, but which was to be the only correct one for the future.

Muntzer and the Peasant War exposed the bourgeoisie, by showing, momentarily, the essential weaknesses and betrayals of the bourgeois classes and their anti-national stance. In the circumstances, Zwingli could have won, but not Muntzer and Gaismair. Yet Muntzer, as a representative of the first proletarian element in the decaying feudal order, was also the one who upheld the most decisive and comprehensive programme for the development of Germany (as a democratic republic). This programme was without doubt seminal and immature, and for its time utopian; but in its entirety it was still an inspired anticipation of the truly national policy of the German working class.

PETER BLICKLE

2 The 'Peasant War' as the Revolution of the Common Man – Theses*

AN ATTEMPT AT DEFINITION

The Peasant War represented an attempt to overcome the crisis of feudalism through a revolutionary reshaping of social and seigneurial relations on the basis of 'the Gospel'. The bearer of the revolution was not the peasant – as a rule he dominated only the first phase of the rebellion, the formulation of grievances and demands. Rather, it was the 'common man': peasants, miners, the citizens of territorial towns, the politically disenfranchised citizens of imperial cities.

The social aims of the revolution, formulated positively in terms of the slogans of 1525, were 'Christian common weal' and 'brotherly love'. Negatively formulated, they were the reduction of the rights and obligations attached to particular estates. The political aims of the revolution developed out of this: the corporative federal state (in small states), or the parliamentary state (in large states with a representative assembly structure). Although the revolution failed because of its incompatibility with Reformation, the results were economic relief for agriculture (with broad regional differentiation), gains in legal security, and a stabilisation and institutionalisation of the political powers of the peasants.

THESES

(1) The decades before 1525 saw a relative economic deterioration for the agricultural enterprises of the day, through factors whose gravity varied regionally, but which were none the less causally related:
  (a) population movements;
  (b) the revival of serfdom rights;
  (c) reduction of usufructs;
  (d) increase in tax burdens.
  All these factors led to noticeable losses of income on every farm.

*Translated from Peter Blickle, 'Thesen zum Thema – Der "Bauernkrieg" als Revolution des "Gemeinen Mannes"', *Historische Zeitschrift*, Beiheft 4, 1975, pp. 127–31.

This meant that simultaneously and as a consequence:

(2) The social units of the family and the village became the focus of a crisis such that

    (a) the opposition between rich and poor was sharpened (through an accompanied numerical growth of the rural lower orders);

    (b) the basic requirements of life could no longer be satisfied (limitations on marriage, abolition of *de facto* freedom of movement);

    (c) the area of village autonomy was restricted (through seigneurial power, partly necessary to implement the innovations mentioned in 1 – e.g. serfdom, reduction of usufructs).

Peasant opposition to the measures mentioned in 1 and 2, at the communal level (village or district) or at the territorial level (countrysides (*landschaften*), estates), led to partial successes. This meant that:

(3) The level of political expectation of the peasants rose, since they were able to establish themselves as a political estate in many territories between Salzburg and Alsace, Tyrol and the Palatinate in the decades before 1525.

(4) The relative economic deterioration, the growing tension in the social areas of family and village and growing political expectations were variables whose importance differ from region to region, but which led overall to similar results. Relations of lord and peasant were extremely strained. Feudalism, which had been able to maintain itself in the agrarian field in a particularly recognisable form, even if it had been strongly distorted because it was deprived of its ethical content, was endangered.

(5) Force of legitimation was one strong support of feudalism, if not its greatest support. Demands were only advanced by the peasants in as far as they could be legally justified. So long as the legal principle of old custom was binding on the peasants, disturbances remained of necessity within the frame of reference of lordship and were limited in their aims to removal of the lords' 'innovations'. Not open to debate were problems caused by exogenous factors, e.g. deterioration of the manpower–land ratio through population growth.

(6) The replacement of old custom by godly law was liberating and in part revolutionary. Through godly law, the needs of the peasants could be presented as ethically justified demands (the Twelve Articles). This aim of realising godly law, for the peasants a non-negotiable demand, and alongside it the Gospel as a concretisation of godly law, left the social and political order in principle completely open. The translation of the Gospel into a concrete social and political order was referred to the Reformers by the so-called moderate wing of the movement (the Baltringen Christian Union, the Lake Constance and Allgau Unions).

(7) Godly law and the Gospel, carried from the towns into the country-side by the preachers, made the Peasant War into a Revolution of the Common Man. The limited coincidence of interests between peasants and burghers, in the shape of similar agrarian problems (farming towns), tax burdens (military levy, pallium), or encroach-ments on communal autonomy by territorial lords (there was an identity of interests here with the miners), was strengthened by a common yearning for a more just, more Christian world.

(8) The authorities became the main opponents of the peasants, the miners and the townsmen (in terms of the definition above) because they closed themselves to 'the Gospel' or, if they were 'evangelical', because they did not follow the common man's interpretation of the Gospel and godly law. It was in this situation that castles and abbeys were seized.

(9) In implementing 'the Gospel' and its consequences, i.e. 'godly law', 'Christian common weal' and 'brotherly love', the clergy were deprived of their economic and political power; the nobility, though their position sometimes remained unclear, were more strongly integrated into communal associations and were deprived of their political prerogatives. Thus, both implicitly and explicitly, the common man became the determining factor for social and political formations. To fill the vacuum of sovereignty which had arisen both in theory and in practice, a programme was drafted which went beyond grievances, or else was put into practice with-out being formulated. Two alternatives were put forward, with fluid boundaries between them, dependent on existing assumptions about the territorial state:

(10) In the area of the small states of Swabia, the Upper Rhine and Franconia, a corporative federal constitution was drafted. Aut-onomous village and city communes, which were formed together into bands (no longer military units, but now political bodies as well), formed a corporative basis. The bands united, without giving up their 'sovereign rights', in voluntary association as 'Christian unions', which in their territorial size corresponded roughly to the duchy of Wurttemberg or to the Swiss Confederation.

(11) A parliamentary constitution was developed in larger territories by estates of peasants, burghers and miners. While retaining the institutional framework (court – i.e. land court, city court, bailiff's court – provincial assembly, committee, government, territorial lord), territorial estates were replaced by countrysides (*landschaften*), which in 1525 meant both the representative assembly and the entirety of the rebels in each territory. Autonomous village, mining, market and urban communes chose representatives by election for the provincial diet, which in turn appointed a representative government (committee), which carried out the business of govern-ment with the territorial lord.

(12) The Peasant War failed as a revolution because the concerns of the common man were not compatible with those of the Reformers. (The Reformers opposed the attempt to use force as a means of realising the godly law.) To override the authority of the Reformers cost the rebels time, energy and unity.

(13) Military defeat made revolutionary change impossible, but did not exclude the path of reform. In parts of the area of rebellion (Upper Germany), the insecurity of the authorities, as expressed for example in committee reports of the 1526 imperial assembly of Speyer, and the refractoriness of the peasants, led in the long term not to restoration, but to co-operation within the framework of a territorial constitution. The existing system was stabilised through greater political integration of the peasants, but was also altered in that it gradually removed exclusive claims to domination of older privileged groups.

JOHN C. STALNAKER

3 Towards a Social Interpretation of the German Peasant War *

The German Peasant War has long been a focal point of early modern German history. The revolutions and expectations of revolution in the later eighteenth and nineteenth centuries drew attention to the only mass insurrection of more than regional scope in earlier German history; the emancipation of the central European peasantry in the nineteenth century called to mind the violent, abortive attempt of their sixteenth-century forebears to better their condition. Since the early nineteenth century, a variety of concerns to which the Peasant War seemed pertinent have kept interest in it lively. The assumption that the 1520s were a formative period in German history, the belief that the Peasant War had important implications for evaluating the stature and influence of Luther, the recently growing concern with the history of the 'common man', the search for a typology of revolution, and the recognition of the frequency and importance of peasant-based revolutions in the Third World: all these have seldom been held by the same historian, but together they have kept the German Peasant War an important and controversial event (Buszello, 1969; Steinmetz, 1965; Waas, 1964; Schulze, 1973; Vahle, 1972).

It is an instructive coincidence that the two most influential monographs devoted to the Peasant War were written on the eve of major political upheavals in Germany, and that each was animated by a spirit of sympathy for the rebels of the sixteenth century while interpreting their rebellion quite differently. Wilhelm Zimmermann saw the insurrection as a primitive expression of the democratic idealism which culmin-

*This article also appeared in a German version, which contains more extensive footnotes: John C. Stalnaker, 'Auf dem Weg zu einer sozialgeschichtlichen Interpretation des Deutschen Bauernkriegs 1525–6', Der Deutsche Bauernkrieg 1524–6 (ed. H. U. Wehler), Sonderheft 1, Geschichte und Gesellschaft, Göttingen, 1975, pp. 38–60.

Author's note
This essay owes more than I am aware to the stimulus of Hans Rosenberg, whose lectures introduced me to the subject more than a decade ago, and whose 'Deutsche Agrargeschichte in alter und neuer Sicht' (1969) set my thoughts going on the topic of this essay. However, here as elsewhere, teachers are not responsible for the vagaries of their students.

ated in the decade of the 1840s, during which his lengthy work first appeared, and of which he himself was an energetic defender. *Der Deutsche Bauernkrieg*, by Gunther Franz, first appeared in 1933. Franz hoped to rescue the Peasant War from the fluctuations of the political *Zeitgeist*. However, one may doubt whether his judgement that the event was not an *Aufruhr* but rather a *Volksaufstand* with *genossen-schaftlich* but not democratic aims was as removed from the political preoccupations of Germany between the two world wars as he hoped (Franz, 1933: 287–8; Vahle, 1972: 265–6). Zimmerman and Franz do not stand alone in their political engagement. Historians have tended to react with intensity to the Peasant War, and in so doing they have often carried their politics with them. Perhaps the ultimate testimony a historian pays to his emotional involvement in an event he is interpreting is to ask, 'Could it have been otherwise?' – and few historians of the Peasant War have been able to refrain from putting that question. Historians of all political complexions have loaded the sins and hopes of German history on to the Peasant War. The conservative fears of Ranke, the revolutionary disappointments of Engels and the liberal sympathies of Lamprecht all found expression in their treatments of the Peasant War; each man attributed to the event an exemplary character and gave it a pivotal position in German history. As we will show, twentieth-century scholars who have contributed to the subject have often done the same, sometimes more circumspectly.

The Peasant War, then, is an event which has long been considered important and controversial. Many talented historians with different views of the historical process and contrasting ideals have devoted their energies to it. One might expect the results to have been a wide-ranging and fruitful debate which would have, if it did not establish a stable consensus, at least provided a constellation of useful hypotheses. The infusion of political engagement can energise and sharpen more than it muddles historical investigation, as the literature on the French Revolution illustrates. But the framework within which the historical debate on the Peasant War has taken place has been narrow. Vigorous polemic has concealed common assumptions which today look either untenable or unprofitable, and which have inhibited historians from seeing or pursuing other approaches.

Among nineteenth-century historians whose interpretations in other respects diverged from one another, it was a common assumption that the Peasant War was directed towards national unification. In the twentieth century this assumption has been sometimes doubted and sometimes qualified, as in the current debate among Marxist scholars as to whether the insurrectionaries aimed consciously at national unification or were directed unconsciously towards that goal (Töpfer, 1963; Zschäbitz, 1964). But the most influential interpretations of the Peasant War in the twentieth century have continued to argue that the insurrectionaries were fighting for a remodelled *Reich* or against the fragmentation of the feudal system (Franz, 1933; Smirin, 1956). Furthermore, historians have tended to focus their attention on those leaders and theorists whose views were most articulate, intelligible and, often, attractive to the historian, and whose plans were most far-reaching, whatever the regional scope of those plans. These revolutionary programmes have been subjected to sober praise or blame as blueprints of new states and societies without the historian having demonstrated that such theoreticians were understood or appreciated by the masses for whom they spoke (Smirin, 1956; Macek, 1960; 1965; Angermeier, 1966). Studies of the 'ideologies' of pre-industrial lower classes elsewhere in Europe have taught us to be wary of the assumption that they see the world with the same eyes as do modern historians (Hobsbawm, 1959; Thompson, 1971). And everything we know about peasants and artisans in the sixteenth century makes it unlikely that any kind of national (as opposed to regional or local) political consciousness could have been highly developed among them (Walder, 1954; Elliott, 1969). The recent book by Buszello, subjecting well-known sources to careful and ingenious reinterpretation, ought to have dealt a death blow to the judgement that a unified German state was the aim of any but a tiny and unrepresentative group of idealists.

Emphasis on the articulate and the educated insurrectionary spokesmen, and especially on the 'nationalists' among them, is the most prominent element in a conception of the Peasant War which has a slightly archaic flavour, and which has made its defeat not comprehensible enough and too portentous. Behind this conception one may perhaps see the continuing influence of the preoccupations of German intellectuals in the first half of the nineteenth century. The political awakening of German intellectuals after 1789, and their need to measure their fragmented and buffeted homeland against the dynamic model of revolutionary France, at the same time both attractive and repulsive, coincided in time with the strong and growing conviction that historical study would clarify the present by explaining the past. This atmosphere helps to explain the awe of those two romantic German nationalists, Leopold von Ranke and Friedrich Engels, before the spectacle of the Peasant War, in which they saw an exaggerated threat to the old and promise of a new social order. The shadow of these historians lies heavily over present interpretations of the Peasant War, not least over their neglect of its rural social origins.

How have the most influential recent and general treatments of the Peasant War dealt with the question of the rural social origins of the insurrection, or, in other words, with the question of the sources of the insurrection in changes in agrarian social structure? The first book to which one must turn in answering this question is Gunther Franz's monograph, republished in its tenth edition in 1975 and still the reigning standard work on the subject. His research has set the standard for his successors, and has been drawn on by many; his interpretation of the event has been widely accepted. For Franz, the insurrection is the result of the collision of two historical tendencies, both of which antedate 1525–6 by many decades. First, the princes (*Landesherren*), and, following them, other manorial lords (*Grund-*, *Gerichts-*, and *Leibherren*), breached local custom in the pursuit of financial or political advantage. Persistent attempts were made to modify tenures and taxes, to extend forms of servitude to peasants who had not been so subjected in the past, to restrict access to forest and streams, to introduce new administrative and judicial norms and controls: in general, to rationalise, centralise and stiffen princely or manorial administrations, to exercise a more uniform and more rigorous control over the peasant population. Secondly, these innovations were imposed on peasant communities whose conception of the norms by which they ought to be governed were becoming more flexible and sensitive: the conception of the 'godly law' was colouring and replacing that of the 'old law'.

The distinction between the 'old law' and the 'godly law' has been accepted by many historians, even by those who have differed from Franz on other matters (Smirin, 1956: 52–62). And there are good reasons for the influence of this interpretation. Based on sympathy with the life and thought of the German peasantry, to whose history Franz has devoted much of his productive career, it makes it impossible to ignore the fact that insurrections have sources in the political norms of communities, however inarticulate such norms may be under ordinary circumstances (cf. Thompson, 1971: 76–9). On the other hand, the categories as Franz uses them are suggestive but not quite satisfactory. They are reminiscent of the vague, ahistorical and well-worn distinction between the 'Germanic' and the 'Roman-Christian'. The historical tendency on which Franz bases so much hangs in the air: he makes no attempt to explain why the 'godly law' should have been an increasingly influential conception in the decades before 1525. Furthermore, the two conceptions of the 'old' and the 'godly' law are so loosely defined that it is not easy to distinguish them from one another and so to verify Franz's hypothesis. Both are divine in origin, imprescriptible, eternal and identical with justice. The 'old law' is in principle more concrete, particular and stable, the 'godly law' more susceptible of generalisation and more flexible, but these are not distinctions which are easy to apply. Apart from the important demand for the abolition of serfdom (*Leibeigenschaft*), there is no definite touchstone for distinguishing them from one another. Thus Franz himself admits a large number of mixed or borderline cases (the Twelve Articles, the Articles of Baltringen, Schwarzburg, Thuringia), and one cannot escape the suspicion that either of the labels, 'godly law' or 'old law', could be arbitrarily applied to many sets of peasant articles. Franz does make a sharp distinction between the movements which carry the 'old law' and those which carry the 'godly law' on their banners: the former is anonymous and spontaneous, the latter conspiratorial with identifiable leaders. Such a distinction would seem to imply sociological differences in the insurrectionary groups, but Franz gives no systematic consideration to this possibility and the hints he gives on the social standing of the rebels allegedly pursuing the 'godly law' do not indicate any regular differences from their brethren pursuing the 'old law'.

Apart from the utility and the validity of this distinction between 'old' and 'godly' law, one must question whether it is possible adequately to account for the Peasant War with an explanation which is so exclusively ideological and political. Franz has insisted on the 'political' character of the insurrection, and in this he has generally been followed by non-Marxist historians. This characterisation is not controversial as such, since an insurrection against overlords with a view to regulating legal relationships must be *ipso facto* 'political'. But the term as used by Franz and his followers has taken an additional and less unexceptionable meaning: it means economic causes are not significant. It means that the peasant rebels were not moved to revolt for economic reasons. They suffered economic injury, to be sure, but it was not primarily because of such injury that they rose in rebellion. It was rather because their sense of justice was aggrieved and their political autonomy was restricted. And why can we draw this conclusion? Because the economic conditions to which the peasantry were subject were generally improving and because those involved in the insurrection, especially in leadership positions, were usually among the more prosperous of the German peasantry.

I do not think this is a tenable argument. The conclusion that the absence of progressive impoverishment of the rebels indicates that economic causes are insignificant is not consistent with recent scholarship on the dynamics of insurrection. This scholarship is filled with disputed questions, but agreement is general on the following three points. (1) Economic change is usually fundamental in causing insurrections. (2) Economic growth can be as disruptive of social contentment and stability as economic decline. (3) In explaining the alienation and propensity to revolt of a particular social group, the absolute level of wealth of that group is less important than the relationship between economic aspirations and expectations, on the one hand, and perception of economic reality, on the other hand, of that group; in other words, rich or poor men with dashed hopes rise in rebellion (cf. Stone, 1972: 14–22).

Therefore, in order to properly evaluate the importance of economic causes for the Peasant War, we would need to have much more refined generalisations on the economic condition of the peasantry than are to be found in Franz's *Der Deutsche Bauernkrieg*, or in the other comprehensive, recent, non-Marxist narrative history of the insurrection, *Die Bauern im Kampf um Gerechtigkeit* by Adolf Waas. In fact, these two books, the most influential, current, non-Marxist interpretations of the Peasant War, are resolute in their determination to ignore economic conditions and the economic background to the insurrection. There are scarcely any statistics or any systematic generalisations on population changes, grain prices, wages, tendencies in agricultural income, or changes in agrarian institutions or practices in either book, to say nothing of judgements as to how the encroachments of overlords affected the economic circumstances of their peasantry. Franz reflects the judgement of older historians when he writes that the economic condition of the pre-1525 peasantry can never be known with any precision, and his own generalisations are consistent with that judgement. Waas does venture some generalisations on the economic situation of the peasantry in the later Middle Ages, but these indicate an antiquated conception of agrarian economic history: although Waas's book is subtitled '1300–1525', he seems not to have heard of the agrarian depression of 1350–1450. When these two historians treat the background to the Peasant War, they deal with either the political or the ideological background, as in Franz's pioneering opening section narrating the *Vorläufer* or the local and regional insurrections in the fifteenth and early sixteenth centuries, and as in Waas's detailed discussion of radical propaganda literature before 1525.

The modern western historical literature on the Peasant War, then, is dominated by older historians, of whom by far the most influential is the doyen of Peasant War studies, Gunther Franz. Its conclusions are solidly grounded in extensive research, especially the research of Franz himself. Its full-dress general works are eloquently written and command the narrative detail. Its interpretation is narrowly political and ideological. It is an interpretation which is characterised above all by a determination to raise the insurrection of 1525–6 above the sordidness of economic motive and to preserve it from contamination with economically grounded class conflict by stressing the importance of political ideas. In other words, it is in a well-established German academic tradition of anti-Marxism (cf. Wehler, 1970).

E. P. Thompson has complained that conservative historians of insurrection have presented us with rebels who have no ideas but only empty stomachs which propel them automatically into political violence (1971: 76–9). The Franz school has given us the reverse: rebels with ideas but no material needs, with full heads but no stomachs at all.

There is no single outstanding figure among the Marxist historians of the Peasant War, at least none of the stature and influence of Franz. From M. M. Smirin has come the most ambitious but also idiosyncratic scholarly work, from Max Steinmetz the most numerous epitomes of the Marxist interpretation (1961; 1967). Disagreement has been frequent and debate lively among Marxist scholars, certainly more so than in the west (cf. Wohlfeil, 1972). However, the premises of the canonical texts – the most fundamental of which are by Engels – are respected. Thus one can speak of a common core or common elements in the Marxist interpretation, despite debate and variety, and it scarcely needs saying that one of those elements is class conflict. However, it is class conflict defined in a restrictive way, and for two reasons. First, as the denotation *frühbürgerliche Revolution* implies, the bourgeoisie play a central theoretical role in the insurrection as the class promoting the economic changes whose objective course is the fundamental cause of the insurrection. That the bourgeoisie are notable in the insurrection itself by their absence has generated some uneasiness, but to minimise or eliminate their role would involve a change in more than the term *frühbürgerliche Revolution*. They are the carriers of the development of capitalism, which causal background gives the insurrection its historical significance and place in the line of revolutions reaching a temporary culmination in the great French Revolution, and distinguishing them from preceding insurrections, mere jacqueries, however formidable in size. Because of this orientation which associates significant economic change with the bourgeoisie alone, agrarian economic and social change has been given less attention than developments in industry and long-distance commerce and has typically been seen as a mere by-product of them (cf. Motteck, 1957).

There is a second and related reason for a tendency in Marxist historiography to give insufficient attention to agrarian social and economic change. The 'classes' whose conflict shapes historical movement are susceptible of refined subdividing and have received them in Marxist analyses from the beginning. But if Marx concerned himself with subdivisions of the bourgeoisie (in, for example, the *18ᵗᵉⁿ Brumaire*), and Engels with subdivisions among the landed aristocracy and princes (in the *Deutscher Bauernkrieg*), modern Marxist historians of the Peasant War have not given the subdivisions among the peasantry the attention they deserve. If 'class' is given its classic Marxist definition, the peasantry must be defined as not one class but as several. Modern Marxist historians know this, but it plays no important role in their analysis of the insurrection or of its causes, perhaps because of their antagonism to the feudal aristocrat and prince, perhaps because the stirring quality of the Marxist historical drama depends on the stark confrontation of oppressive lords and suffering peasantry. Whatever the reason, their depiction of the changes in rural society which precede the insurrection have taken a form which is familiar to us, because we have seen it before in the works of Franz and his school: that of a personal duel between lords and peasants. It is characteristic that the title of chapters or sections in recent Marxist works on the rural background to the insurrection, including a work of economic history, are cast in purely political terms; 'the implementation of feudal seigneurial demands', 'the offensive of the feudal lords against the peasants', 'the strengthening of feudal repression in the German village', etc. (Motteck, 1957, and Smirin, 1955). Just as in Franz and Waas, impersonal economic forces and their rural social consequences in the decades before 1525 are either absent altogether or not integrated into an analysis of the causes of the insurrection. However, although the historiography of the Peasant War has been little influenced by their work, other historians in the past generation presented us with a transformed picture of the central European countryside in the fourteenth and fifteenth centuries.

Since the 1930s, the approach of economic historians has changed. Primary interest in the development of economic institutions has been replaced by interest in the measurement and explanation of economic productivity. In consequence, the older belief in the steady continuity of institutional development between the high Middle Ages and the Industrial Revolution has been qualified by awareness of marked discontinuities in the productivity of the European economy, in which the period from approximately 1350 to 1450 has a notable place (cf. Rosenberg, 1969). Wilhelm Abel was a pioneer in this application of modern economic theory to the history of the pre-industrial past, and especially in its application to the history of agriculture (Abel, 1955, 1966, 1967). He and his pupils continue to be among the most convincing spokesmen for an interpretation which has become the new orthodoxy, and may be very briefly summarised as follows.

The agrarian economy of the fourteenth and fifteenth centuries contracted rapidly and markedly, while at the same time undergoing major structural changes. Population fell and tended to regroup in larger communities. Cities attracted migrants from the countryside more powerfully than in the past, and the relative balance between villages and hamlets shifted towards the former. Wages rose to unprecedented heights because of a shortage of labour, and landlords found it difficult to find peasantry to accept tenures or labourers to accept employment at costs they considered reasonable. The price of grain fell more sharply than did the prices of demand-elastic specialised foodstuffs, industrial materials and industrial products. Arable land contracted; forest, waste and meadow expanded. After approximately 1450, there was a gradual reversal of these tendencies. Population began to grow rapidly, the chronically depressed prices of grain rose and the 'scissors' movement of prices and wages was reversed.

The new orthodoxy has not gone unchallenged (cf. Kelter, 1953). There are risks in applying tools created for the analysis of industrial economies to a period as early and as undeveloped as the later Middle Ages. Most agricultural production was not destined for the market in the fourteenth and fifteenth centuries and for long afterwards. The sources available are limited in quantity and quality. Therefore the implications of this data for economic history are ambiguous in ways which do not trouble historians of later periods, and not everybody has accepted Abel's conclusions. In view of the responsiveness of pre-industrial demographic patterns to prosperity, the validity of placing as much emphasis as Abel does on population decline as a cause of structural economic changes has been questioned, as has the logic of a decline of both grain producers and grain consumers causing a sharp fall in grain prices. As regards the economic developments themselves, and apart from their explanation, Abel has presented a complex picture. Overall economic contraction is set against higher *per capita* wealth, relative urban growth and a corresponding tendency towards more market-orientated and specialised agricultural production. Better terms for peasant lessees and higher wages for labourers is set against the uncertainties and instabilities, not all of them economic, of the period. Other historians have drawn a different balance of these contrasting elements than has Abel. Some have disputed the optimistic connotations of the phrase 'the golden age of craftsmen'. Others have found more rational resettlement and less depopulation than Abel in the deserted fields and villages of the period. I think it is accurate to say, however, without evaluating the validity of these objections, that they amount to limited modification and qualification of the approach and the conclusions discovered by Abel and others, the fundamentals of which stand intact.

In the two centuries preceding the insurrection of 1525–6, the German agrarian economy had been jostled by a powerful wave of contraction succeeded from about the middle of the fifteenth century onwards by an equally powerful expansive wave. What implications do these contrasting waves of economic change have for the long-term social origins of the Peasant War? In other words, what effects have these economic changes had on the size, income, political position and social prestige of the different social groups in the countryside? How have the relationships of these social groups changed? How have the organisation of production and the forms of social life changed? And how do these changes help us to explain the insurrection of 1525?

First, it has been noted that Abel himself is not particularly interested in these questions (cf. Rosenberg, 1969: 133, 139–41). His larger studies on agriculture have not dealt with them in any systematic way. The latest, magisterial history of agriculture contains some ingenious attempts to measure the effects of economic tendencies on the fortunes of individual landed aristocrats or of 'ideal typical' peasants. But beyond these two systematic generalisations he does not go, perhaps in part because he is restricted by the division of the series of which that volume is part. Secondly, the historical literature which bears on these questions is fuller for the contractive phase of the agrarian economy than it is for the fifteenth- and early-sixteenth-century expansive phase. In the no-man's-land between the 'medieval' and the 'early modern' periods, the monographic literature thins out and up-to-date general surveys do not exist. We lose the guidance of the magnificent *Economie rurale* by Georges Duby in the fifteenth century. The single important exception to the diminution of specialised historical literature on the agrarian economy and society of the post-1450 period is the topic of *Gutsherrschaft* and *Gutswirtschaft*, which has been thoroughly explored.

But these institutions develop in eastern Germany, which is almost untouched by insurrection in 1525–6. Thus both the geographical and the chronological choices by historians of pre-1525 agrarian society and economy indicate their lack of interest in the Peasant War.

Two bodies of historical literature have been surveyed. The first comprises the histories of the Peasant War, whose living historiographical tradition is two centuries old and still vigorous, although split into two sectarian wings. The second is a recent and remarkable reinterpretation of the agrarian economy in the later Middle Ages. These two topics would seem to be closely associated. The putative bearing of agrarian economic cycles on a peasant insurrection is obvious. And one would think that the greatest central European mass insurrection in the countryside would have some implications for the history of the agricultural economy. But, in fact, histories of the one subject pay no attention to histories of the other, even when – as in one instance – they are both written by the same man (Lütge, 1963). Conservative historians of the Peasant War shun any inquiry into social and economic causation as tainted with Marxism, and the Marxists, fixated by feudal oppression, are not Marxist enough not to emulate them. On the other side of the street, the newly prestigious proponents of *histoire structurelle et conjoncturelle* will not deign to speak to their elderly relative, *histoire événementielle*, and what might have been a useful conversation does not take place.

What follows is a preview of the conversation as it might some day be held, or, in other words, a sketch of the social implications of agrarian economic change in the later Middle Ages as they bear on the Peasant War. It is briefer and more solidly based where it touches the more thoroughly investigated pre-1450 period, lengthier and less solidly based on the period between approximately 1450 and 1525. It is intended to be hypothetical and suggestive. It ignores regional variations until near the end of the essay.

The agrarian depression hit hardest those families and institutions dependent on the sale of grain produced with hired or dependent labour. Therefore the bonds of the manor loosened, or rather continued to loosen, since the tendency to shift from direct cultivation to leasehold antedated 1350 and may have antedated 1300 in some areas (Bog, 1958). The demesne shrank, often on poor terms for the manorial lords because of the shortage of men and the constant depreciation of money. The largest manorial landholders suffered greatly, but were aided in the struggle for survival by political influence, sometimes by more systematic management practices, and by their very size, which permitted them to undergo considerable losses of land without going under. The smaller manorial landholders lacked these advantages, and there may have been a marked diminution of property and turnover of personnel among the medium-sized nobility.

Leaseholds tended to be smaller in size than in the past. The former large lessee was investing his capital elsewhere. The social unit of production best fitted to survive the hardships and respond to the opportunities of the period was the substantial peasant farm. A considerable proportion of its production was for family consumption, and the household was insulated from the market-place as regards the basics of life. Relying largely on family labour, the farm was also insulated from the prevailing high labour costs. On the other hand, the farm was large and well-situated enough to provide a satisfactory guarantee of dues to the manorial lord. The family had taken advantage of the depopulation to concentrate and extend its holdings, and it was devoting more of its resources to the more profitable products of pasture and woodland (Hasel, 1967: 140ff.).

At the other end of the social scale, landless labourers and cottagers may have been proportionally less numerous and better off than in the past. Opportunities in the city were more plentiful; deaths from disease may have given unexpected inheritances to some; and for those who chose to work in the countryside and could evade the wage maxima imposed by the authorities, wages were high.

Peasants with substantial land-holdings emerged about 1450, on the edge of the period of agrarian expansion, well armed to do battle in the succeeding period. They too had suffered during the agrarian depression, but their relative political and economic position had improved because of the flexibility of the substantial peasant farm: small enough to have mitigated the effects of low grain prices and high wages, yet large enough to have responded to the relatively stronger pull of urban markets. The flexibility stood them in good stead in the economically expansive post-1450 period too, in which they were able to build on the advantages gained in the preceding century. The manor had become a less influential institution in governing the lives of the peasantry and the village more influential; the substantial peasants tended to control the autonomous institutions of the village. The grain market revived, from which peasantry who held much land were better able to benefit than were others in the village. The products of pasture and field, from which substantial peasants had profited in the period before 1450, continued to be profitable after 1450. The needs of towns, especially of middle- and upper-income townsmen, continued to sustain the market for meat, wool and wood (Saalfeld, 1971).

The substantial peasantry prospered because of the expansive tendencies of the post-1450 period, but these same tendencies also strengthened enemies from various quarters who threatened their new prosperity. These are, in reverse order of social eminence, the rural poor, the landed nobility and the territorial princes.

The rural poor

The steeply rising population curve generated a plentiful supply of agricultural labour and eventually dampened its price. It also first restored the price of grain and then drove it to new heights. From both of these developments the substantial peasant benefited. But this population growth also restored the numbers of the marginal men and families on the edges of the peasant villages and largely outside its political structure, those in possession of a few acres or a garden or no land at all (Steinmetz, 1965: 35–9; Blaschke, 1956). The economic interests of these families were sharply opposed to those of the substantial peasantry (Sabean, 1972: 36ff., 114ff.). They were, on balance, employees, purchasers of grain and debtors, against the employers, sellers of grain and lenders among the substantial peasantry. The two groups had different interests also on the regulation of inheritance and on the use of the village common lands. Especially the latter became a flash point as the villages filled up with people again and the village social structure became increasingly differentiated. Forest, meadow and waste-land had been plentiful since the depopulation of the fourteenth century and had increasingly been put to commercialised use. The rural poor wanted restoration of the days when common lands had served local and subsistence needs. Their interests were met by maximising open access to common lands and by carving what they saw as surplus into subsistence arable plots. The substantial peasants wanted to regulate access by criteria weighted according to ownership of animals and the holding of arable land and to maintain the commons as a grazing and wood preserve. At issue were both who was to control the commons and what sorts of economic purpose it was to serve.

The landed nobility

The 'decline of the nobility' is still enshrined in textbooks and general treatments, crystallised in such phrases as Maximilian I, 'the last knight', and in such images as Franz von Sickingen dying amid the rubble of his fortress in the Landstuhl. In fact, not much in the way of systematic investigation of the German nobility between 1450 and 1550 is available, and it seems likely that the adaptability of the German nobility to new conditions of political and military organisation and technology will turn out to be greater than has sometimes been assumed (Müller, 1939; Rössler, 1965). Two considerations relevant here support this supposition.

First, the degree of autonomy and of local or regional influence of the landed nobility depended on the policies and fiscal needs of their territorial princes. The indebtedness of princes was on balance rising between 1450 and 1500, and perhaps the most important source of supplementary income involved the shifting of 'sovereign' rights into the hands of the landed nobility, sometimes *en bloc* in return for grants by diets, sometimes piece by piece by the pawning of *Amter*, sometimes informally by encouraging ill-paid aristocratic service in return for rights to exploit subjects (Droeger, 1966; Cohn, 1965: 75–139, 162–4).

Secondly, the economic tendencies which encouraged and made more profitable the farms of substantial peasants also encouraged a restoration and a stiffening of manorial controls. The plenitude of labour, the reversal of the 'scissors' movement between wages and grain prices were favourable circumstances for higher ground-rents and other obligations from peasants to lords, and for a restoration of demesne lands, whether arable or pasturage.

The territorial princes

The burgeoning officialdom of late-fifteenth- and early-sixteenth-century territorial princes impinged directly on sensitive areas in the life of peasant communities, such as when access to forests was more strictly regulated and inheritance laws modified. This larger central administration also had to be paid for, as did the more frequent warfare and more active diplomacy of the period, and the peasantry typically bore a disproportionate share of the burden.

The weight of the princes on their subject peasantry varied with the character and ambition of particular princes, but it also varied with some objective factors. The capacity of a prince to protect his peasantry depended heavily on the amount of his income, because this governed the political leverage of the landed nobility. His financial incentive to protect his peasantry depended on the sources of his income (Droeger, 1966; Kötschke, 1953). The basic division here is between income derived from manorial and other dues paid by the prince's own peasants on his domanium, on the one hand, and income from tolls, subsoil rights and direct or indirect taxation, on the other hand. The higher the proportion of a prince's income which was derived from manorial lordship and related rights on the domanium, the less was his incentive to limit the rights of manorial lords, and the more inclined he was liable to be to exploit his own peasantry and permit his nobility to do the same with theirs. Princes with a smaller domanium, in contrast, had more of an interest in protecting their peasant subjects as a source of taxation and – although this was of declining importance – of troops.

The tendencies just sketched are general, and their consequences varied from region to region. The easiest to generalise about is the north-east. This region has caught the imagination of nineteenth- and twentieth-century agrarian historians, both because of the general fascination with Brandenburg-Prussia and because the agrarian problems of nineteenth- and early-twentieth-century Germany were most starkly evidenced there. Monographic literature on the region is plentiful, and generalisations may be advanced with some confidence (Rosenberg, 1969: 95f.; Carsten, 1954: 89f.; Boelcke, 1957: 11 ff.).

A distinctive combination of circumstances made possible the peculiar east-Elbian institution of *Gutsherrschaft* and practice of *Gutswirtschaft*: the substantial size of the territories, relatively light population density and paucity of substantial towns, the weakness and financial needs of princes, the frequency of a concentration of the various lordship rights (including those adhering in theory to the prince) in a locality in the hands of its squire, the shallow roots of peasant custom (no *Weistümer*), and the coming into being of markets for east-Elbian grain which were both substantial and distant. In this environment the peasantry, once the beneficiaries of the exceptional privileges needed to populate a colonial area, were gradually hedged round with restrictions on movement, increased labour services, and, eventually, diminished landholdings. The framework of legal and semi-legal aristocratic control over peasantry was already well established by the end of the fifteenth century. In the sixteenth and early seventeenth centuries the regime of reconstituted serfdom was consolidated, peasant expropriation began and the economic bulwarks in the form of earnings from grain export were built.

Therefore, the purest and clearest case of *feudale Unterdrückung* in central and central-eastern Europe in the decades before 1525 is to be found in east Elbia. It is there that the generalisation of the scholars of the Soviet Union and the German Democratic Republic on the tendencies of the decades preceding the Peasant War have the most obvious applicability, and it is also there that there is no insurrection in 1525. The single exception is Prussia, which is accounted for by the protracted crisis of the Teutonic Order, whose slackening grip necessitated exceptional concessions to the landed aristocracy and was accompanied by exceptional unrest (Hubatsch, 1960: 139 ff.). In general, the east-Elbian social structure which was emerging by 1525 was notable for its simplicity, its rigidly hierarchical and oppressive character and its stability.

The opposite corner of Germany, Swabia and Franconia in the south-west, was opposite also in its dominant sociological and political traits (Cohn, 1965; Bader, 1950; Ott, 1970). It was the heartland and point of origin of the Peasant War, a region characterised by dense population, flourishing cities, political fragmentation and the confusing overlapping of unevenly defined and unevenly consolidated political sovereignties. The pressure of sundry lords on the peasantry was clearly a major feature of the seventy-five years preceding the Peasant War, but the phrase *feudale Unterdrückung* misses the point. Like the French Revolution more than two centuries later, the insurrection in Swabia and Franconia involved the collision of 'two rising classes': ambitious lords and prosperous, assertive peasants. Furthermore, it was a collision sharpened and to an as yet unknown degree shaped by the disturbing influence of the numerous and dissatisfied rural poor. The substantial peasants had secured an enviable position in the villages and *vis-à-vis* their landlords during the agrarian depression of the fourteenth and fifteenth centuries. Now reaping the fruits of that strategic position with the agricultural prosperity of the later fifteenth and early sixteenth centuries, they were threatened from two quarters: from above by the intrusion of landlords and princes, from below by the growing mass of landless or nearly landless rural poor clamouring for a share of the agricultural prosperity. The essential elements which the social scientists have taught us to expect in an insurrection are here: confidence, hope, 'rising expectations', confronted by formidable threats to those expectations.

The nature of the social conflicts in the countryside which precede and lead to the insurrection of 1525 remain to be more closely defined. The following considerations seem to me relevant to their closer definition.

(1) One of the virtues of Sabean's work on Upper Swabia is to have emphasised the tensions within the villages between prosperous and poor peasants. This suggests the question as to how intra-village tensions related to the pressures of lords on villages or groups within villages. One would suspect that princes or landlords would use intra-village tensions to justify authoritative intrusion in the affairs of the village. One might also expect to find instances of *ad hoc* alliances of convenience between the overlords and the village poor against village notables.

(2) Pitz has argued that late-medieval agriculture moved in the direction of rationalisation and market orientation (Pitz, 1965: 355–67). If this generalisation is accurate and applicable to the enterprises of the prominent in the insurrection, then the question may be asked as to the significance of the economic character of substantial peasant agriculture in producing the insurrection. Perhaps an economically more advanced agriculture made the peasantry particularly resentful of the imposition of manorial or princely burdens which were both heavy and irregular, and thus disruptive of the rational planning which now had a larger place in the operation of substantial peasant farms. The incompatible needs of predominantly subsistence and predominantly market-orientated agriculture might also be seen behind the conflicts within the village on the use of common lands. If there is anything to these hypotheses, they would indicate that the explosive juxtaposition of capitalist and pre-capitalist economic forms can be found within the peasant village, and without invoking the bourgeoisie.

This essay does not pretend to account for the whole of the insurrection of 1525–6, which, once under way, set into flames every local and regional grievance. The urban revolts in the north-west, the special influence of the mining populations in Thuringia and the southern Tyrol, and much else are not touched. Nor does this brief and hypothetical sketch pretend to be a substitute for the detailed research on the social and economic conditions in the areas with which it does deal. Such extensive research has not yet been done, but the recent, suggestive monograph by Sabean has shown that detailed analysis of the rural economy and social structure which the great Frenchmen have made us familiar with for the seventeenth and eighteenth centuries are possible in fifteenth-century Germany, albeit with less precision and more necessity for resort to hypothetical assumptions (cf. Sabean, 1972, ch. 4). Such an approach, I think, promises to take the discussion of the Peasant War out of familiar paths and on to fresher terrain.

HEIKO A. OBERMAN

4 *The Gospel of Social Unrest* *

In spite of intensive research, it has proved difficult to set aside terms
and concepts that have been current since the time of the Reformation.
Thus we continue to speak without further reflection of the *German*
Peasant War, although this limitation has long since proved untenable.
For a period of almost two centuries the so-called *tumultus rusticorum,*
best translated as 'social unrest' or 'countryside agitation', was a
phenomenon which extended across all of Europe, from Italy to the
Low Countries and from southern France to Bohemia.

We also continue to speak of the *Peasant* War even when our sources
suggest that the term *rustici* must be used in a more differentiated way
and be defined as 'country folk' or, when viewed from the humanist
perspective, be translated as 'uneducated' or 'simple folk'. Furthermore,
throughout the later Middle Ages and in the first twenty years of the
sixteenth century, part of the urban population pursued the same
political and social goals as the peasants. These townspeople not only
offered the peasants 'solidarity', as it is often put, but they decisively
participated in and supported the consequent revolutionary movement.
Hence we find in the *Artikelbriefe,* or peasant manifestos, the common
political platform of town and country. We read in one *Artikelbrief*
that the poor must suffer under 'great hardship (burdens) which are
contrary to God and all justice. These burdens are placed upon the
poor by secular and sacred authorities in *city and country*' (Kaczerowsky,
1970: 15). The Muhlhausen Articles of September 1524 demand the
reform of the city council at the urging of 'the weavers (of St Jacob)
and other craftsmen in various city districts' (Franz and Fuchs, 1942:
47, No. 1128). The Erfurt Articles of 9 May 1525 are the result of a
meeting of 'all craftsmen belonging to the various districts of the city
of Erfurt to discuss the need for social reform' (Luther, *Werke*, vol.
18: 534).

Particularly in this sensitive area of research, ideological considerations tend to obscure our grasp of historical reality. Historians from

*A German version appeared as follows: Heiko A. Oberman, 1974,
'Tumultus Rusticorum: Vom "Klosterkrieg" zum Fürstensieg', *Zeitschrift für
Kirchengeschichte,* 85, pp. 157–72.

East Germany emphasise the Peasant War as a *German* event because they want to be able to compete for historical glory with the French and Russian Revolutions. In regard to the *Peasant* War as an affair of town and country, however, Marxist research with its ideological presuppositions has indeed the edge. It is not Marxism but National Socialism that has most distorted the proper perspective. In the Nazi effort to play the *völkische* peasants off against the *klassenkämpferische* workers, Hitler is presented as the fulfilment of the Peasant Revolt (Franz, 1933: 481).

Finally, the expression Peasant *War* covers no more than that military phase which developed only after May 1524 (Forchheim, 16 May), with its dual climax in Muhlhausen on 25 May 1525 and the flight of Gaismair a year later on 2 July 1526 (Waas, 1964: 38). But the roots of this movement had long been present in European history as a non-violent impulse for reform, as what might be called 'the Gospel of Social Unrest'. Indeed, it is true that the early 1520s saw a radicalisation across the board. The fundamental Reformation concepts of 'freedom' (*Freiheit*) and the 'Priesthood of all believers' (*Priestertum aller Gläubigen*) became slogans that electrified and mobilised peasants everywhere. But Luther and the Reformation are merely accelerators. Far from freeing the soul by means of a sublimation of worldly *gravamina*, as Marx, Engels and Marcuse have put it, the Wittenberg and Zurich Reformations brought a clearly traceable tone of impatience into the political petitions and polemical pamphlets of the time.

The pre-Reformation rebellious 'hordes' (*Haufen*) and 'mobs' (*Rotten*) had appealed to the old common law and rights. They congregated around preachers of repentance who summoned the people to prepare for the coming Kingdom of Peace. They banked on a non-violent reform from above. Hence *conversio cordis* and *patientia mentis* were extolled as the most prominent virtues, i.e. a personal disposition of penance and a patient awaiting of the coming Kingdom of Peace and Justice.

The new ferment of reformation implied political radicalisation by a biblical and spiritual opposition to the secular power of the Church, with its tax privileges in both city and country and its Rome-orientated economic policies. Yet, during the time of the so-called Peasant *War*, peasant leaders repeatedly and explicitly distanced themselves from any use of violence, while, on the other hand, long *before* Luther's call to reformation, armed clashes were frequent. There were other rebellions in 1478 (Salzburg), 1489/90 and 1513/15 (Swiss Confederation), 1499 and 1502 (Vorlande), 1514 (Württemberg, 'Poor Conrad'), and 1520 (Tyrol, planned) (cf. Stolze, 1926: 39–40). It is true that the problem of the use or non-use of violence did not become thematic until after the rebellions of 1512–13 in rural and urban areas – from Deventer to Regensburg and from Swabia to Saxony – when the call for godly justice had fully taken the place of the old common laws and rights. The term 'War' is an overdramatisation that distorts our historical perspective and tends to isolate the events of 1525.

Therefore, in all its three parts, the term 'German Peasant War' is to be used with caution and according to its differing contexts.

II THE NEW HORIZON OF EXPECTATION

When we make the difficult, but for our modern understanding necessary, attempt to distinguish within the maze of programmes and tendencies of this epoch between reform attempts and revolutionary movements, we have to point to the changed horizon of expectation. On the eve of the Reformation an important change took place. Earlier the appeal to old common law and custom against the irresistible spreading of centrally administered territories, the precursors of our modern states, was a cry of distress and a plea for help from those below to those above. This plea was grounded in a trust in the authorities which, given the circumstances, remains for a long time surprisingly shock-resistant.

However, where the appeal to the new godly law penetrates, the injustice experienced because of unbearable tax burdens, encroachment on the common pasture land and further disenfranchisement of free men starts to spark off intensified reflection and action. At this point we have left the plane of longing for *restitutio* and for a return to the multiple forms of an earlier, regional autonomy. We now hit upon a new awareness of all men being equal under the just will of God, which is seen as equally binding, embracing and obligatory for the entire society: city and country, peasants and city dwellers, ecclesiastical and civil authorities. What had been operative in the self-understanding and legislation of both imperial city and city-state for two centuries, namely the joint and equal responsibility of all citizens and residents to the will of God, caused tangible reverberations among the rural population in the last decades before the Reformation.

One can concur with earlier research which held that the German city riots of the year 1513–15 are to be traced back to peasant disturbances. It is to be borne in mind, however, that the basic structure of the peasants' programme did not arise *ex nihilo* in the country. Instead, their programme is rooted in the idea of the God-willed balance between rights and duties which had long been tested in the cities (Moeller, 1962: 33; Kiessling, 1971: 126 and cf. 312, 360).

It has been argued that the peasants were too unrealistic in their dreams about a new society with justice for all. The one point of criticism in Marxist studies on Muntzer is that he was utopian in his aspirations. But we would be missing the point if we regarded the appeal to godly law and the vision of an ideal rural state as political utopianism. The designation 'utopian' is a mere *vaticinium ex eventu*, a prophesy from hindsight. This is as ludicrous as dismissing the ideals of the late-medieval city-state with its religious covenant-theology as a utopian dream, merely because in the 1530s the city-state could no longer extricate itself from the clutches of the princes' absolutism (cf. Brady, 1973: 20). It would be just as unfounded to deny the rural people of the territories the realistic demand to align their living conditions, in the realm of existing political and economic possibilities, with the tested judicial structures of the city. In the *Bundschuh* movement, for example, the freedoms of the cities – with their own election of pastors, their tax and market privileges – provided a realistic basis for incorporating its concept of freedom in the sense of a covenant community interpreted according to the Old Testament. This occurred years before Luther's fundamental Reformation writing, *The Freedom of a Christian*, had been printed and rapidly and widely circulated.

Here we touch upon another assertion that even today haunts the literature on the Peasant War. It is felt that Luther gave birth to the idea of freedom, but that this idea was then misunderstood by the peasants. This interpretation is based on the earliest Counter-Reformation propaganda, which even predates Cochlaeus. How such a misunderstanding was possible has been reconstructed by Hans Hiller-brand (1972: 118 ff.). It argues that the revolutionary Luther, with his pseudo-prophetic sense of calling and his impatient attitude towards Church and Pope, could not but evoke *tumultus*, social unrest and subversive action. In the humanist circles influenced by Erasmus, it was exactly this charge which prepared for the break of many humanists with Luther, years before Erasmus publicly attacked Luther in his 1524 treatise on 'The Freedom of the Will'. Since 1521 *tumultus*, not only as *Uffrur* but more generally as 'agitation', to an increasing extent is reason for concern on the part of the city fathers (cf. Naujoks, 1958: 56). This kind of propaganda did not come unexpectedly. As early as 1521, when the first rumours about armed mobs reached Wittenberg, Luther forecasts that he and his interpretation of the Gospel will be held responsible for the revolutionary freedom movements.

Our modern resources grant us a better insight into the social status and educational level of the peasant leaders and *Rottenpastoren* (usually leadership did not emerge from the peasant class, but from the pastors, nobles, artisans and innkeepers; cf. Gerlach, 1969: 144–75; Endres, 1974: 162f.). It has thus become highly improbable that the peasants either warped Luther's ideas or deluded themselves about them. This is especially clear when one bears in mind that for over a century the *libertas christiana* had been a current issue and a central question in pub and market-place. With the peasants, Luther's concept of freedom did not fall into a vacuum to be distorted by their fanatical enthusiasm. For those who no longer expected reform from the feudal establishment, the higher obedience towards the *iustitia Dei* had already started to imply freedom from the 'old law' obligations in dealing with temporal authorities. There the ground had long been prepared by 'the Gospel of Social Unrest'.

That does not mean, however, that Luther functioned as nothing more than a catalyst. Whereas Reformation research likes to present Luther as a biblical scholar who influenced people through his publications, Luther at that time functions primarily as a symbol, a beacon, a sign of the times, a means to read the timetable of God. Admittedly a shift *did* take place: the appeal to godly justice is transformed into an explicit appeal to the Gospel, which, as it is put, is now at last proclaimed clearly and without additions. Further, Luther's proclamation of the priesthood of all believers highlighted the contrast between the justice of God and the existing inequality between the priests and the laity and provided a rationale for abolishing this inequality (Kaczerowsky, 1970: 10).

The right to free election of pastors is not a new demand (Kurze, 1966: 465f., 471f.). It is now, however, clearly founded on Reformation principles. According to the Twelve Articles, a pastor has to be elected who will proclaim the Gospel on the basis of Scripture alone (Kaczerowsky, 1970: 10). And that means here: a Gospel not moulded in the cast of canon law. In a parallel context, from the side of the cities, the Hallenser Articles of 6 May 1525 state that every congregation should be allowed to call a minister, since Christ has freely proclaimed the Gospel and has 'made us free to know it' (Franz and Fuchs, 1942: 216f., No. 1345). This freedom, intended by God for all men, to elect a pastor and to hear the Gospel, joins with a third demand: the civic incorporation of clerics, i.e. the end of their extra-legal status, which later is put into practice in the cities won for the Reformation (Moeller, 1972a: 195–224; 1972b).

Friedrich Engels, the historical engineer of Marxism, has advanced the thesis that the resistance by the cities to feudalism was a merely conservative opposition, the conservative heresy, as he called it (Engels, 1970: 48f.). The real opposition was the radical heresy of the peasants. He argues that the bourgeois heresy deviates from the plebeian heresy because of the different economic conditions and hence motivations. It seems to me crucial, however, to see that for both town *and* country it is godly justice and not merely economic betterment that provides the key for the basic propulsion and highest motivation. Both see godly justice as the guiding line, indeed as the law for Church *and* society. One of its major characteristics compared with later conceptions of justice is the inner connection between *iustitia coram Deo* and *iustitia coram hominibus* between the vertical and horizontal dimensions of justice. This city ideology provides the breeding ground for the early reformed tradition by virtue of its emphasis on the idea of covenant and an ethic of common rights and duties (Endres, 1974: 160).

Yet it is by no means the achievement of the Reformation to have first exported this urban theology beyond the city walls to the villages and the countryside. The desire of the peasants for social change is based on ideas which were indigenous and vital to the late-medieval city long before it had been influenced by the Reformation.

Admittedly, the effort to put these models, determined by the 'justice of God' concept, into practice also in the countryside was to be frustrated by the prevailing political, economic and cultural conditions there. As a reaction, these attempts often led to a return to the city, as in the case of Tabor, Munster and Geneva. Conversely, since the beginning of the seventeenth century we can note time and again 'a trek into the wilderness' which in the case of the poor German country folk, becomes 'a trek into the Americas'.

Animosity against the cities is often said to be a major thrust in the peasants' programme. One can indeed point to some peasant writings of that time, particularly to Gaismair's appeal to remove the walls of the cities and make them into villages (cf. Gaismair's *Landesordnung* in Kaczerowsky, 1970: 79). This evidence does not, however, contradict the fact that the peasants claimed the urban freedoms and privileges for themselves. When Gaismair calls for the destruction of the city walls, this is the necessary response to the challenge of a city unwilling to extend its human rights to the countryside, thus hoarding the treasures meant for all. To use Engels's terminology, the conservative heresy is to be found just as much with the peasants, in so far as they were motivated by anti-urban tendencies. To sum up: the programmes of the peasants which aimed purely at re-establishing the past were not realised and were, in hindsight, reactionary. The later history of social emancipation, e.g. in the battle for freedom in the Netherlands, shows that a movement based on the idea of godly justice can become political reality only when it joins forces with the emancipatory tradition of urban rights.

III   THE PEASANT WAR IN THREE CONTEMPORARY TESTIMONIES

The collections of documents on which our picture of the Peasant War is based deal mainly with the events of 1525. This is understandable since this year represents the final phase of the war, with the princes' expedition to level punishment on the peasants as its spectacular climax. But because of this limitation in the selection of sources, essential impulses from the early stages have remained unconsidered.

Perhaps the earliest attempt to understand the Peasant War historically by placing it in the history of the Reformation was made by Desiderius Erasmus. For him the history of the Reformation up to 1525 is a drama in three acts. The first is the campaign of humanism; the second the battle around Luther; and the third and final act is the armed clash between the princes and the peasants: *prodierunt in scenam nobiles et agricolae*. For the humanist from Rotterdam, however, this is not merely a chronological succession of three acts, but rather a spiritual descent towards catastrophe. After the main event of the century, the rebirth of the *studia humanitatis*, there follows the rough, uncouth battle over religious doctrine. According to Erasmus, the intemperate Luther had kindled this fight, which consequently, and because of him, grew into a fiery and bloody confrontation (Allen, 1926, VI: 153).

As if at a central newsdesk, Erasmus in his European correspondence is able to survey and assess the entire complicated situation. Thus his assessment of the motives present in this drama is of particular significance. Although taking part only as a 'spectator' (Lötscher, 1943: 234–6), he shows understanding for the unbearable economic position of the peasants. He views the Peasant War not as a rebellion against the princes and secular authority, but as resistance provoked by monastic exploitation:

> Monks are roughly treated in many places, no doubt because many are insufferable, others because they cannot be corrected by other means. They are provided with too many privileges, too many exemptions . . . Although it seems terrible that the peasants destroyed certain monasteries, the wickedness of the latter provoked them to it, since they could not be controlled by law. (Allen, 1926: 156–7)

It is a reaction against the evil doings of the monks who enjoy their privileges and seem to be beyond the control of law.

In short sentences, Erasmus sketches 'the state of the nation' as follows: the Franciscans and Dominicans have been expelled from 's-Hertogenbosch, the capital of Brabant; in Antwerp, despite prohibition by king, regent and rural magistrate, 'hedge-sermons (*Hagepreken*)' are being held outside the city walls; the majority of the people in Holland, Zeeland and Flanders are driven by hatred of the monks (ibid.: 155). Spurred on by Luther's writings, the rebels have brought about a situation which is now completely out of control. Urban culture is mortally threatened.

In Germany, according to Erasmus, a similar fury against the monks has erupted. The cloisters of nuns and monks have been destroyed. The magistracy intervenes in some places to moderate things by introducing a stricter control of the cloisters, but it too is of the opinion that the monks are a pest, no longer to be endured (ibid.: 150). On 5 September 1525, the tumult of war has come so close to Erasmus's study in Basel that he can hear the cries of the wounded. The bloody end is near. The peasants are drowning in their own blood. Then he comments cautiously, but with scarcely veiled criticism: 'The princes react with the usual measures – I fear that they only increase the misery' (ibid.: 160; Lötscher, 1943: 236).

In contact with humanist, i.e. urban circles, Erasmus has seen the Peasant War from the perspective of a city dweller. Averse to everything which threatens his academic peace, especially when it develops into tumult, he sees his cause, that of the *bonae literae*, endangered. The basis and responsibility for this, however, do not lie with the people (*infima plebs*), but rather with the monks and their intolerable claims. For Erasmus, the Peasant War is a *Pfaffenkrieg*, i.e. a war against the priests and cloisters. In Erasmus's opinion the war is an understandable, in its motivation justified, rebellion by city and country. In responding to it, the city magistrates have reacted more reasonably (*moderatius*) than the princes, who do not appear as a party until the last phase of the war.

Erasmus's perspective from the city distorts the picture. In the country not only cloisters but also castles and manor houses were stormed as symbols of subjugation. Nevertheless, his perspective offers a correction of our contemporary tendency to view the Peasant War mainly as a war against princes and nobles. Erasmus's interpretation should thus not be ignored. Erasmus's judgement for the initial phase of the Peasant War is relevant and noteworthy in spite of all its local peculiarities throughout the Low Countries and Germany. In contrast to his friend Bonifatius Amerbach, who sees in the peasants only murderers using the Gospel merely as a pretext (Hartmann, 1947, III: 18; Lötscher: 220), Erasmus does not hesitate to emphasise that the complaints (*gravamina*) of the peasants are legitimate. But, in the last analysis, it is for him the cause of the *bonae literae* which is the most important. This cause stands or falls with the *pax Christi*, with peace and order, which is now being threatened in a diabolical way. He could have taken over without alteration the concluding sentence of Amerbach's report: 'If God does not squash this revolt, we shall all perish' (Hartmann, 1947, III: 19).

Another contemporary document grants us a close-up of the military situation, and is one of the first reactions to the Twelve Articles of the Peasants, the upper-Swabian manifesto which became a prototype for the articles of the peasants all over Germany (de Vocht, 1928: 417f.).

This source is a letter of April 1525 to Rutger Rescius from the ambassador of Margrave Philip of Baden, commissioned to report to the regent of the Netherlands, Margaret of Parma, about the situation in southern Germany. The ambassador emphasises how numerous the Swabian peasants are – 120,000 with daily additions; how disciplined – 600 officers; how pious – with daily sermons by many chaplains; and how self-confident. He writes further that it is assumed that they have made solemn alliances with many cities. They could even afford to refuse an offer of alliance from Duke Ulrich of Wurttemberg. They wish to have nothing to do with the duke, since he has only his own, worldly interests in mind, whereas they themselves represent the 'cause of the Gospel and Christian freedom'.

In this report, with its assessment of the Twelve Articles, three points are of prime importance. (1) The Articles demand justice not only for the peasants, but explicitly also for other Christians. (2) The Articles are aimed against the Church, the bishops and prelates, with only a few directed against the princes. (3) The attempts by the bishops and princes to raise an army have failed because no one was prepared to run the risk of having to kill family members, their own flesh and blood.

This diplomatic report certainly brings us closer to the real situation than we are allowed from the perspective of Erasmus's armchair assessment. Indeed, the judgement of both agree that the goals of the programme for change went beyond the concerns of the peasants themselves, and that, above all, these goals signify a religious revolt against the ecclesiastical establishment. Furthermore, the diplomat does not see the Peasant War as a regional rural rebellion, but as a revolt by both city and country which is well-organised and, by means of a successful policy of alliance, has been made both secure and unstoppable. He sees it as apparently unstoppable because, according to his view, it is not simply a *Pfaffenkrieg* directed against the monks, but a civil war which sets citizen against citizen and brother against brother.

Our correspondent obviously wants to present and report his data free of value judgements. He is impressed by the seriousness of the peasants in practising the *negotium Evangelii*. At one point he reveals his own standpoint when he writes that the peasants boast (*sese iactitant*) that they are evangelical. But his view is characteristic in that he does not regard the peasants as a blind rabble led by the Devil, but much more as sober and secular; he envisages a revolutionary project with a considerable chance of success. This document warns us not to view the Peasant Revolt as a utopian movement which from the beginning was destined to fail. In many areas it was touch and go. If the Emperor's troops had not been available after the victory at Pavia, the balance of power would have looked different; and if the trend towards centralism, which was favourable for the princes, should have been politically weakened, German parochialism would have been a stumbling block not only in the path of the peasants.

Finally, we turn to a third document, written by one of the peasants' leaders. It is an evaluation of the final phase of the Peasant War. Written by Christoph Schappeler in Memmingen on 2 May 1525 and directed to Zwingli, it brings us even closer to the event itself. Schappeler, co-author of the Twelve Articles, shows himself to be well informed concerning the abuses in the country. Far better than anyone else known to us from that time, he penetrates the psyche of the underprivileged class and describes with a gripping rhetoric what it means for the peasant to have to groan under crushing tax burdens (Zwingli, *Werke*, 1914, VIII, 2 (Köhler): 325). When he tends to be more critical of the movement, it is on the basis of his own observations and because of his involvement in the revolt from its very beginning. Schappeler's new attitude over against the consequences of the Twelve

Articles cannot yet have been occasioned by Luther's 'Admonition to Peace on the Twelve Articles'. What he describes is the radicalisation of, in principle, a fully justified resistance.

From close quarters, he reports how the poor people were torn by conflicting claims of obedience to God, to the civil and ecclesiastical authorities and to their feudal lords, who were hostile to the Gospel (ibid.: 325). They decided, however, to obey God more than men. But when the resistance developed into a blind destructiveness, no trace of the Gospel was to be found any more. After they initiated bloodbaths and destruction, their appeal to 'justice' became a pretext (*praetextus*) and an attempt at self-justification.

In the apocalyptic end of the revolt, Schappeler sees a just punishment for all because, as he says: we, the leaders of the revolt, have sinned against Jesus Christ in that we have 'embraced the Gospel and doctrine of salvation impatiently and clumsily'. We have used the Gospel *sinistre et impatienter* for our own needs (ibid.: 326; Lötscher, 1943: 230 and n. 61).

As a man of the moderate centre and a man of the first hour, Schappeler is outflanked by the 'left' because, as he sees it, the peasants have ignored the conditions stipulated in the final clause of the Twelve Articles. 'Wol man vns mit dem Wort Gots für vnzimlich anzaigen, wolt wyr daruon abston . . .' (Kaczerowsky, 1970: 14): 'We do not want to use force but are prepared to cede to anyone who can prove us wrong on the basis of Scripture.' When the Articles are no longer a basis for negotiation, but rather a programme which must be pushed through immediately and with violence, one proceeds *sinistre* and *impatienter*.

According to Schappeler's interpretation, the Peasant Revolt is programmatically a justified movement for liberation, grounded in Christian doctrine. In its concluding phase, however, it degenerates into an economic battle and a war of interests. The fault for this lies not with the monks or princes, but with the peasants' impatience which threatens to transform southern Germany into a Sodom and Gomorrah, into a place of destruction as a sign of God's wrath in the last days (Zwingli, *Werke*, 1914, VIII: 326). We pray for forgiveness and ask that we who started because of faith will not perish without it.

IV   IUSTITIAE PRAETEXTU: JUSTICE AS PRETEXT OR MOTIVE

Now we turn to our final question. Do the Twelve Articles, as has been argued from Friedrich Engels to Hans Hillerbrand, present a social programme in religious dress which we can strip off so that we are left with a hard core of economic interests? I believe not. Rather, what initially was not a pretext, but a genuine and original motive rooted in a knowledge of the justice of God, could not be realised. The original vision of justice for all collapsed under the weight of ungovernable fanaticism. Schappeler's prayer is at the same time an assessment: 'God forbid that the formerly righteous should perish as unbelievers.'

No other contemporary document and no modern presentation confronts the reader so directly with the awesome turn from initial hope to final, terrible shock. Neither fact-filled diplomatic dispatches nor the armchair wisdom of a scholar can, it seems, replace daily, direct contact with the combatants themselves.

According to its own sources, the Peasant War was a religious revolt of people in town and country who, on the basis of godly justice, pressed for improved social conditions. And they did so not only for the benefit of one social group, but for the benefit of 'all Christians'.

The accusation of a merely simulated thirst for godly justice, *iustitiae praetextu*, was raised in one form or another during that time by each party against the other: against the old believers, the Lutherans, the anabaptists and finally against the peasants themselves. Modern research has made significant progress due to its recognition of the genuine motives of the parties concerned, but this is a task which is yet to be undertaken as far as the Peasant War is concerned. We are quite aware that our emphasis on Schappeler's letter and on the diplomatic dispatch, more than Erasmus's report of the situation, can give rise to the suspicion that one is trying to interpret the entire Peasant War from a limited, regional viewpoint. As a justified correction in this regard, we can accept Hans Hillerbrand's thesis that

> there can be little doubt that the famous Twelve Articles convey an utterly erroneous picture of the relationship between the Reformation and the peasant uprising. The bulk of the peasant documents does not echo the sentiment of that document. The majority of the grievances are concretely economic or social' (Hillerbrand, 1972: 125).

The main thrust of present research is oriented towards economic and social history, hence providing an insight into a large number of elements that go into the making of history. Yet this should not tempt us to permit biblical ideas, Christian apocalyptic ferment and the horizon of religious expectation on the part of the rebels to be relegated to the background, since it is only through these means that the birth and spread of the Peasant War are to be understood.

In its differing expressions, varying from Luther and Carlstadt to Muntzer and Hut, the Reformation movement attempted to influence, to strengthen or to regulate the religious factor operative in the long history of social agitation in town and countryside, to redirect 'the Gospel of Social Unrest' (Oberman, 1973: 205–14). The term 'religious factor' is open to the charge that it is used in a modern and thereby anachronistic way when it is not clearly seen that at that time the religious factor reaches far into the other domains of life, so that social conditions and factors are also included. We have noticed the cohesion between horizontal and vertical justice. The two most prominent religious traditions, apocalypticism and mysticism, go even further in making it a programmatic point to fuse the outer and the inner orders, the world of the soul and the world of the senses. The so-called 'religious factors' then embraced a much larger range of experience than applies for most of us today. Yet, it cannot be denied that there is a second sphere not covered by the religious factor. Not only Luther, but also Schappeler and Muntzer, speak of a development in the programme and action of the peasants which is no longer in tune with the Christian faith. The religious factor itself, however, is for all three so much an uncontested category and a common criterion that the purely social demands of the peasants are characterised with surprising unanimity as *que sua sunt querunt*, 'the self-serving quest for gain'. By all three this is regarded as the selling-out of God's cause.

The characterisation of the Peasant War implicit in the condensed formula *iustitiae praetextu*, under the cloak of righteousness, is therefore not only an out-group judgement, conditioned by ignorance or class distance. It is also an in-group self-analysis and self-criticism which stems from a mixture of disappointment and solidarity.

In its initial thrust and programme, the so-called Peasant War is for both its moderate critics and its radical leaders basically a religious movement. It seems to me that we have no right to question this any more than in the case of the movements originating in Wittenberg, Geneva and Trent. This conclusion itself is not unimportant *vis-à-vis* Marxist interpretations in eastern Europe and a recent sociological trend in Reformation history in the United States. But beyond this, there are two more points to which I want to draw attention by way of conclusion. I have found it a sound rule for my own work to illustrate a historical movement on the basis of its extremes, but to interpret it from its mean. In our case this rule helps us to see that Thomas Muntzer serves as an excellent illustration of the apocalypticism on the edges of 'the Gospel of Social Unrest'. Except for the very last stages of the uprising, he remains a marginal figure who would never have played such a prominent role in our modern presentations if he had not been singled out for attack by Luther's verbal bombardment. If any single figure should be named, it is not Muntzer but Hus, who fathered the movement both in its moderate and more radical manifestations. For the bloody climax not only the monks, the princes, and to an extent Martin Luther, but also Muntzer has to carry part of the responsibility. In his hands, and because of his apocalyptic impatience and misreading of the eschatological timetable, 'the Gospel of Social Unrest' became transformed into the assembly call for the elect, for the children of righteousness to take up arms in the final battle against the children of darkness and wrath.

The enormous religious potential in an extensive lower-middle-class layer of society in central Europe was squandered. This potential proved to be badly missing when, half a century later, it was most needed, at a time when the religious impetus of the Reformation and Counter-Reformation movements issued in a new scholasticism. That seems to me the real drama in what we misleadingly call the German Peasant War.

FRANCIS RAPP

5 The Social and Economic Prehistory of the Peasant War in Lower Alsace*

This article poses the following questions:

(1) Was Lower Alsace overpopulated, and were the peasants short of land?
(2) Were the peasants in any way able to take part in the economic boom that occurred in the towns on the Upper Rhine?
(3) If the answer to the second question is yes, then we must pose another: were there exceptions, or set-backs? If so, how did these difficulties work themselves out?
(4) Finally, what connections can we discern between these economic and social expectations of the population and the uprisings that occurred prior to 1525?

It is based on research in the *Archives departmentales du Bas-Rhin* and the *Archives municipales de Strasbourg*, *Archives de l'Hôpital de Strasbourg*, and the archive of the *Sankt-Thomas-Kapitel*, Strasbourg; detailed references to these may be found in the original German text.

I

If I am not mistaken, then the documents that I have consulted would lead me to suppose that in the half-century before the great uprising of 1525, peasants and wine-growers in Lower Alsace were not short of land. There is hardly a trace of overpopulation in the records: rather the opposite seems closer to the truth. It is generally thought that deserted areas were a sign of population stagnation. Shortly before the Peasant War of 1525, we still hear of such deserted settlements, even if they are no longer so widespread a phenomenon at this late date. In the Kochersberg region alone two settlements come to mind. Ittlenheim, in which two houses were still inhabited in 1508 and which was not totally deserted until a number of years later; Kleinatzenheim, some-

---

*Translated with edited references from F. Rapp, 'Die soziale und wirtschaftliche Vorgeschichte des Bauernkrieges in Unterelsass', in *Bauernkriegs-Studien* (ed. B. Moeller), Gütersloh, 1975, pp. 29–45.

what closer to Strassburg, where at the same time there was at least one family still living and which was no longer marked on Specklin's regional map of 1576 (Humm, 1971: 124, 126).

Yet the phenomenon of deserted settlements does not indicate a particularly significant reduction in population, and it is now thought that the former inhabitants of deserted villages and hamlets migrated to larger and safer fortified settlements in the region. Concentration of population is thus used to explain the disappearance of numerous small settlements in wine-growing areas of Lower Alsace (Humm, 1971: 45). If this is the case, then the population of still existing settlements should have been relatively high at the beginning of the sixteenth century. But not even this can be clearly affirmed from the sparse records that remain. At the foot of the Vosges in the shadow of the Odilienberg lie the villages of Ottrott and St Nabor. In the former, the 1525 fine was levied on 16 hearths, and in the latter on 10. Somewhat to the north lay Marlenheim and Nordheim with considerably more people comprising 77 to 80 hearths or houses respectively. However, neighbouring Kirchheim only had 21 houses. In the rich ploughland of the Kochersberg region, Hohatzenheim only had 28 hearths in 1453, and thirty years later this was even reduced to 23 (Humm, 1971: 37). Very close to Strassburg, at Itenheim, the town authorities swore in only 36 adult males. Strikingly high population figures were available only for a few villages lying to the north of Strassburg, such as Weyersheim zum Turm with 300 houses, or Wantzenau with 200 houses, just like Honau on the other side of the Rhine. Inside walled settlements such as Brumath and Neuweiler, there were 200 and 150 houses (Humm, 1971: 38).

One could indeed object that these population figures are nevertheless relatively high, if one takes into account the productive capacity of the agrarian economy at that time. The land did not produce enough even for the meagre population that existed. But if this were the case then all the suitable land available would have been cultivated as fully as possible. Yet the records often give evidence of waste fields called *egerden*, even in the fertile Kochersberg region. In 1512 at Breuschtal, which admittedly had little fertile land, the diocesan administration was even forced to intervene. They issued a decree deploring the fact that Breuschtal had turned into an area of waste fields since many of its former inhabitants had become huntsmen and woodmen. Consequently they ordered every peasant who kept a horse to sow a field each with winter and summer cereals. Peasants with two horses were ordered to cultivate twice the amount of land and so on. 'But he who has no arable or horse shall clear wood or scrubland.'

The bailiff was ordered to confiscate uncultivated fields and apportion them out to more hard-working tenants. The possibility of living on wild-life and fish from water and woodland was correspondingly curtailed. In a substantial region, land was therefore so uncultivated that the authorities found it necessary to legislate against this. The valley concerned was admittedly rather inaccessible and possibly less attractive, but if the population of the more inviting lowlands had indeed increased substantially, then surely some of this surplus would have found its way into the upland valleys.

In those settlements nearest to the larger towns there were clear signs of heavy demographic concentration. The citizenship records of Strassburg contain very many names of peasant sons, but also older people who had made their ploughs over to their heirs and settled inside the town wall (Wittmer-Meyer, 1948–61, docs. 6309, 7815). They added to the steady flow of immigrants into the town who came from the most varied of south German districts, above all from Swabia. Yet we must remember that not all Swabian immigrants became town-dwellers. They also settled in the villages. In hamlet (*Flecken*) Westhoffen, near Molsheim, at the end of the fifteenth century there lived a certain Michel Snyder from Ulm, and a few years later a certain Balthazar from Dinkelsbuhl. In the wine-growers' township of Borsch, south of Westhoffen, people from Esslingen had settled at about the same time. If rural settlements attracted immigrants like this, then we may suppose that they were not yet overpopulated. Those laymen and clerics, craftsmen and farm labourers who came from a seemingly overpopulated region like Swabia especially seem to have regarded Alsace as a land of opportunity (Rapp, 1974: 313f.).

As an aspect of the relative population density I would also finally like to examine horizontal mobility. Not only was it in the towns that inhabitants had often not been born or brought up, but frequently also in villages and markets, peasants, wine-growers and craftsmen were immigrants. If we return to Westhoffen, we encounter, apart from the Swabian Diebold from Boersch, Cuntz from Mosbach, Peter Appenzeller, Hans from Stollhofen and Gangolf from Brechlingen. We could also find similar examples for settlements in regions of arable farming. There seemed to be something unstable about the peasantry, a trend which the authorities regarded with mixed feelings. Their attitude was that in order to provide more effective supervision, subjects were to remain tied to specific pieces of land. Nothing good could come from travelling folk, beggars and mercenaries.

Where there is room to move about, there is still spare space. At the beginning of the sixteenth century, Lower Alsace was not heavily populated. So it is highly unlikely that any shortage of land caused the Alsace peasantry to rebel.

II

We may thus assume that, on the whole, the country people had enough land at their disposal. But was it still enough to live on – and how?

As regards subsistence farming which had no contact with marketing, the records say little that is specific. Yet there were at least two areas in Lower Alsace where there was definite agrarian production for the market. This applied above all to the wine-growing region which stretched alongside the Voges, from Landgraben in the south to the Palatinate in the north, and to the east into the foothills of Kochersberg between Breusch and Zor. At no other period in the history of Alsace was the area of wine-growing so large as around the year 1500 (Barth, 1959: 39). In the vicinity of Molsheim, in Sulz and Wolxheim it was difficult to find tenants to take on arable to pay the *Etter* tithe, since all land that was not completely infertile was devoted to viticulture. The region had thus developed its own monoculture.

The second area which was closely integrated into a market economy was the 'ploughland', comprising above all, though not exclusively, the Kochersberg district to the east of the wine-growing foothills (Rapp, 1967). The figures given in peasants' contracts from this district show that two thirds of the sown land was devoted to wheat. There was a third region of cattle and pasture producing for a market to the north-east of Strassburg. This has hardly been researched into, and we can only mention it here briefly. We will restrict ourselves to wine and cereals, which provided the greatest volume of trade.

How did the peasants and wine-growers produce any surplus? Did consumption at home together with the various rents, interest payments, tithes and taxes swallow up the lion's share of what grew in the fields and vineyards? Of course, it is highly speculative to attempt a clear answer to these questions. Yet there are a number of points that can be made to clarify the problems posed. The average vineyard produced fifteen to twenty measures (*Ohm*) of wine. The average ploughland usually produced about two quarters (*Viertel*) of cereals, wheat or rye. Records of tenancy contracts specify the number of pieces of land, and whether they are freehold or leasehold. Those fields which the landlord held as heritable fields were assessed only lightly for the rent, which seldom exceeded 2 pfennig of Strassburg currency. A measure of wine cost 35 pfennig on average, and a quarter of wheat was worth at least the same. Most of the land was owned by nobles, rich burghers and above all the Church. But before the Peasant War this land was seldom farmed with paid labourers and serf labour service. The accounts of farm managers and bailiffs show that such farms seldom made profits, and sometimes even made losses. Most landowners rented out their land on conditions that varied according to whether it was for production of cereal or viticulture. Wine-growers demanded long-term contracts, usually with fixed rents over twenty years.

In order to be able to meet his obligations, the tenant often received a loan in advance from his new landlord, who in return was guaranteed the opportunity of first purchase on a fixed amount of the wine that was eventually produced. As regards the rent, it was usually just under four measures per field, or about one quarter of the average harvest.

The tenancy contracts in the Kochersberg wheat-growing district tell much the same story. Half a quarter of cereals were usually demanded as rent in kind (Rapp, 1967: 444). But most contracts were for shorter periods than in the wine-growing region. Of 142 contracts, 99 were for nine years; 23 for eighteen years; and 6 for twelve years. Added to these rents were a host of other payments which reduced net profits to a mere fraction. The tithe had often been rented out to the community or other well-off landlords by the original tithe-lord in return for a lump sum for several years in advance, so that the average amount paid did not necessarily correspond to a tenth of the production in any one year (Rapp, 1974: 243). We must also include the taxes levied by the territorial ruler. For example, the spring and summer tax (*Bede*) levied on the inhabitants of a relatively poor Breuschtal village came to 20 pounds Strassburg currency. One may assume that assessments were even heavier in the richer farming areas. Yet it is practically impossible to work out more specifically how this tax burden affected individual peasant households beyond the point where local assessments had been made.

Yet the records do show that, on average, rents and taxes did not consume all that was produced in a year of relatively good harvest, when there was usually a surplus which could be marketed. For example, the Mittelbergheim wine-grower Hans Zimberman rented a field from the Strassburg Hospital in 1480. He promised to pay not only four measures (*Ohm*) of wine in rent, but also to supply the hospital as far as possible with another five measures of wine for purchase according to current rates at Mittelbergheim. The hospital was thus seeking to purchase some of its wine at the wholesale market price. We can obtain an impression of the life and work of specific wine-growers by examining the rent register of parish rector Agram at Wolxheim. This register contains important notes from around the year 1500. Rector Agram cultivated his own church land with two servants. He produced a quite handsome surplus of red and white wine which he sold in Strassburg. He kept a close eye on price movements and tried to sell his wines at the most favourable time. When he failed to achieve this, he tersely noted the fact.

> On 20 July [1517] I was offered 18 gulden and 14 schillings a large measure [*Fuder*]. On 25 April I was offered 24 gulden for it. Prices have steadily fallen in the meantime.

Even if not all wine-growers had the opportunity to keep orderly accounts and a planned economy like rector Agram, we can assume that they all knew something about a marketing system through which they were keen to maximise their profits. Self-sufficient subsistence farming no longer played a part in the substantial wine-growing districts. The records also show that cereal prices were often higher in wine-growing districts than in the ploughlands or even the town (Rapp, 1974: 438). Marketing was thus essential for farmers in those districts.

Cereal farmers were also active in marketing their produce, which turned the main town of the region (Strassburg) into a major centre for foodstuffs. In a court case that went on appeal to Rottweil, Claus Banwart of Truchtersheim, a village in the centre of the fertile Kochersberg district, declared that in 1504 he had found buyers for 400 quarters of wheat and cereals at good prices. One can understand why peasants valued their tenancy contracts highly, if they could make such profits. The desirability of these contracts can be seen in agreements giving compensation to tenants who passed their contracts on to a third party before the agreed time for renewal. This compensation was the equivalent of the net profit that a tenant might hope to make out of his tenancy, and it was called the 'improvement' (*Besserung* or *melioracio*). At the beginning of the sixteenth century, a farm renting at 60 quarters a year was worth a *Besserung* of about 100 gulden (Rapp, 1967: 445). This was a significant sum, considering that the well-known cathedral preacher and doctor of theology, Geiler von Kaysersberg, was paid only 120 gulden a year. Many Kochersberg peasants kept close contacts with Strassburg merchants, above all those dealing in cereals. When Diebolt Dossenheim from Truchtersheim, a friend of bailiff Florenz Rummler, celebrated his wedding in the Strassburg Dominicans' refectory, his guests included not only a number of village mayors but also several grain dealers. Among the wealthiest peasants it seems to have been the custom to let a member of the family settle in Strassburg as a grain dealer. Claus Banwart of Truchtersheim, whom we have mentioned already, appears in records from 1517 as a citizen of Strassburg and grain salesman (*venditor annone*). The move to Strassburg was often easy since some peasants traditionally had town houses around market places, especially in districts near residences of the larger merchants and nobility. Even if these were exceptions, we may assume that most prosperous peasants had regular contact with tradesmen which encouraged them to produce for the market rather than merely for their own immediate needs.

Among the hundreds of sacks of grain leaving Strassburg for other destinations, there was certainly a large number which had been purchased directly from producers. A similar system operated in the wine-trade. Documents and chronicles are full of evidence demonstrating the prosperity that involvement in this flourishing commodity trade brought with it. Jacob Wimpfeling is a case in point here. In the wine region at Sulz-Bad, where first his uncle Ulrich and then he himself were priests, he was able to observe the ways of his parishioners:

Wealth has made them presumptuous and insolent. I know peasants who spend so much on christenings and weddings of sons and daughters, that one could buy a house, fields or even a little vineyard with the equivalent sum. With their wealth they are really wasteful of food and clothing. (Barth, 1959: 115)

In like manner, Thomas Murner described peasant pride while mocking the frilly shirts of Kochersberg people (Pfleger, 1923). Many houses also displayed the prosperity of their owners. The main room of such a house in Furdenheim was eighteen feet broad, thirty long, and it had eight windows. A Truchtersheim peasant, Dossenheim Claus, had twenty-two horses in his stables when he died in 1504. He had employed four labourers who addressed him as 'master'. We thus obtain an impression of his wealth and self-confidence. Did the rural inhabitants of Lower Alsace really have no grounds for complaint? Therefore did the Peasant War come upon them from out of the blue? Certainly not.

III

What we have said up to now about the peasantry depended on the assumption that there was an average of moderately prosperous productivity. But if we look at the price curve in more detail, we can see that there were increasingly severe fluctuations after 1460. Low prices became increasingly lower and high prices went steadily higher. During the first half of the fifteenth century, the price of a quarter of cereal almost invariably fluctuated between 40 and 90 pfennig. In the second half of the fifteenth century, it went as low as 26 pfennig and as high as 160 pfennig. Similar fluctuation in wine prices tended to coincide with that in the grain trade. Extreme price fluctuation could only do damage to the rural population. If the harvest was abundant, prices were depressed. If crops were meagre, producers had nothing left to sell, despite high prices. Rents and taxes may have seemed relatively light when there was high production; but they soon became oppressive when productivity fell. Since rents were relatively inflexible and not related to actual production, the matter could easily get out of hand.

Those who managed to store grain, and to a lesser extent wine, at times of lower prices and plenty, and who then sold it at times of dearth and high prices, did stand to gain substantially. Yet most of these people were townsmen, and above all religious corporations, which must have added significantly to popular hatred of the clergy (Rapp, 1974: 237–65, 435–41). Occasionally a peasant did manage to accumulate a significant amount of surplus grain in his barns. For example, the village mayor of Lampertheim in the ploughlands sold grain for 100 gulden to the inhabitants of Marlenheim in the wine-growing region. Wine-growers were in a worse position than grain-growers since at that time wine seldom kept for long, deteriorating rapidly. A policy of storage could not be used effectively against unfavourable price fluctuations. And when no money came into the house because a poor harvest had produced nothing to sell, then the real fear of famine made people desperate and angry. There were at least four such periods of crisis just prior to the Peasant War: 1480–83, 1490–92, 1500–3, and last but not least, 1516–19.

During such bad years some peasants and wine-growers gave up hope. At such times estate books of ecclesiastical and charity foundations record many new tenancy agreements replacing contracts that had still not run out. Tenants fled when they could no longer bear the burden of arrears. Successors had to take on predecessors' debts, which handicapped them from the outset. They often did bad business, became bankrupt and the farm went from bad to worse under frequently renewed management. Sometimes the tenant did not give up immediately and instead asked for more time to pay. Lienhardshansen Jakob who rented a farm in Holtzheim from Kloster Sankt-Marx was more than two years in rent arrears by 1511. He promised to pay this off by next Christmas and pledged four of his horses. A year later his debts were even greater and he had to let his landlord have the use of a further two horses as security for the debt. In 1513, another peasant took over the tenancy of the farm which Jakob's family had managed for three generations. Thereafter we do not know what happened to them. Perhaps bankrupted tenant farmers like him swelled the ranks of beggars whom townspeople feared and against whom authorities tried to take strict measures.

The difficulties that the rural people experienced did not always end so drastically. Wine and grain producers often suffered only temporary set-backs. They retained the hope of pulling themselves out of such crises by taking loans from wealthier neighbours or townsmen. There are very few traces in the documents of common mortgages, but 'mutual aid' existed in the form of grain provided for sowing. Jews who had been driven out of the towns were given a bad name as creditors in the countryside, although there is little concrete evidence (Rosenkranz, 1927: 23). Loans in the form of annuities fill hundreds of pages in the estate records, cartularies and memorial books. The peasant had to pay interest on what he borrowed at a standard 5 per cent in the fifteenth century. Usually this amounted to paying as many shillings in interest as had been borrowed in pounds. In order to avoid the law against usury, the debtor had to show that he had immovables to cover the value of the sum borrowed. These could serve as security and in theory provide income to cover annual interest payment. The debtor was empowered to return the capital sum to the creditor and to repurchase one half or the whole of the annuity (Rapp, 1974: 245ff.). Yet it was very rarely achieved: Quite to the contrary, the burden of annuity payments grew steadily heavier. Some districts suffered from over-indebtedness. In Westhoffen in the wine region most of the inhabitants had to pay annuities. On one day in February 1508 alone, eight wine-growers from Westhoffen came to the administrator of St Thomas

Foundation in Strassburg to make annuity agreements. Communities in their capacity as corporations were also forced to take on similar burdens. Reitweiler and neighbouring Gimbrett in the Kochersberg district had borrowed 1,300 pounds (about 2,500 gulden) from twenty different creditors – merchants, patricians, vintners and even clergy, all from Strassburg – bringing an annual 120 gulden revenue into the town. If one examines the indebtedness of the residents of Westhoffen, then one can see that the situation in Gimbrett in 1496 was not exceptional, and the position only became worse the closer it came to the Reformation era. One could certainly be allowed to talk of over-indebtedness. A map showing where these annuities were levied covers the wine-growing region up to the mountains, right to the Kochersberg foothills and close to the walls of Strassburg (map in Rapp, 1974: 531). It is also significant that the richest peasants were also buyers of annuities who gave credit to worse-off peasants in return for a few shillings annual rent or more commonly some measures of 'fine, white wine' delivered to their houses by their debtors. Many creditors were inefficient in collecting their annuities. Some were lazy, some negligent, and yet others did not possess the means to insist on their rights. In 1504 the monastery St Claren zum Werd collected only 133 of the 344 pounds that the rural population owed it. Confiscation did occur, although excommunication was usually first attempted, since most annuities had been sealed by ecclesiastical notary in the spiritual court. Even the village mayor suffered excommunication when he had failed to coax one of his subordinates to pay his debts. A memorandum from 1430 claims that probably twenty, thirty or even forty peasants were excommunicated in one case alone where an ecclesiastical foundation acted to recoup debts. If that failed, then the debt contract allowed the creditor to take the law into his own hands after one year had elapsed. He could invoke the law of distraint, confiscate and use the debtor's goods and property. For example, the monastery of St Marx had all the horses in two villages impounded, because several pounds of rent had not been paid. Creditors could turn to the infamous 'bloodsuckers', mercenaries who ransacked and plundered rural districts indiscriminately. On return to the town, creditors would then auction the booty. The grievances of the hamlet of Rosenweiler in 1462 give us a clear picture of brutal distraint, which occurred there because of an unpaid petty debt owed to a sculptor and the church of St Nicholas in Undis. That such methods also harmed the ecclesiastical authorities as landlords was indeed appreciated by Bishop William of Honstein, though not until after the Peasant War of 1525. Naturally many a landlord found it unwise to insist on rents so high that they took all or even more of the produce from the field that had been designated as security for the debt. Fritz Kiener (1904) called such demands folly. I would rather see them as examples of ignorance. Assessing, accounting and some level of education were not totally separate things. Anyway, debt invariably accumulated as each crisis increased the number of debtors.

Let us recapitulate. In theory, severe fluctuations in prices and production allowed the possibility of high profits. Yet only very few people could take advantage of this in practice, above all townsmen who then lent their profits back to nigh-bankrupt peasants and wine-growers. In the countryside there were very few peasants rich enough to give credit in this manner. The majority of peasant farmers regarded economic developments fearfully rather than with opportunism. Day-labourers lived in perpetual fear of the day when a wine-grower would only hire thirty instead of sixty hands because of a poor harvest. The peasants and wine-growers, whose businesses were run with great economic uncertainty, easily throttled by high rents combined with uneven productivity, were as terrified of good harvest years when grain and wine prices collapsed, as they were of years of dearth when, despite favourably high prices, they had nothing to sell. Even if some houses were spared this evil fate, most people lived in fear that it might well strike them next. For not even the substantial peasant farmer could be sure that he safeguarded himself against all eventualities. In this way the decades before 1525 saw poorer people being driven into acting rashly because their economic situation left them with hardly anything to lose. The better-off rural inhabitants also began to show increasing signs of unrest.

IV

Is it possible to establish any links between the economic situation described above and the conspiracies of the Bundschuh peasant up-risings?

The first connections seem naturally to emerge from recorded grievances and plans of reform. In the first Bundschuh movement of 1493, the third grievance dealt with indebtedness. It demanded aboli-tion of the ecclesiastical legal office which drew up and enforced annuity contracts at law; abolition of the court of appeal at Rottweil which handled many of these cases, and expulsion of Jews who lent money on promissory notes (Rosenkranz, 1927: 23). After the 1513 Bundschuh, demands for reforming the credit system became even more urgent. Annual payments on annuities should be suspended as long as they were not converted into simultaneous repayments or mortgages combining interest and capital which could be paid off in twenty years at 5 per cent (Rosenkranz, 1927: 125–234).

There were also direct links between the economic situation and the exact timing and location of uprisings. The mere fact that these con-spiracies coincided with a marked increase in price fluctuation is significant. We can observe much closer links when we examine the record in detail. Let us consider the Bundschuh conspiracy of 1517 which covered most of Lower Alsace and the Ortenau region across the

Rhine in Baden. The 1516 harvest was poor. In the following winter prices rocketed. Hoards of peasants came to the towns demanding credit. Lists of defaulters fill pages of memorial and account books. The year 1517 was no improvement, and prices stayed high until the summer of 1518. They were highest in wine-growing districts, where producers were faced with catastrophe. The 1516 harvest in the autumn was so poor that a large measure (*Fuder*) of wine cost 24 gulden, and the 1517 harvest was economically even worse. This time the vines were so full of grapes that prices collapsed. The income which indebted wine-growers had expected to make from selling the new harvest in order to repay their debts on the old disappeared overnight. At the same time the grain harvest had been poor and wine-growers were faced with even higher bread prices. It was at this moment that Joss Fritz organised his third uprising. He collected supporters near Bretten on 22 April 1517 to discuss plans. On 13 July he was operating from the heart of the wine district at Oberehnheim. The revolt was planned for 8 September after wine-growers had convinced themselves that harvest prices would collapse with the expected glut of ripening grapes. After storing their meagre sheaves of corn in half-empty barns, they had hoped to riot but were in effect betrayed on the day before the event was scheduled to take place. As the professional revolutionary that he undoubtedly was, Joss Fritz knew how to exploit the situation (Rapp, 1974: 438–40).

However, the case of Joss Fritz is a warning not to over-simplify the complex relationship between economic situation and revolutionary action. Who knows how things would have developed in 1516, 1517 and 1518 if someone like Joss Fritz had not been there in effect to agitate tirelessly and organise for violent action? It is well-known that Joss Fritz used religious slogans for this, and after all, anticlericalism was religious in its way. I point this out in order to show that the importance of non-economic aspects in the behaviour of specific human beings does not escape me. I would be cautious of assuming too hastily that the Peasant War was an economic revolution, as that excellent local historian, Fritz Kiener, already suggested as early as 1904. But even if the economic situation itself had not necessarily produced conspiracies without Joss Fritz, it is true to say that without this economic situation Joss Fritz would not so readily have found peasants and wine-growers to listen to him. Like the Peasant War of 1525, so the earlier uprisings are phenomena which are impervious to monocausal explanation. Yet the economic situation is a necessary factor in our understanding of the Bundschuh uprisings; and I hope that this view is clearer as a result of our essay into the Alsatian past.

RUDOLF ENDRES

6   *The Peasant War in Franconia**

We must ask what differentiated economic and social structures of
Franconian peasants and burghers from similar ones in other regions?
How high were demands and duties levied by territorial states? What
specifically verifiable connections existed between uprising and Lutheran
movement? What were the political aims of the rebels? From which
sections of society did the rank and file as well as leaders of the movement come? How did their opponents on the side of the territorial
rulers behave? Above all, what was the role played by the powerful
imperial city of Nuremberg, which had already gone over to the
Reformation? Finally, what were the consequences of the Peasant War
in Franconia? At least to some extent I shall try to answer these
questions.

A full survey of the material needs of life among the Franconian
rural and urban population at the beginning of the sixteenth century
has not yet been undertaken. But we can say that like neighbouring
Thuringia, Franconia was a region of pure tenant farming (*Grundherr-
schaft*) with extensive splintering of feudal holdings and relatively
favourable land-holding rights of peasants under hereditary copyhold
(*Erbzins*) with personal freedom. By the early sixteenth century, serfdom had been confined to a few districts on the edges of southern and
western Franconia. It had become merely a levy in kind and exemption
was easily purchased at 3 florins for a man and 4 florins for a woman
or 10 per cent of their wealth. Serfdom was therefore not a cause of the
uprising, quite contrary to some other regions (Tischler, 1963: 67, 88ff.;
Blickle, 1967). Therefore thesis seven of Max Steinmetz, following
Engels, that the base of society before the Peasant War was made up of
serfs and unfree peasants, does not apply in this form to Franconia.

Furthermore, in the Franconian countryside economic and social
differences were very great, not only between geographically distinct
districts, but also between neighbouring villages and even within the
same community. What Gunther Franz has said about Swabia and the
Upper Rhine also applies to Franconia, namely that minute farms of a
size merely an eighth to a sixteenth of the original, together with

*Edited translation of Rudolf Endres, 'Der Bauernkrieg in Franken', *Blätter
für deutsche Landesgeschichte*, 109, 1973, pp. 31–68.

cottage gardens, were predominant in the village (1969: 292). It was due not only to the practice of partible inheritance, but also to a general population explosion since the mid fifteenth century creating land hunger and a steady increase in land prices. This produced a large group below the peasantry, ranging from the pettiest tenants, settlers without fields, day-labourers, lodgers and living-in servants to the most varied of village craftsmen and rural migratory workers (Franz, 1970: 210ff.). In the spring of 1525 there were about 1,000 casual labourers working in the vineyards around Kitzingen, a town of about 500 households. They were very active in the uprising. In Saxony it has been estimated that the groups below the peasantry, which can really be classed as immiserated, comprised between one quarter to one half of the total rural population (Blaschke, 1956). In Thuringia, a half of all the rural taxpayers were without property, and in poorly situated villages this was even as high as two thirds.

There was a similar situation in Franconia. Even in the villages of the prosperous local district of Burgkunstadt in the upper valley of the river Main, 8 per cent of all rural households had nothing to declare for taxation in 1525 and 4 per cent had wealth totalling less than 25 florins. In other words, one half of rural households belonged to the large sub-stratum of propertyless or very poorly endowed (Dietz, 1925: 72). In reality, the number of immiserated was probably greater than these figures suggest since they do not even include single men and maid-servants or unmarried members of families.

According to Kitzingen town council, for every one burgher with a fortune of 1,000 florins there were twenty others with far less. In smaller townships there was a more even social structure. Those with a modest amount of property were relatively far more numerous than the very rich or very poor. In the minute imperial city of Heidingsfeld, near Wurzburg, the number of poor households was 10 per cent, whereas in the metropolis of Nuremberg at the time of Albrecht Durer about one third of the estimated 50,000 inhabitants belonged to this sub-stratum.

Not only were immiserated people in the countryside and small towns often disastrously deprived of a precarious livelihood, but so also were numerous, small and divided peasant farms and cottage gardens which were operated at bare subsistence levels. They were hit especially by new tax demands from landlords and territorial overlords, by bad harvests and wars, by reduction in use of common land and by novelties often of the most diffuse kind. The richer peasants, however, noticed these varying financial burdens much less, and instead they suffered more from the contradiction between their relatively good economic position and their relatively poor legal and political status. In the Burgkunstadt district, 15 per cent of householders had fortunes of 100 florins or more, and for half the rebellious peasants of the Nuremberg countryside who were put on trial by the town council, tax values ran at over 100 florins. Some were even worth 500 florins and more (Buck, 1971).

What were the burdens of Franconian peasants generally like? To start with we must distinguish between land dues and personal services. Land dues were divided into landlord rents and territorial overlord taxes, which could, however, overlap. First came rents and annuities, usually paid in kind to landlords. Then came tithe, divided into a great tithe and a controversial small tithe which included 'blood tithe'. Tithes covered nearly all kinds of produce. Third came a quit-rent (*Handlohn*), to be paid on all feudal property whenever there was a change of ownership. Its size varied, although it averaged 5 to 10 per cent. This also became due, payable as death duty on the death of either the feudal landlord or his tenant. It could also be levied in order to pay off siblings, which was regarded as a novelty in the territory of Bamberg. Apart from these landlord dues, peasants still had to pay a great variety of taxes, which could even include such items as water-rent, forest, cheese or acorn levy.

We will not delve further here into a very complex and confusing variety of burdens, except to draw attention to the fact that on average 30 to 40 per cent of all produce was paid in rents and taxes. Naturally this led to great difficulties in years of poor harvest, when peasants were even known to pledge their seed-corn in order to try and escape short-term bankruptcy, which then ruined them in the following year. In Franconia there were especially poor harvests immediately before and after the Peasant War – in 1502–3, 1505, 1515, 1517–24, 1527, 1529–34 and 1540–41.

Peasants in the territories of Bamberg and Eichstatt were particularly troubled by new labour services and restrictions on use of common land. The rulers' extensive hunts not only did extensive damage to fields and crops, but were also accompanied by laws protecting game and by new services to be performed for the hunt, above all keeping dogs or making payment in lieu of them. Sometimes a whole hunting party with all their dogs had to be lodged, fed and supplied with beaters for up to a week at a time. This could be very oppressive indeed for a small village community which suffered the presence of a large hunting party of noblemen perhaps two or three times a year.

Similarly there was a massive increase in sheep farming organised by the territorial authorities for the ruler, above all in the region of the Franconian Alp. Some communities had to suffer the presence on their lands of four to five herds, each comprising a thousand or more sheep. In Upper Wiesenttal, Hollfeld even supported eight sheep-runs. It meant total exclusion from the common, and it was very harsh to poor villagers. By close cropping of the hillsides, sheep destroyed the water tables of highland villages. The sudden increase in sheep-rearing in Franconia was linked to a boom in near-by cloth manufacture, above all at Nuremberg and Nordlingen. A relatively substantial increase in population produced greater demand for cheap cloth like *Loden*, which was produced from lower-quality local wool. The masters of the Nuremberg clothmakers' guild boasted in 1530: 'It is true that by the grace of God our cloth of Nuremberg is held in these times in considerable esteem' (Bog, 1968: 73).

New dye-works and fulling mills were built, and the cloth was baled in eight warehouses for Nuremberg cloth, which had been finished under the supervision of more than one hundred city guildmasters, plus almost as many in the suburbs of Wohrd and Gostenhof. The bad effects of the cloth boom were soon felt in poorer quality, increased complaints and the appearance of new enterprises run by underqualified staff. In Nordlingen, where the guild of Loden makers went back to the fourteenth century, numbers of manufacturers rose from 106 to 257 between 1500 and 1540. Income increased from 141 pounds in 1450 to 1,359 pounds in 1520 (Endres, 1963: 144). During the boom the Nordlingen clothing industry used about 5,000 hundredweight of wool a year, which exceeded the capacity of local sheep-farmers in the Ries district. The Nordlingen wool exchange thus attracted representatives from all over Franconia, from Hohenlohe, Nuremberg, Bamberg, Coburg and Windsheim. For example, Langheim monastery had important sheep-runs and sold wool directly to Nuremberg, making its tenants in Buckendorf and Weichenwasserlos transport wool as labour service. The boom in local cloth manufacture misled a number of peasant communities into sheep-rearing in the hope of making quick profits, with the result that they could no longer produce enough to pay their rents in kind. The bishop of Eichstatt was forced to decree that a peasant must not keep more than thirty sheep, and a cottager was restricted to fifteen. However, territorial rulers did not limit the size of their own sheep-runs, much to the disadvantage of their subjects' traditional rights and usage of common lands.

Complaints and demands of numerous communities to have their woodland rights re-established are connected with the appearance of forestry decrees that territorial rulers were beginning to issue from the later fifteenth century onwards. Rulers attempted to protect woodland against indiscriminate exploitation by villagers and townsmen, although those who suffered from the new regulations did not see the matter that way. During the Peasant War rulers like the margrave Casimir, who had made concessions over forest use while under duress, repudiated them immediately afterwards. This Franconian ruler had conceded that all wood for building purposes could be taken from the forests free of charge (cf. Pfeiffer, 1972).

A symbolic rather than economic measure was to fish out forbidden stretches of water, using as justification biblical references to the free use of woodland and game. Uprisings often started in this way, as, for example, in Forchheim and Eichstatt. Rebels seem to have regarded fishing as a symbol of freedom, and as giving them the opportunity to share the diet of their landlords and masters, a diet which the 'poor man' could only ever afford, if at all, on feast days (Heimpel, 1964). Demands for free access to hunting seem to have had a similar significance to fishing, although most people would have been satisfied with the right to hunt small game only. In a territorial assembly decree of late April 1525, the margrave Casimir even admitted that any game found outside the forests could be shot by his subjects, but the meat had to be handed over, although skins could be kept.

To landlord rents were added a growing number of indirect as well as direct taxes to territorial authorities. After 1500 this included imperial taxes. The most important indirect tax was *Ungeld*, a levy on wine and beer and occasionally also on meat and flour, averaging 10 to 20 per cent. It was first imposed on the towns, and from there it spread slowly into rural districts after the fifteenth century, against much peasant opposition. In the districts around Rothenburg, shortly before the Peasant War, an additional extensive wine and beer tax was levied, ostensibly as an emergency tax to pay for the reconquest of Rhodes from the Turks, together with a substantial cattle tax called *Klauengeld* levied from 1522 at between 42 pfennig and 1 florin for each ox brought to market. Especially objectionable were extraordinary land taxes, such as the impost (*Bethe*), to pay off territorial rulers' debts, which was assessed generally at 5 to 10 per cent on movable property. It was levied with increasing regularity all over Franconia so that it began to look like an ordinary, regular tax over which not even the territorial Estates could wield much influence.

Ecclesiastical territories had also created an investiture tax (*pallium*) during the course of the fifteenth century, collected when a new bishop came to power in order to cover his expenses at accession, such as his annates and provision to Rome. It usually ran at 10 per cent of the total value of all ecclesiastical fiefs, excluding the fees for reinvestiture with the holding. On a number of farms where the bishop was not also the direct landlord, investiture tax ran at anything up to 10 florins.

At times of war, a territorial ruler levied his own muster tax (*Reissteuer*) in order to raise the appropriate troops, and he also collected Turk tax for the imperial war effort until the imperial circles took over the task, although he still pocketed one third of the proceeds for all his trouble. The towns also levied taxes for the right of citizenship, and various defence and guard duties, from which nobles and clergy were exempted, much to the envy of the burghers.

We must also remember that each time there was currency reform, as happened, for example, in Franconia in the 1470s, tax levels were kept at old currency values, which often meant that, in practice, burghers and peasants paid up to one third more. Whenever taxes were paid in inflated silver coins instead of gold currency, rulers like those of Wurzburg, Nuremberg, Ansbach and Bayreuth demanded a surcharge of up to one quarter. This monetary measure was caused by the general debasement of silver coinage, which, for example, amounted to 26 per cent in Nuremberg between 1440 and 1500. Long before bullion imports from America, silver inflation drove out gold, which increased in value (Nef, 1941; *Cambridge Economic History*, 1952: 430–92). Since payment could be made in gold or silver, it was understandable that tax-collectors added a surcharge on debased silver coins in order to cover their losses. Such monetary policy was operated by the bishop of Wurzburg when he increased the price of the gold gulden from 60 to 63 kreuzers.

Even more disruptive than currency manipulation was, for example, the Wurzburg *Guldenzoll*, an extraordinary tax on wine to pay for territorial state debts. It was granted for the first time in 1397, and thereafter several times on a limited basis until, in 1468, Bishop Rudolf von Scherenberg succeeded in turning it into a perpetual tax granted by the Emperor. From then on, one gulden extraordinary tax was levied on every large measure (*Fuder*) of wine travelling by land or waterway through the Duchy of Franconia. The citizens of Wurzburg demanded immediate abolition of this tax since it increased the price of wine and reduced wine merchants' profits. Ebern community also protested against this tax, whereas Ohringen community demanded that proceeds should go to upkeep of roads under their own sole direction, which would have increased village autonomy against the power of the territorial state. Wurzburg even suggested that tolls should be traded against the better communal upkeep of roads.

Let us examine the extraordinary tax burden of the bishopric of Bamberg just before the Peasant War. Investiture tax was levied in 1501, 1503, 1505 and 1522. War tax for the Swabian League against the Duke of Wurttemberg came in 1519, and in 1523 against Franz von Sickingen, to be followed by a Turk tax in 1524. We can thus estimate the burden of tax over and above the rent which subjects had to pay. It is thus quite feasible that when people in Rothenburg complained of paying over half of their income in rents and taxes, they were probably telling the truth. High taxes, as such, were not the real problem, but rather their cumulative effect, especially when they were levied too frequently at times of poor harvest. There were clear signs of rebellion when the margrave Friedrich IV imposed 800 florins imperial tax on Kitzingen town in 1512 in order to provide aid for the Emperor Maximilian's war against the Venetians, especially when the town only had 500 households who, over a decade later, were to pay the margrave Casimir's particularly brutal fine of 1,300 florins after the Peasant War (Böhm, 1893: 5, 116).

Everywhere in Franconia rebels' grievances are directed against small tithes with no biblical justification, as well as against novel and arbitrary levies of territorial rulers. Uprisings in Franconia were usually only directed against excessive and unchristian tax demands imposed by putative territorial states and not against the territorial state as such.

But what the rebels regarded primarily as economic demands were taken, in the last resort, by ruling princes as a political challenge, even though it took many of them a while to realise the fact. For it was precisely via their economic policy and not through any attempt to revive serfdom, as generally implied by Waas (1964: 60), that Franconian territorial rulers tried to consolidate and extend their state power. It was certainly not by chance that the right to levy taxes became the cornerstone of territorial state power in Franconia. Later on it was also significant that territorial rulers' main objection against rebellious subjects turned around their failure to pay taxes during the course of the uprising.

If we take into account the burden of land taxes and not just the rents that peasants and small burghers had to pay on the eve of the Peasant War, then it seems that the general economic climate was even more unfavourable than we would otherwise have assumed. Contemporaries, even on the side of the ruling princes, understood this too, as brought out by the conclusion of the Imperial Assembly held at Speyer in 1526, and also by the remarkable declaration of the Swabian League after crushing the peasants, that it would no longer come to the rescue of lords who caused their subjects to revolt because of any new taxes they imposed (Franz, 1963: no. 209). The margraves had after all described the economic situation in their Franconian territories around the turn of the century as follows: 'Where one has enough to live on, there are at least fifty poor country people who barely manage to provide enough daily bread for themselves out of what they produce' (Höfler, 1849: 53). In 1523 the Wurzburg territorial assembly refused to grant the ruling bishop a Turk tax, because his subjects were already paying so many dues that any new burden or poor harvest could cause an uprising.

To these economic problems can also be added popular envy and hatred of the privileged, above all clergy and nobility, who were exempted from paying most of the new taxes, thereby gaining further economic advantage which they exploited ruthlessly. In towns such as Rothenburg, ordinary townspeople hated the few patrician families who controlled the town council. Some town communities wished to strengthen their freedom from territorial state control, notably Forchheim and the episcopal cities of Bamberg and Wurzburg. Wurzburg and Mergentheim even hoped to obtain the status of imperial free cities during the course of the Peasant War. It was the mayor of Rothenburg who reminded Wurzburg citizens of their supposed imperial free status which he claimed their bishops had tyrannously usurped. Mergentheim wished to drive out its overlords, the German Order.

People regarded the imperial tax levied for the Swabian League in early 1525 as outright provocation, since the money was not to be used against foreign enemies, as were the proceeds of Turk tax, but rather to put down rebellious peasants in neighbouring territories, with whom there were vague feelings of sympathy and understanding. When Bishop Conrad von Thungen also called up the local militia as well as levying imperial tax, demanding that his subjects fight in person against approaching rebel bands, his demands were rejected not only as economically unacceptable but also as unchristian (Fries, 1883: 107, 279; Cronthal, 1887: 26).

Concrete economic and social problems among large sections of the rural and urban population, together with various socio-psychological factors, provided grounds for the uprising in Franconia. What sparked it off was preaching of the Gospel. The traditional church in Franconia had, as elsewhere, been severely criticised for its worldliness and corruption. Ecclesiastical authority was questioned specifically within the context of a wider and more general social criticism. The final touch was given by a number of misunderstood Luther pamphlets wherein the rebels confused temporal and corporal freedom with the true freedom of the Gospel, providing religious belief in God's justice as a catalyst for the social and political upheaval that followed (Böhm, 1893: 26).

The Reformation began to take significant hold in Franconia as from 1521, the year in which Count Georg von Wertheim, who later joined the rebellious peasants, asked Luther to send him a preacher. At the same time Dinkelsbuhl approved the new communion. The town also subsequently joined the rebels. In the summer of 1524 Nuremberg introduced an evangelical system of worship. From 1521 there was a strong evangelical movement, including several preachers inclined to Luther in the districts around Ansbach. In the three Franconian bishoprics, Luther's teachings spread rapidly among clergy and people. Luther's earliest and most enthusiastic followers included a number of cathedral canons who were humanists. Even the suffragan bishop of Wurzburg, Johannes Pettendorfer, adopted the new teachings in 1525. To start with, ruling bishops like Weigand von Redwitz and Conrad von Thungen only prosecuted priests who married, and otherwise tended to let the new religious movement have a free hand.

Thomas Muntzer's stay in Nuremberg also had its repercussions in the city and surrounding districts. By the summer of 1524 the town council was beginning to scrutinise Muntzer's pamphlets circulating in the city. In October 1524, in the company of Heinrich Pfeiffer, Muntzer himself arrived in Nuremberg, after being driven out of Allstedt. On 29 October the town expelled Pfeiffer after he had attempted to have two of his tracts printed. We cannot be certain how long Muntzer stayed, although he later claimed to have refused invitations to preach in the town since he had only come in order to arrange for the printing of his works. The journeyman printers of Johann Hergot secretly produced Muntzer's *Ausgedrückte Entplössung* on the advice of Hans Hut, but it was confiscated by the town council in early November after Schleupner, the preacher at St Sebald, had declared the tract to be highly subversive. Muntzer's *Schutzrede*, which was ready for printing at Hieronymus Holtzel's press in December, was also confiscated by the town council. Yet Muntzer's views soon became well known, as was made clear by the trial of the 'three godless painters' (Pfeiffer, 1971: 154–8). A former preacher from Jena, Martin Reinhart, who was born in Eibelstadt, distributed Muntzer's revolutionary writings in Nuremberg and was accordingly expelled. Even the margrave Casimir ordered the strict supervision in his territories of booksellers who were known to have handled Muntzer's works (Hoyer, 1970: 1597ff.). In the following year, several rebel weavers in Eichstatt claimed to have heard Muntzer preach in Nuremberg. One of the weavers even dressed up as a preacher and gave a sermon against the authorities and all taxation. The 'peasant from Wohrd' was a priest from the Ries district who gained popularity when he preached in the Nuremberg suburbs of Wohrd and Thon in the guise of a simple layman inspired by the Word of God. In the summer of 1524, he preached in Kitzingen to neighbouring peasants against paying tithes, annuities and taxes. The town council did not expel him until the margrave Casimir had begun to threaten them. Nuremberg council finally ordered two hangings on 5 July 1524 in order to cow the common people into submission. The victims were Ulrich Aberhan, innkeeper at Wohrd, and a cloth-worker called Hans from Nuremberg (Schornbaum, 1952: 488f.; Staatsarchiv Nürnberg, Ratsverlass 704: 19).

It is difficult to find direct links between the evangelical movement and the peasant uprising in Eichstatt, but such links are clearly discernible in the neighbouring bishoprics of Wurzburg and Bamberg, as recognised by contemporaries such as Conrad von Thungen and the Bavarian chancellor Leonhard von Eck, who warned his master 'not to tolerate the evil of Lutheranism in any sermons, since it is the sole cause of this rebellion' (Jörg, 1851: 290). Even the margrave Casimir blamed the peasant uprising on ignorant and boorish preachers. The uprising in Rothenburg was less due to the presence of Andreas Bodenstein, called Carlstadt, who had been expelled from Electoral Saxony, than to a radical reformer called Dr Johannes Teuschlin who led burghers and villagers in a boycott of tithe and cattle tax. There are also clear links between reform movement and peasant uprising in the bishopric of Bamberg. The uprising in Forchheim, which came in the spring of 1524, and which had been brutally put down with the help of mercenary troops, had been influenced by the evangelical sermons of Jorg Kreutzer, who was finally captured in the autumn of 1525 and expelled.

Of crucial importance to the great uprising in Bamberg during April 1525 were the sermons of Kustos Johann Schwanhausen, which were printed and circulated by Georg Erlinger, also a follower of Luther. From Schwanhausen's programme of reform it was easy to deduce refusal to pay tithes and secularisation of church property, and under his influence Bamberg subjects withheld taxes, above all the investiture tax. Schwanhausen soon had to flee to Nuremberg. He also claimed to have preached only against the existing social order, and not against an overall concept of godly authority as such, which shows that he was indeed a true follower of Luther. After he returned to Bamberg by demand of the rebellious burghers, which was promptly sanctioned by the bishop, Schwanhausen played no further part in the events of the uprising, in contrast to many other preachers who had appeared as spokesmen of rebel peasant bands. As a pure Lutheran, Schwanhausen was only interested in spiritual salvation and not concerned with any revolution on earth.

Naturally the religious question, above all the demand for 'simple, pure and unclouded sermons of God's Word' (Franz, 1963: 408) played an important part in the course of the Peasant War in Franconia, although demands like the free election of parish priests, abolition of the clergy's privileged legal status and destruction of the existing ecclesiastical authorities are really much more questions of politics than of belief. It is true that the religious question had often sparked off uprisings, but rebellious movements soon took another turn and pushed social, economic and political issues much more into the foreground, which rebels themselves regarded as well in tune with holy writ.

Popular hatred, which Steinmetz has labelled 'bourgeois heresy', was rife especially against nunneries, monasteries and the houses of the German Order. The bishops of Bamberg and Wurzburg even conceded that monasteries be deprived of property; that a number of them be turned into seminaries for preachers or even schools for burghers; but above all that their revenues were to be used to pay off territorial state debts to relieve ordinary subjects of some of their tax burden. This latter point overthrows Steinmetz's thesis thirteen. The peasants of the Ries district also offered their ruler, Count Ludwig von Ottingen, opportunity to use monastic property to pay off his debts and thus reduce their land taxes. He refused. However, a number of ruling princes thought along the same lines as the peasants regarding secularisation of ecclesiastical property. In the bishopric of Wurzburg alone, thirty-one monasteries and nunneries were plundered and even pulled down by peasant bands, although this was often not done just out of hatred and greed but rather because the peasants really needed the provisions that the monks and nuns had stockpiled. For according to many of the nobility, monastic authorities had notoriously overtaxed their peasants. They claimed that although monastic foundations had originally been endowed by nobles, in recent years they had accepted more and more commoners, above all peasant children, whose striving was not for a godly life but merely to 'screw as much as possible out of the poor, for which they will undoubtedly suffer the wrath of the Almighty' (Cronthal, 1887: 30f.).

Demands to secularise the Franconian bishoprics, which would have altered the whole politics of the region, are not recorded for Bamberg or Eichstatt, and in Wurzburg the issue was only really debated by some of the rebels right at the end of the uprising in the company of Count Wilhelm von Henneberg, who thereby hoped to gain substantial amounts of territory. With the help of Philip of Hesse and rebellious peasants in Wurzburg, Wilhelm von Henneberg hoped to conquer the bishopric, thereafter proclaiming the margrave Casimir as Duke of Franconia with the ostensible help of the Ansbach chancellor, Georg Vogler (ibid.: 78). But in actual fact the bishops of Wurzburg and Bamberg were recognised specifically as rulers by the rebels, as indeed were the margraves in Ansbach and Kulmbach-Bayreuth. Bishop Weigand von Redwitz of Bamberg was even begged on bended knee to take over sole control of the territorial government and to abolish the hated co-administration of the cathedral chapter, while the Wurzburg rebels were even prepared to keep their cathedral chapter on as a co-administration. In Bamberg the chapter had become too powerful and a threat to the local government of the town and surrounding districts. After much hesitation the bishop agreed, thus annulling his election oath not to enter into direct negotiations with his burghers and subjects except in the presence of representatives from the chapter. Without knowing it, the rebels thus offered him the chance of secularising the bishopric along East Prussian lines, although Weigand had too much integrity to lend himself to any such policy. All over Franconia there were demands to abolish the economic and legal privileges of the clergy, and insistence that they carry out their communal duties and services (Franz, 1963: 315, 408; Fries, 1883: 229f.; Cronthal, 1887: 30ff.).

Rebels' treatment of the nobility, however, varied. During the first uprising in Easter week 1525, Bamberg rebels still insisted that they 'had no quarrel with any noble folk', which showed that this revolt was concerned specifically with urban matters of town self-government. A second wave of uprisings after 15 May, however, brought serious reprisals against the nobility, whose privileged status was abolished in favour of equality with burghers and peasants. This had been demanded right from the start by rebel bands in the Tauber, Odenwald and Neckar districts, symbolised by making noble folk go on foot just like peasants: 'And all ecclesiastical and secular people, noble and non-noble, shall from now on obey the common laws of burghers and peasants, and they shall no longer behave in any other manner than the common man' (Zweifel, 1878: 356f.); and similarly, according to a rebel decree from Ochsenfurth, 'Henceforth, the nobleman shall no longer keep an armoured horse, since such behaviour is not justified' (Fries, 1883: 148). The Thannhauser peasant band even wrote to the margrave Casimir inviting him in true Christian manner to join them, but only on foot as was seemly among good Christian brothers (Jäger, 1892: 122). Yet there was never any talk of depriving the nobility of their property or of taking widespread social measures against them. Instead, nobles were offered protection, once they had defortified their houses and agreed to co-operate with rebellious peasants. Ochsenfurth records show that rebels reimbursed a noblewoman, Clara von Ehenheim, at Willenzheim, for cattle that the rebel camp outside Wurzburg had stolen from her, since she was able to prove that she had already complied with their wishes and destroyed the fortifications around her home (Böhm, 1893; 82f.).

In attempting to abolish the special position of nobles and clergy, rebels in Franconia worked to create a uniform group of subjects within a centrally run state system that would guarantee a fair economic position for all its members, as can be seen from the proposal to use tithes for the benefit of poor people. In other words, the demand was for a welfare state (*Sozialstaat*) (cf. Angermeier, 1966). Only at the end of the uprising did the Bamberg and Wurzburg rebels demand stricter control over the territorial administration and greater say in decision making. In Bamberg, there was to be a government made up of representatives of knights, burghers and peasants who would preserve peace and justice in the bishopric and deal with grievances. The peasants also demanded control of all the castles in the territory, insisting that they be staffed by non-nobles. Wurzburg wanted a collegiate administration by the estates made up of nobles, burghers and peasants which would meet the bishop four times a year to settle important affairs of state. Attempts to limit a territorial ruler's prerogative power were still very traditional late-medieval ones, except that rebel peasants began to exclude the clergy in their demands. But we must stress that nowhere in Franconia were there actual plans to replace ecclesiastical or secular principalities with a peasants' republic of the kind advocated as democratic and social by the followers of Thomas Muntzer, despite the fact that social and economic conditions were very similar in Franconia to neighbouring Thuringia, where Muntzer was most active (cf. Smirin, 1956; Bensing, 1966). In Franconia the institution of the princely territorial state was not challenged. Its authority as such was not doubted, but only specific privileges and material grievances, without thereby even questioning the basic right of the state to levy taxes. This contradicts the basic point that Waas makes about Franconia (1964: 35), since in this region the Peasant War was less of a political but much more of an economic and social movement calling upon biblical support.

It is also significant that Franconian uprisings kept to the confines of territorial state boundaries, above all to the bishoprics of Bamberg and Eichstatt, or to the margravate of Bayreuth. In the northern part of the bishopric of Wurzburg, the Bildhauser rebel band was still forbidding its members to attack fiefs held by Saxony, also ordering the restitution of property taken from neighbouring Bamberg. Only in the south-western part of Franconia was there agreement between rebel bands that cut across territorial loyalties and boundaries, above all among the Tauber, Neckar and Odenwald bands who lay before Wurzburg and were stiffened by contingents from the western districts of Ansbach territory. At the same time, numerous peasants from around Dinkelsbuhl and Crailsheim joined bands from Ellwangen and Jaxt. The margrave Casimir repeatedly ordered rebel leaders of various peasant bands in the Ries district around Dinkelsbuhl and Thannhausen to return those of his subjects who had joined them. Although the peasants encamped outside Wurzburg called themselves common country representatives of the Duchy of Franconia, or country representatives of Franconia (*gemeine Landschaft*), this did not imply the whole of Franconia, as Buszello interprets it (1969: 42f.), but just the districts west of the Steigerwald, actually only covering the territory of the bishopric of Wurzburg, whose subjects were in general control of the peasant camp (Endres, 1967: 168ff.). The Wurzburg band did not behave offensively or aggressively against other territories, nor did it seek a supra-territorial political rearrangement. Admittedly after the conquest of Liebfrauenberg, representatives of the rebellious peasants openly told the Nuremberg council that they would move on to the city, but at the same time leaders of the united peasant bands in Wurzburg promised in writing to stay aloof from the internal affairs of the bishopric of Bamberg. Even the assembly at Schweinfurt failed to produce an alliance or agreement to unite rebellious peasants throughout Franconia. Bamberg representatives refused to combine with anyone, fearing that such a move would jeopardise agreement with their own ruling bishop. All peasants of Wurzburg could not even come to agree-ment, and local prejudice or, as Engels called it, provincial narrow-mindedness predominated (MEW, 7: 412). There is no evidence that Franconian rebels wished to establish a united, national state from the bottom upwards, as Steinmetz, in thesis 31, would wish to see it. The Heilbronn programme of Wendel Hipler, proposing co-ordination of individual peasant movements at least in south Germany, and the utopian imperial reform proposals of Friedrich Weigandt were excep-tions outside the general run of the movement. They do not reflect the attitudes of 'the common poor man' in Franconia, who did not think of a new order in a grand manner but only of narrow regional or even local reforms. The Peasant War was thus certainly no 'part of the Germans' struggle for the Empire', as Buszello has perhaps rather too sharply pointed out (1969: 145).

There was also only a very limited amount of co-operation between rebellious peasants and burghers, probably occurring for the first time in Rothenburg, which certainly has a bearing on future developments. Most of the smaller territorial towns and markets were forced to join the 'plebeian masses' or peasants, and some even took over local leader-ship of the rebels, as happened with the Bildhauser band. Examples of this came from Kitzingen. The peasant armies that were annihilated by the Swabian League near Konigshofen and Ingolstadt consisted to a large extent of burghers from small towns in the Tauber and Neckar valleys (Merx, 1907: 153). Large towns were, on the whole, suspicious and opposed to the peasants. Ansbach town stayed neutral, and in Bamberg town the peasants were forced to encamp outside the walls. In Wurzburg the gates were only opened after besieging peasants had threatened to burn all vineyards in the vicinity. Even after joining the uprising. Wurzburg and Bamberg towns each retained their own mercenaries for protection against peasant excesses. In Bamberg, peasant bands who were on their way to plunder Michaelsberg had to run the gauntlet through lines of ill-disposed burghers. In secret, Götz von Berlichingen was offered 20,000 florins to move his Odenwald band out of Wurzburg. There was only really a genuine alliance of the peasants with the urban poor, the *Gärtner* (gardeners) in Bamberg and the so-called drunken rabble in Wurzburg, who were much more dependent on plunder and drink, above all if it could be taken from the homes of cathedral chapter canons.

Of decisive importance to the nature of the whole uprising was that no links were forged between the rebels and the broad proletarian mass in Nuremberg, although there was certainly a significant amount of discontent in the city and its extensive landed territory. At the height of the uprising in Franconia during the first half of May 1525, it was touch and go as to whether the common people in Nuremberg would rebel and join the peasants. The town council was well aware of its precarious position at home and abroad. It tried to recruit new mercenaries from the region around Lake Constance. When this failed, the council finally turned to the Swabian League for help, threatening to withdraw its own troops to defend the city against the peasants.

Peasant leaders came from all social groups among the people, not only from rich peasants of villages or upper layers of town society. There were officials of territorial princes, such as Kastner Contz Dietmann von Kronach, who was condemned to die after the uprising but actually bought himself free for 800 florins; the mayor of Rothenburg, Ehrenfried Kumpf; and the wealthy mayor of Wassertrudingen, Wilhelm Wagner, who claimed to have joined the rebels only to save his fortune of over 1,500 florins. In Kitzingen there was the optician Jacob Schmidt, and above all the rich miller of Hallstadt, whose place on the river Main was used for co-ordinating the latest news carried by rivermen between Frankenwald and Lower Franconia (Jäger, 1892: 159f.). Yet there were also more dubious types among them, including renegade clergy like the priest of Cannstadt who was executed in the Hallstadt camp for encouraging boys to set barns alight. Some local priests led their parishioners into the uprising, as, for example, the priest of Hollfeld who encouraged them to take castle Thurnau, or rector Michael Schrimpf, who acted as chancellor to the Bildhauser band. The abbess of Bamberg's convent of Clarissen nuns complained that the abbot and monks of Bamberg's Michaelsberg monastery had all gone over to the peasants' camp and done more damage than the others. Some leaders were craftsmen, like the carpenter Hans Schnabel of the Bildhauser band or the cloth-maker Heule in Eichstatt. Leader of the radicals in Wurzburg was the plumber and street-musician Hans Bermeter, nicknamed 'Linck', who had a prison record for theft and had been expelled from the town on a number of occasions. He was finally captured in Nuremberg 1526 and beheaded after the council had first refused to hand him over to the bishop of Wurzburg. But ordinary peasants and fishermen from the suburbs of the towns were also among the leaders, whom the margrave's bailiff, Wolf von Rechberg, called 'a lot of useless rabble who have nothing and contribute nothing' (Staatsarchiv Bamberg, Ansbacher Bauernkriegsakten, Tom. 3, f. 218).

Among the poor in town and country occasional radical and communistic demands were made, as in Wassertrudingen, whose wealthy mayor was told, 'You great fool, you must share your wealth with us and everyone must be as rich as everyone else.' In Wurzburg, peasant rebels publicly proclaimed, 'that if we are all to become brothers, then let's start right away making the rich share with the poor and redistribute above all what the rich have taken from the poor by trade and retail.' These lower orders could also act spontaneously, especially where the wine and beer cellars of castles, monasteries and inns were concerned, as happened at the sack of the monasteries of Auhausen and Bildhausen. Wine generally played an important role in Lower Franconian uprisings. While the rank and file of peasants expected immediate improvements in their economic and social position, their leaders, especially in the towns, such as Hippler or Weigandt, held completely different views. The more radical of the Lower Franconian peasants therefore felt betrayed by their leaders, got rid of them and continued to plunder more monasteries and castles.

In the bishopric of Bamberg the course of the uprising was quite different. Two hundred castles were pulled down in the space of ten days, although in some cases only roofs were destroyed. The nobility were driven out, often in ludicrously calm and orderly fashion. Actions were carefully supervised by rebel headquarters, first near Hallstadt, later near Bamberg town. Local peasant bands received strict orders as to which castles they were allowed and forbidden to plunder, and they were made accountable to headquarters for what they took apart from foodstuffs. For the latter they usually paid, and all the rest they were ordered to deliver into their main camp. Problems arose with castles near territorial boundaries where peasants did not know whether the place was on Bamberg or margraviate territory, for only the latter was not to be touched. Cases in point were castles at Rabenstein and near Kups, a fief of the Franconian margraves of Brandenburg lying in the bishopric of Bamberg. This led to a lively exchange of letters between the local band and peasant headquarters until the problem of ownership and overlordship had been clarified. When the peasants of castle Ermreuth, which was a fief of the margraves occupied by the Nuremberg patrician Muffel on Bamberg territory, plundered it, they had to make restitution of all damage, since they had disobeyed orders from central headquarters. The latter were usually very efficient in controlling actions by local rebel bands. The villagers of Gossweinstein drew up an extensive list of all that they had taken from the castle, including those items that they decided to leave the owner, sufficient for her use as a common noblewoman (*gemeines edelweib*). It can hardly have been the 'spontaneous' action or direct class struggle of ignorant peasants to decide in detail what constituted the necessities of a 'mere nobleman's' way of life, especially when it included details such as beds for guests, the best pieces of jewellery and tin, and five trunks of linen. Events such as these in Gossweinstein were by no means exceptional happenings in the bishopric of Bamberg, but the situation was quite different in Lower Franconia where there was much less discipline leading to excesses like in Kitzingen where graves were disturbed and the head of St Hadelogis was used for bowls (Endres, 1971: 121ff.).

In many cases an immediate cause of looting and destruction was provided by fear of gaining nothing for oneself, as well as the threat, or often only the rumour, that neighbouring peasant bands would take on the task for themselves. Kronach town called upon its neighbouring nobility to pull down their own buildings and thereby forestall any action from the peasant band at Hallstadt, for, if the latter did arrive, the damage done would be far greater. In all, twenty-five castles were pulled down before the peasants could set about the task themselves. Auhausen and Heidenheim monasteries were plundered by local peasants only when they knew that the peasants of Ries would otherwise do it. The plunder fell into the margrave Casimir's hands, although he did not return it to the Church, and he continued to draw up his own monastic inventories, ostensibly for protection against the peasants, but in fact to enrich his own treasury (ibid.).

The margrave Casimir's role during the uprising was one of sheer opportunism. The peasants believed right to the end that he was their ally since he had introduced the Reformation in all his territories and had even met nearly all the demands of the rebels at a territorial assembly in Ansbach on 1 May 1525. This applied even after his victory over the peasants from Ries at the battle of Ostheim on 8 May. He made a week's truce with the peasants from upper Aisch on 19 May, which left him a free hand to deal with rebels in the southern borderlands. In order to play for time, he also made a truce on the basis of the Twelve Articles with the Jaxt peasant band, seemingly on highly unfavourable terms. Along with the Counts of Henneberg, Hohenlohe and Wertheim who had pacts with the rebels, the margrave Casimir was invited to attend the peasant assembly at Schweinfurt, where a decision was taken to seek an agreement with him. Wilhelm von Henneberg played a similar game, and he watched unperturbed as the Bildhauser peasant band plundered church property. Once it was certain that the Swabian League would win, he immediately changed sides and executed 130 rebels, including three parish priests. Bishops Conrad von Thungen and Weigand von Redwitz acted differently. Under conditions of considerable personal danger, each tried to negotiate directly with their rebellious subjects to overcome the grievances that arose. But when the territorial assembly that he had called failed, Conrad fled from the Marienburg in Wurzburg, an act of treason in the eyes of his subjects. However, Weigand von Redwitz stayed to the end in the Altenburg at Bamberg, in contrast to his cathedral chapter canons, who either fled or made alliances with the rebels. On several occasions Weigand tried to negotiate directly with the Hallstadt peasant band, but was turned away by the rebel commanders out of fear for the influence he might have on their rank and file. Weigand immediately accepted the offer from Nuremberg to mediate, and it seems that right to the end he was prepared to make concessions and genuinely redress grievances. He was not responsible for the wholly superfluous punitive expedition of Swabian League troops into his territory, which he tried to prevent. Up to now Bishop Weigand's reputation has suffered because of a general misinterpretation of the role that he played in the Peasant War.

The reaction to the uprising shows clearly how great were what Max Steinmetz in thesis 32 has called the inner contradictions in the class alliance of the reactionaries. The margrave Casimir travelled through the countryside on a sadistic campaign of revenge. For example, he blinded sixty Kitzingen citizens on the cynical pretext that they had refused 'to look upon him' as their lord (Gross, 1855: 114ff., 137 ff.). His brother eventually reminded him that he would have to seek his own livelihood if he slaughtered all his peasants. Bishop Conrad of Wurzburg also set up his own courts of punishment, which decreed well over two hundred executions in the bishopric, including almost one hundred in the town of Wurzburg alone, although for these the bishop was not solely responsible. He also imprisoned another two hundred citizens, of whom some were even tortured (Hoyer, 1952: 435ff.). Perhaps it was not without good reason that, a few years later, Bishop Conrad sought and obtained absolution from the Pope in Rome for all the irregularities that had occurred during the suppression of the uprising. Conrad and his entourage were above all keen to suppress all signs of Lutheranism, which they regarded as the real cause for the lack of obedience and loyalty among his subjects (Merx, 1907: 155).

By way of contrast, in Bamberg very few executions took place in reprisal, and they were nearly all perpetuated by the Swabian League. Nuremberg arbitrators gave warning to Bamberg rebels to plead for Bishop Weigand's mercy in good time, since this ruling prince was known to be 'no bloodthirsty man'.

Surprisingly, Bishop Weigand, whom Georg Truchsess von Waldburg considered more of a monk than a territorial ruler, took no reprisals against the Protestants, although his cathedral chapter tried to blame them solely for causing the uprising. No burghers and peasants were interrogated for their religious views. To start with, even Lutherans at court were left in office. Weigand did not begin to harden on the question of religion until 1527–8, and this was probably due to the problem of the anabaptists (Endres, 1971: 132ff.).

Weigand speedily handled the problem of compensation in order to forestall reprisals taken in revenge. Already on 3 July 1525 he made an agreement with those of the nobility, and shortly after with those of the chapter, who had been hit by the uprising. A commission of two bishop's representatives, two nobles, two masons and two carpenters was appointed to assess the amount of damage done to buildings. For lost property, nobles had to draw up an exact list on their 'noble honour and faith'. The Bamberg nobility claimed about 170,000 florins in damages. To pay for this, Weigand ordered an extraordinary wealth tax of 5 per cent to be levied only on rebels, including those who were tenants of the nobility and cathedral chapter. The chapter had demanded a higher rate of assessment at 20 per cent. The money collected was insufficient, and in the autumn of 1526 a hearth tax of 3 florins and a poll tax of 1 florin was levied. In 1527 a final composite tax made its appearance. Every hearth paid 1½ florins, and on top of this 1 florin had to be paid on every 30 florins of wealth. Weigand showed considerable understanding for the position of the ordinary poor, as can be seen in the way that he tried to protect them from excessive fines, which led the margrave Casimir to comment that such mercy would only set off another uprising (Jörg, 1851: 633).

In Wurzburg, Bishop Conrad eventually followed the example of Bamberg, and on 29 November 1525 he made an agreement with chapter, nobles and common country (*Landschaft*). But nobles' compensation granted by a mixed commission ran as high as 273,209½ florins and 1 ort, which was to be recouped by a massive house tax of 8½ florins, to be paid in three instalments with no exemptions at all. Hence the poor paid at the same rate as the rich and were thus much harder hit by the tax. Apart from this castle tax, fines for rebelling were levied on the urban population for a period of three years, at a rate that was equivalent to annual land tax. In two years it brought 54,205 florins into the bishop's coffers (Staatsarchiv Würzburg, Standbuch 487, f. 487). Wurzburg town itself was fined even more heavily with a supplementary 10 florins per hearth to be quit of punishment by troops of the Swabian League. The town had to hand over all its ready cash, silverware, rents and properties to the bishop. Anyone who could not pay the fine either fled or was driven out of the bishopric. This included substantial numbers of people, as can be checked in the lists that Bishop Conrad ordered to be drawn up a few years later to see what had happened to them (Denzinger, 1848: 113ff.).

The town of Kitzingen was punished hardest of all. Since 1443 it had been held as a pledge for debts by the margraves of Franconian Brandenburg. Casimir fined its 500 households a total of 13,000 florins, which was far more than the much larger town of Bamberg paid to its rulers. On top of this came a customary castle tax of 2½ florins per hearth and a weekly poll tax of 15 pfennig per citizen to rebuild the destroyed monastic church. Refugees who had left the town were ordered to return within a given period of time, after which their families were expelled and property confiscated. Of the sixty citizens who had been blinded on Casimir's orders, only those who paid an extra 10 per cent of their wealth were allowed to remain in their homes (Böhm, 1893: 94–162).

Considering these massive fines imposed on peasants and burghers, it is important to examine any economic consequences that occurred as a result of reaction to the uprising. This is just as controversial as assessing the political, legal, religious and confessional consequences of the Peasant War. For the nobility the consequences seemed clear enough. As Wurzburg town scribe Cronthal wrote, 'many a house, castle and property was assessed for damages far beyond its worth. Many old and patchy rats' nests were assessed by their noble owners at such high damages that they were able to replace ugly old hulks with handsome new palaces' (1887: 111f.). Cronthal wrote this perhaps not only out of hatred and envy as a citizen who had been seriously hit by having to pay such fines to the nobility. Many a petty nobleman was undoubtedly relieved to be rid of his old cramped turret or tower, which he now replaced, at no cost to himself, with an up-to-date and more spacious building.

Bearing in mind that every new episcopal election meant substantial investiture tax, the sum total of all the fines which were levied after the Peasant War in the bishoprics of Wurzburg and Bamberg, the former being harder hit than the latter, can be roughly estimated to have equalled two or three investiture taxes, that is the equivalent of what Bamberg had to pay at the beginning of the sixteenth century when its ruling bishops had died in quick succession. With this background it is not surprising that the demanded sums of money could be collected within four years of the event. Yet since the fines often had to be literally squeezed out of the population, as, for example, in Kitzingen and in the Wurzburg area, we have to be wary of drawing any conclusions as to the socio-economic condition of the population on the eve of the Peasant War from the size of the fines.

Undoubtedly it was the poor people in the countryside as well as in the towns who were hardest hit by these collective fines to buy off reprisals from troops of the Swabian League, tax for rebuilding castles and extra land taxes for territorial rulers. A rich peasant whose farm was worth several hundred gulden could quite easily pay castle tax of

8½ florins as well as various other fines, but for the majority of the population these fines were a real threat to their existence. A labourer earning an average 15 pfennig a day was paying the equivalent of his whole earnings for half a year just for this one castle tax. The representative of Hesse at the Swabian League, Eberhard von Radenhausen, probably assessed the situation accurately when he reported to Philip of Hesse from Franconia that 'the peasants have been so heavily fined, plundered and burned-out that it will take them many years to get over it' (Merx, 1907: 152).

Although it must be used with caution, tentative comparison of social statistics in the local district (*Amt*) of Burgkunstadt for the years 1524 and 1527 shows us the social consequences of the Peasant War and its aftermath. In these years the number of households worth more than 100 gulden remained static. They had little problem paying fines. The number of middle-sized and small households worth between 26 and 100 florins decreased by 4 per cent. But instead of seeing a corresponding increase in the number of poorest farms worth less than 25 florins, this latter group itself decreased by 14 per cent. Many of the poorest farmers had either become totally destitute or had even fled from their homes (Endres, 1971: 135).

These unmistakable economic difficulties for Franconian peasants and small burghers in the years immediately after the Peasant War were not only due to the high fines that were imposed, but were probably even more due to further day-to-day burdens such as some of the following extraordinary taxes. As soon as all the fines had been paid in Bamberg and Wurzburg, they were immediately followed by an extraordinary land tax in 1530. In 1532, Turk tax was levied as wealth tax of 2 per cent. In 1537, Turk tax was paid as a combined 1 per cent wealth tax and 2 florins hearth tax. Turk tax reappeared as a 1 per cent levy on wealth in 1543, and imperial taxes were imposed in 1542, 1544, 1547 and 1548 at rates of 1 to 2 per cent on all wealth. To this we must add years of poor harvest, above all 1527, 1529–34 and 1540–41 with attendant price rises and food shortages, leading many peasants into bankruptcy (Endres, 1968: 27ff.). The ruin of these peasants was thus not just due to the Peasant War and its immediately consequent period of reaction, as Friedrich Engels implied – at least not in Franconia (MEW, 7: 409).

Peasant War and Reformation are seen as the focal point of a German 'early bourgeois revolution' in Marxist-Leninist historiography, according to which the complex of class struggle in the transition from feudalism to capitalism grew out of a genuine revolutionary situation encompassing the broadest levels of an emergent nation. Crass social differences created by inherent contradictions in feudalism led to increased activity of the masses in the countryside just as among the plebeians in the towns. Hence the moderate as much as the radical wings of the early bourgeois revolution demanded reorganisation of society and state, in which the moderates were eventually dragged along by the radicals to making greater revolutionary demands.

But the actual conflicts that took place during the Peasant War in Franconia only contain very little of value to the above theory, and no monocausal explanation, from whichever angle, is valid. The causes, motives and sequence of events were far too complex and many-sided. The reform movements and uprisings of peasants and poorer burghers in Franconia were certainly very closely linked. But there can be really very little or no justification for seeing a revolutionary change to the predominant ecclesiastical, socio-economic and political system, let alone of seeing 'a national German unity arising from destruction of princely power' (Steinmetz, 1961: 51). There was no unity above the level of the territorial state, nor agreement between burghers and peasants. In Franconia the traditional order was not to be overthrown, but only to be improved or re-established on the basis of Holy Writ. That is why demands were made to abolish burdensome intermediate layers of society, such as the privileged clergy and nobility, to secularise monastic land, the rich rewards from which were to be distributed among ordinary people. The chief aims of the rebels in Franconia were to create centrally governed, more socially cohesive territorial states in which the Gospel could be freely preached; subjects would pay less taxes and be protected from arbitrary levies. That no radical-revolutionary demands appeared was due not only to the lack of alliance between rural and urban proletariat, nor merely to an underdeveloped level of class-consciousness and organisation among the broad mass of the proletariat (subjective conditions which are indivisibly tied to objective ones), but rather due to the complicated patchwork of small territorial states in Franconia, which created very local, narrow-minded attitudes; to the absence of an effective revolutionary like Thomas Muntzer, who could carry the masses along with him; and not least also to the disunity of princely opposition, whose mutual rivalries made any kind of co-operation at a Franconian level quite impossible (Bensing, 1966: 251). This poses an interesting question for Marxist ideology, as to whether it is a law of earlier history that individuals can deputise for classes before the latter have emerged fully developed.

KARL CZOK

7   The Socio-economic Structure and Political Role of the Suburbs in Saxony and Thuringia in the Age of the German Early Bourgeois Revolution*

I

It was primarily its commercial establishments which made the suburb an indispensable component of the town: the various mills, forges, copperworks, smithies, baking ovens, rope-making workshops, cattle- and slaughter-yards, sandpits and brickworks, bleaching grounds and bath-houses (brothels), vineyards and hopgardens, inns and unharnessing yards, as well as sheds, barns and stables, fields and gardens. The economic structure of the suburb was thus determined both by trade and commerce and by agriculture and gardening. It represented, above all in the larger towns, an essential economic area. Without the suburb, further economic development of the town would have been checked, as was seen at a later date in towns which were forced into a strait-jacket by fortifications. Even then new suburbs always sprang up. Even when war, fire or other catastrophes, the building of fortifications or urban expansion destroyed them, as in Augsburg in 1377, Leipzig in 1546 and 1631, or many times in Stralsund between the sixteenth and the nineteenth centuries, it was usually not too long before they were rebuilt, in the old or in new places. Whether large or small towns were involved, it was primarily socio-economic factors which influenced the rise and development of suburbs (Maschke and Sydow, 1969: 80ff., 96ff.). Thus in the Leipzig west-suburb (the Rannisch suburb) during the sixteenth century there were several mills, a barber's, and cattle- and slaughter-yards, all based on old custom. There had been two or three brickworks in various suburbs of Leipzig since the thirteenth century. The two town-council brickworks before the Petersgate and

*Edited translation of Karl Czok, 'Zur sozialökonomischen Struktur und politischen Rolle der Vortstädte im Sachsen und Thüringen im Zeitalter der deutschen frühbürgerlichen Revolution', *Wissenschaftliche Zeitschrift Karl-Marx-Universität Leipzig*, 24, 1975, pp. 53–68.

efore the Ranstadter Gate between 1471 and 1490 often produced ʌer 500,000 bricks and 250,000 tiles annually. A depiction of the town council's brickshed in Peter's suburb in the oldest city view of Leipzig from 1547 shows a large two-storeyed building, although suburban houses were usually one-storeyed. With its large area it is easily recognisable as one of the largest places of production in the urban area. During the events of April/May 1525 in Leipzig, insurgents gathered in the brickshed to discuss the imminent conflict of Duke George of Saxony with the Thuringian peasants. There were also brickworks in the suburbs of Chemnitz and Weimar and in numerous other towns.

In Leipzig the tanners were concentrated in the Hallisch suburb, where the river Parthe supplied the water they required. Here there was a tanning mill and the tanner's fields could spread themselves out. Similarly, in Chemnitz, a necessary part of linen production, the city bleachery and bleaching houses, stood before the Monastery Gate. In the suburb Old Chemnitz, besides the mills, there was a clothmaker's fulling mill and a metal refinery (Kunze, 1958: 24ff.). These commercial establishments did not owe their development so much to the fact that they stood on the main road, but rather to special conditions of location resulting from geographical factors and from peculiarities of production. Thus in 1492 the Chemnitz town council decreed that bakers who, because of poverty, could not build their bakery or coal-pit from stone, should conduct their baking and business outside the town; the same was decreed for the smiths and the bath-house owners (Uhle, 1922: 11).

The development and growth of the suburbs in terms of size and socio-economic structure in the Thuringian-Saxon area can be followed more clearly in the fifteenth and sixteenth centuries. The question of their exact time of origin must remain unanswered for Leipzig, Dresden, Chemnitz, Erfurt, Muhlhausen, Weimar, Rochlitz, Colditz, Wurzen and others. In individual cases, it can be shown that many suburban layouts with a mixed commercial structure (trade and agriculture) existed even in the thirteenth century. In Muhlhausen in Thuringia, for example, suburbs around St Peter's and St Nikolai are mentioned in 1220. However, only in the fifteenth and sixteenth centuries is it clear that, for example, Colditz and Muhlhausen each had five suburbs, Leipzig, Chemnitz and Halle four each, Weimar three, and Magdeburg, Rochlitz and Wurzen two each. In Pirna we know so far of only one suburb, the Shippersgate suburb. Their number was thus dependent neither on the size of the town, nor on the number of main roads and city gates.

In Leipzig, according to the Turk tax register of 1529, there were six city gates, but only four suburbs. But these four had already attained substantial dimensions, for the total number of suburban houses was only a hundred less than those in the inner city (Table 7.1).

Table 7.1   *Residential houses in Leipzig 1554* (Feige, 1965 : 165).

Inner city		Suburbs	
1 Grimma Quarter	152	Grimma	160
2 St Peter's Quarter	158	St Peter's	130
3 Hainisch Quarter	145	Rannisch	99
4 Hallisch Quarter	118	Hallisch	86
Total no. houses	573		475
No. taxpayers	1937		918
No. of houseowners	527		344

The suburb of Grimma at the eastern exit of the town had more houses than the corresponding quarter of the inner city. There was also a multiplicity of rented houses in the suburbs (119 in all), whereas the inner city had only sixteen. The number of lodgers in the houses outside the city (436) was twice as high as those within the walls (217). This leads to the conclusion that the many smaller suburban houses had to house considerably more people than the roomy two- or three-storeyed houses of the inner city. In Dresden in 1454, on the other hand, each house in the inner city had on average just over seven residents, whereas on average only four people lived in each suburban house (Kunze, 1958 : 54).

Smaller towns also revealed a considerable growth of their suburbs within a few decades, as can be seen in the cases of Frankenberg, Oederan, Leisnig, Mittweida and Colditz (Table 7.2). Linen-weavers,

Table 7.2   *Houses in and before the city of Colditz* (Colditz, 1965 : 107).

Year	Inner City	Suburbs
1506	49	47
1540	51	113
1548	50	98
1551	58	133
1595	59	214

tanners, smiths and potters are the artisans often represented here, who also pursued gardening, agriculture and animal husbandry as a second trade – although more cows were kept in 1551 inside the city of Colditz (109) than in the suburbs (41). Rapid growth of the suburbs must have been a general phenomenon of the development of towns during the fifteenth century. Muhlhausen in Thuringia had only two small suburbs in 1220, but in the fifteenth century it had five with over 3,000 residents (Vetter, 1910 : 37). In two towns which were developing as princely residences, Dresden and Weimar, the number of suburban houses and dwellings was also growing. In Weimar the inner city doubled its

number of houses between 1507 and 1557, whereas its suburbs grew
five times as big.

The growth of the number of residents, and in particular the growth
of suburban houses, in Chemnitz can be traced in large measure to the
development of linen-weaving and the cloth industry. In 1466 there
were 132 houses in the suburbs, but in 1495 this number had risen to
196, and in 1531 to 238 (Kunze, 1958: 54, 63). Corresponding to the
needs of linen production, the suburbs extended largely along the river
Chemnitz and the stream beds. Thus the city bleachery and the bleaching houses, for example, lay before the Monastery Gate, and the
clothmakers' fulling mill by the mills before the Old Chemnitz Gate.
In 1400 the mayor and town council decreed that the linen-weavers
should keep watch for two days and nights before the city. In 1474 we
hear of Chemnitzers who had pieces of field before one of the gates in
order to earn a living: these are all poor folk, and can hardly raise as
much as they require for their weekly upkeep in the gardens that they
have, and by following their trade (ibid.: 53). This indicated the varied
social structure of the city and its suburbs. The fact that there was a
more or less considerable drop in wealth from the one to the other has
long been known. Already in 1910, Vetter had demonstrated this
statistically for Muhlhausen in Thuringia from 1418 to 1553 (63ff.).
While the total amount of taxable wealth in the inner city rose in this
period from 55,531 to 64,704 marks, the overall wealth of the suburbanites fell from 6,296 to 3,834 marks (allowing for a reduction of 90 in
the number of suburban residents liable to taxation) (ibid.: 37, 73).
Similar figures have recently become available for other towns in
Saxony and Thuringia (Table 7.3).

The land-tax register of 1554 provides information about the percentage of taxpayers in Leipzig who were without any wealth (Table
7.4). From this one can deduce that only a few of those without wealth,

Table 7.3   *Wealth structure in Weimar, 1542.*

Wealth in gulden	Inner city	Suburbs
1 – 25	41	49
26 – 50	41	20
51 – 75	21	5
76 – 100	22	6
101 – 150	18	2
151 – 200	17	1
201 – 300	16	—
301 – 400	10	—
401 – 500	8	—
501 – 600	3	—
601 – 700	2	—
701 – 800	1	—
Total	200	83

Table 7.4   *Those without property in the city and suburbs of Leipzig (1554), expressed as percentage of taxpayers.*

City district Quarters:	Total taxpayers	Propertyless – %		
		Independent	Menial	Total
Grimmaisch	466=100	6·9	59·7	66·6
St Peter's	584=100	3·9	65·0	68·9
Hainisch	496=100	4·0	63·7	67·7
Hallisch	391=100	5·6	56·0	61·6
Total inner city	1937=100	5·0	61·9	66·9
Suburbs:				
Grimmaisch	346=100	46·2	17·6	63·8
St Peter's	246=100	44·7	9·8	54·5
Rannisch	174=100	48·3	10·3	58·6
Hallisch	152=100	28·9	23·0	51·9
Total suburbs	918=100	43·4	15·0	58·4
Total inner city and suburbs	2855=100	17·3	46·6	63·9

5 per cent in fact, lived independently in the inner city, that is, poorer master craftsmen or day-workers, while menials, apprentices and maids – the dependent poor – were more strongly represented with over 60 per cent. In the suburbs the relationship was reversed. Here there were over 40 per cent of the independent poor, and only 15 per cent of the dependent poor residents. This result is fairly obvious, in so far as the rich Leipzig merchants, some printers and many master craftsmen employed several apprentices, maids, servants, day-workers and journeymen, while only a few residents of the suburbs could afford such employees (Table 7.5). It is also interesting that of twenty-six couriers (*Boten*) who offered their services in 1554 in this city of trade fairs, twenty-five lived in the suburbs (Prochno, 1933: 32). However, the bulk of the master craftsmen of Leipzig also lived and worked there. Of the citizens who were taxed on wealth of up to 100 gulden, only

Table 7.5   *Distribution of menials (apprentices and maids) in the quarters and suburbs of Leipzig 1481, 1502, 1506* (Wustmann, 1889: 70, 102).

Year	Quarters				
	Grimmaisch	St Peter's	Hainisch	Hallisch	Suburbs
1481	232	352	281	342	110
1502	173	228	218	222	68
1506	289	387	334	332	117

112 were from the inner city, but 247 came from the suburbs (Feige, 1965: 192). Whereas each of the inner city masters employed as a rule two or three journeymen, the suburban masters employed *in toto* only twenty-one persons designated as menials.

That the various suburbs of a town could have a completely different social structure can be shown in many cases, for example by a comparison of the Leipzig suburbs of Grimma and St. Peter's. In the first were found most of those persons who were designated in the Turk-tax book of 1529 as destitute (*nihil habet*), that is, they were so poor that they were unable to pay any tax (eighty-six entries in all). Only six of these were registered before the Petersgate, and none in the other two suburbs. In the suburb of Grimma lived as well most of the day-workers and linen-weavers, the majority of whom were propertyless (see Table 7.6).

Table 7.6 *Selected independent occupations without and with wealth in the suburbs of Leipzig 1554* (cf. Feige, 1965: 238ff.; Prochno, 1933: 26ff.).

Occupation	Grimmaisch Suburb		St Peter's Suburb		Rannisch Suburb		Hallisch Suburb		Total Suburbs	Total city overall
Day-worker	27	12	21	3	7	1	—	—	71	83
Mason	10	8	10	12	2	3	3	1	47	52
Linen-weaver	10	4	7	1	2	3	—	—	27	41
Carpenter	9	20	4	3	5	—	1	3	45	49
Tanner	—	—	—	—	—	—	6	12	18	51
Knacker	15	9	2	—	4	—	3	—	25	?

Parts of Grimma were torn down in 1494. When the suburbs were set alight in 1456 at the command of Duke Maurice of Saxony, it was Grimma which suffered the greatest destruction, as the oldest city view of Leipzig shows. Of the four suburbs in this city of trade fairs, Grimma was probably the poorest, but it was also the most heavily populated. The streets and houses before the Petersgate, on the other hand, lay in the protective shadow of castle Pleissenburg. Here there were many hostelries and almost as many corner inns as houses, as well as much monastic property and various persons who were taxed on owning substantial property.

The situation in Halle was probably much the same, if one compares the suburbs Glaucha and Neumarkt. Glaucha was a predominantly proletarian residential quarter in the sixteenth century. Thomas Muntzer preached here in 1522–3 in the Marienkammer of the Cistercian monastery and found a large audience among the plain folk (Neuss, 1958: 18). In the Halle suburb of Neumarkt, which was linked to the Augustinian monastery of Neuwerk, artisans such as masons, carpenters, tailors, butchers and bakers predominated among the residents. But there were also grocers, peasants and gardeners (ibid.: 103). In Colditz the residents before the Barbers' Gate were better off than those before the Nikolai Gate. In Weimar such folk lived before the Jacobsgate, which was the area of heaviest taxation; they were mostly small traders and bakers. In Erfurt, too, the suburbs lying between the inner and the outer walls had a varied structure. On the one hand, the city squires and patricians had their vineyards and hop-gardens there, on the other hand, weavers worked there, as well as other artisans who were forbidden to have workshops in the inner city because of fire danger, such as smiths and bakers. Here, too, lived numerous labourers, day-workers, beggars, serfs and bondsmen (Neubauer, 1914: 13ff., 45).

The social structure of the suburban population in both the larger and smaller towns of Saxony and Thuringia was determined by various groups of people who belonged to differing social strata, and by other factors closely connected to the socio-economic relations of each individual town.

The artisans were a relatively numerous group: masons, carpenters, smiths, tanners, weavers, shoemakers, butchers, bakers, fishermen and linen-weavers are named most frequently in the sources. To these must be added those working in agriculture and gardening, such as peasants, gardeners and vintners. A part of the master craftsmen were socially independent, had modest wealth and owned their own small house. There would scarcely have been any great social difference between these and the poorer masters of the inner city. They were close to the lowest stratum of the bourgeoisie.

Numerous suburban artisans found themselves in a completely dependent social position, for they depended on the merchants and rich master craftsmen of the town, the more so with stronger development of the putting-out system and manufactures. This has been convincingly shown for a large part of Saxony by the work of Arno Kunze (Kunze and Aubin, 1940: 42ff.; cf. Heitz, 1961), and more recent research has even shown that in a suburb of Gorlitz (Lunitz) early forms of manufacturing developed, with master craftsmen working together as employees of the same enterprise (*Meistereien*). In nine large work-shops, merchants and rich master craftsmen employed impoverished master clothmakers, journeymen and assistants just like proletarians.

Clearly these dependent and poor independent master craftsmen stood socially close to the plebeian classes, to whom belonged, on the one hand, day-workers, labourers, journeymen, apprentices, maids and couriers as productively active persons, who could be employed both in the inner city and the suburbs. On the other hand, there were beggars, riff-raff, the poor and the diseased as unproductive folk, who were a burden to the entire urban population and were often banned by the town council and the citizenry to the outer districts. Finally, serfs and bondsmen were often mentioned as living in the suburbs. These could belong either to the property of secular or spiritual feudal lordships that lay before the gates, or could be refugees, who wanted to enter the city from the countryside. For some the suburbs were only a transit route, but for many they were the end of the road.

The social differences between all the groups of the suburban populace were of no such great significance as those on the inside of the great towns, where deep-rooted social conflicts and differences of status existed between the patricians or ruling families, the bourgeois middle class and the plebeian classes. In a position as outsiders, sharply distinguished from the citizenry, the suburbanites were oppressed by their lack of political and constitutional rights. This, in turn, worked on them as a leveller, whether they were master craftsmen, journeymen, apprentices, day-workers or beggars. A graphic example of the social and economic disadvantages, and of the lack of political rights of the suburban population, is found in the clash between the citizens and suburbanites of Jena in 1404, where the latter complained that their burdens were too high, that they could not brew or draw wine or beer, that they had no control over civic finances, although they mostly paid tax, and that the town council never answered their complaints (Maschke, 1973: 368).

Nearly all residents of the suburbs were constitutionally disadvantaged or completely without rights. In Halle they were not counted as free citizens, but as subjects of the council, who were called 'neighbours' and obliged to do labour service like the peasants, as for example by the building of fortifications in 1536. In most suburbs the town council exercised complete jurisdiction. In Muhlhausen in Thuringia the suburban population also had a position similar to that of the peasants. According to the city statutes there, if a citizen wounded a suburbanite he had to pay a 6-gulden fine and endure four weeks' house arrest; in the reverse situation the suburbanite lost his head (Bemmann, 1915: 9). Just as underprivileged were the 'folk before the gates' in Erfurt, though since the end of the fifteenth century they did have the advantage of living for the most part in the protection provided between the two rings of walls, similar to those who lived within the protection of the 'boundary-ditch' in Muhlhausen.

Certainly, there were suburbs with very varied constitutional arrangements, as for example in Leipzig. Here individual lanes and parts of streets were under the council, that is under city law. If they were able to pay at all, their residents were taxed by the council. Other parts of the suburbs belonged to the monasteries, especially St Thomas. The so-called Altenburg, however, with fifteen hereditary houses and six rented houses, belonged to the rich bourgeois Preusser family. This was an independent community with its own judge; the hereditary court was controlled by the Preussers, but supreme jurisdiction was under the territorial ruler. The community fell into the city's possession in 1544. However, the council was responsible for policing the suburbs, enforced by a constable (*Gassenmeister*). There were similar differences in the constitutional position of individual suburbs or parts of suburbs in Halle, where Glaucha and Neumarkt became administrative towns during the sixteenth century.

It emerges clearly from investigation of the economic, social, political and legal relations in the suburbs that the territorial ruler, the town council, the church and the bourgeois upper class each ruled there according to special circumstances. These were linked to the possessions and property they owned there as persons or institutions: economic establishments, above all mills, fulling mills, bleaching grounds, workshops, land and property, all of which were often leased to individuals or corporations (e.g. guilds). In the interests of preserving their rule, it could at no stage be a matter of indifference to them what occurred economically or politically in the settlements before the town. There were also military considerations for the territorial ruler or the town council, and at times these were uppermost. They intervened mercilessly in the life of the suburb on such occasions; whoever settled there was never secure against arbitrary behaviour. Its population must therefore have been subject to more unpredictable economic, social and political changes. That this influenced the socio-economic relations and the class struggles of the entire city is only understandable. Thus it is not permissible to regard the suburb merely as an appendage of its town.

Marx's statement that the capitalist era can be dated from the sixteenth century is closely linked to the process he described of primitive accumulation, that is, the process of separating the producer from the means of production. This development, which involved in the first place the expropriation of the rural producer, the peasant (MEW, 23: 753f.), was clear in the German Empire during the sixteenth century, especially in the suburbs. For they were exactly points of concentration for those who were already expropriated – labourers, day-workers, apprentices, couriers, carters – or for those who in fact faced expropriation, as did the continually growing number of eternal journeymen and impoverished masters. To this must be added those whose activity indicated a proletarian status: brickmakers, sanders (*Sandwerfer*), market-hands and sweepers, handlers of lime (*Kalkmesser*), domestic stokers (*Stubenheizer*), doorkeepers, unloaders, donkey drivers and others. The putting-out system and early manufacturing spread itself often with less restriction in the suburbs than in the inner city, so furthering the process of primitive accumulation. When one counts in the numerous poor immigrants and refugees from the land and the peasant suburban population, there emerges all in all a very heterogeneous society, which was forced into an outsider position by its location. It is understandable that it did not refrain from participation in conflicts and class struggles (cf. Czok, 1975).

II

During the German early bourgeois revolution the suburban populace played a prominent role alongside the peasants as a political driving force in the socio-religious conflicts and class struggles. It is well known that Marxist historiography sees in the Reformation and Peasant War the first act of the early bourgeois revolution in Europe. In all of these revolutions, from the German, Dutch and English up to the French Revolution, the suburban population belonged to the progressive driving forces. If the early bourgeois revolution was first of all given the task of removing feudal restrictions (dependence, labour service, services, dues and territorial splintering), of furthering capitalist developments, and of breaking the predominance of the Roman Catholic Church and reforming it in a bourgeois sense, all these concerns were also mirrored in the struggle of the suburban population. Their socio-economic and geographical position, lying as it were between town and country, led them to take sides at once with insurgent peasants and citizens.

Many residents of the suburbs took an active part in the popular reformation movements in the first half of the 1520s; indeed, in many cases, they even helped set these in motion. After Martin Luther presented his programme of church reform in his writings of 1520, and as more and more preachers adhered to his teaching, the suburbs of Leipzig, Halle and Muhlhausen became starting points for popular reformation movements. The pulpits of the Leipzig city churches were closed to the young preachers of the Reformation, but after 1522 they found an ever more attentive audience in the small suburban churches and chapels. Master Froschel from Wittenberg made his confession by preaching in four churches in the suburbs, with the result that he won a great following and was finally cited before Duke George. He was driven from the town because an open-air sermon in October 1523 had nearly caused a riot. But there was soon a successor to Froschel, Andreas Bodenschatz, who attracted even greater crowds, including an increasing number of citizens from the inner city, so that the suburban churches could no longer hold the crowds. Finally, 105 citizens and residents from all parts of the city petitioned the council to place one of the two large city churches at his disposal. The petition was signed by some of the richest citizens as well as by poor master craftsmen, who in May 1525 under the influence of the Peasant War joined citizens of the inner city in a conspiracy (Gess, 1905, no. 630). In Altenburg in Thuringia, seventy-seven citizens also composed a similar petition in 1522 and presented it to the council. The Leipzig demands, however, were passed on to the duke, who sharply rejected them. But despite frequent opposition from the territorial ruler, the reformation movement which had first struck roots in the suburban populace could not be checked.

Adherents of Lutheran teachings also appeared in Halle in 1521, but it was not until Thomas Muntzer preached in the Marienkammer of St George's monastery in the suburb of Glaucha, a predominantly proletarian district, that this following grew into a popular reformation movement. Among his friends was, for example, a suburbanite, Michael from Steintor. Muntzer finally became the spiritual author of a disturbance of suburbanites, journeymen and salt-miners at the end of 1522, which was directed in the first instance against the Neuwerk monastery, but also against the town council and against Cardinal Albert of Mainz and his clergy. About 300 insurgents marched to the town hall and wanted to break down the doors, throw the council from the town hall and strike them dead. Then they marched to the Moritzburg and held rebellious and blasphemous speeches: 'they shit on such a bishop, and into his pointed hat as well' (Neuss, 1958: 79). Doubtless the popular reformation movement in Halle received an essential impulse from this which culminated in a rebellion in 1525, and which forced concessions from the cardinal for as long as he was in peril.

Everywhere the suburban population must have participated in the numerous parson storms and stormings of monasteries, even if this does not always appear clearly in the available sources. Many monasteries lay on the fringes of the town or directly in the suburbs. Certainly 'those before the gates' took part in the storming of the clergy of St Severus and St Mary in Erfurt alongside students, apprentices and peasants; the same in the storm of the Wittenberg Franciscan abbey in 1521 (Eitner, 1903: 17ff.; Müller, 1911, no. 10). In March 1522 it was largely clothmakers' apprentices who broke into the Grunhainer manor of the Cistercians in Zwickau, and in 1523 rebels stormed St John's monastery in Halberstadt, which lay in the suburban area (Wappler, 1908: 17ff.).

The clearest evidence of how a reformation popular movement turned into a socio-political action with the prominent participation of sub-urbanites is found in the events of 1523 in Muhlhausen in Thuringia. Here Heinrich Pfeiffer preached in the Nikolai church in the suburb of the same name. One of his sermons in April led to a rising, with strong participation of the suburban population, who, as associate citizens, were strongly disadvantaged compared with the full citizens, since they were placed on the same minimal legal footing as the peasants. They expected an improvement in their position from the newly elected citizen committee and the 'eight men', who now ruled beside the town council as a form of second government. On the occasion of the September rebellion in 1524, three of the five suburbs, besides the nearby quarter of St Jacob and the linen-weavers' guild, presented the council with Twelve Articles. Later, when the 'Eternal Covenant of God' was created under the influence of Thomas Muntzer, numerous suburbanites also joined it: of the hundred members whose names are known, fifty-eight belonged to the inner city, but forty-two came from the Muhlhausen suburbs and sixteen of these were property-less (Lösche, 1960: 151ff.).

Suburban residents also contributed substantially to the radicalisation of the popular reformation movement in Magdeburg, which had two independent suburbs, Neustadt and Sudenburg, which were not included in the city fortifications and stood under the lordship of the archbishop. However, the impulse here does not seem to have come from the suburbs, but from the Lutheran pastors of the city church. When Luther was in Magdeburg in 1524 to oppose radical tendencies, the suburbanites turned up to his sermons in droves, but he could not hold them in check. The radical movement now moved into Neustadt, which was under the rule of the archbishop. The bailiff of its mills (*Mollenvogt*), Sebastian Langhans, an eyewitness and chronicler of these events, reported graphically on what followed in Neustadt (Langhans, 1962, reprint: 144ff., cf. 7f.). He reported a disturbance in the monastery chapel of St Agneten, in which 'many loose apprentices and all kinds of common rabble' took part inside the church; and another row in the Lorenz church. Finally, he mentioned numerous suburbanites, who wanted 'to elect a new council according to their pleasure' and did not recognise the legal jurisdiction of the archbishop, for they wished, as the bailiff wrote, 'to be their own masters, and not to obey authority any longer'. There was also a disturbance in the Franciscan abbey, in which the smiths' apprentices especially took part, and the entire Neustadt community refused to pay the cathedral provost their meadow taxes. The movement was constantly in action from the summer of 1524 until the spring of 1525; indeed, it was activated by lay preachers who appeared in the Neustadt church and had all the features of a popular reformation movement.

Intensive participation of the suburban population was also seen in the revolutionary events in Saxony and Thuringia during the Peasant War, which represented the highpoint of the early bourgeois revolution. Their economic and political position in the transitional zone between city and country had clearly increased their activities to the point where they readily understood, out of their own experience, the aims and demands of the peasants and the petty bourgeois opposition within the walls. This was clear with the rising of the suburbanites in Erfurt under their own banner on 28 April 1525. Certainly, the destruction of Mainz property in the suburbs and before the gates is, in the main, to be attributed to them. How far they participated in the rebellion in the inner city is difficult to discover in detail, but certainly they would not have absented themselves. The Articles of the city of Erfurt, however, take little notice of the interests of the suburban population. Certainly, the abolition of compulsory guild membership would have been a wish of those commercially active in the suburbs, and 'those before the gates' especially requested the right to sell their own wine (Franz, 1963: 540ff.). As in Erfurt, the suburban population of Muhlhausen formed a considerable part of the revolutionary element. It was the same in Altenburg, when a storm of the monastery and of clerical houses unleashed a rebellion which extended well beyond the town itself. Citizens, suburbanites and peasants – and in particular linen-weavers – acted together both inside and outside Altenburg and contributed to the spread of the peasant movement into the districts of Altenburg and Borna (cf. Czok, 1975a: 5ff.; 1975b: 155ff.).

The events of the first days of May in Leipzig show especially impressively the co-operation of citizens and suburbanites in a petty bourgeois–plebeian revolutionary movement directed against the territorial lord, the city government and traditional ecclesiastical institutions (Czok and Steinmetz, 1975). If the popular reformation movement rested on a broad base in 1524, the class forces were polarised through the influence of the Peasant War and the military preparations of Duke George against the Thuringian rising. The movement in Leipzig was split. Under the influence of the peasant rebellion and the stubborn stand of the duke, one of the richest Leipzig citizens, Martin Leubel, turned from the movement back to Catholicism. A large part of the wealthy men of property, however, remained true to Luther's moderate Reformation. But another part, largely petty bourgeoisie and plebeians, among them numerous suburbanites – the number of 300 adherents was mentioned – wished to force developments further. Many gathered in secret meetings, in inns and in the brickworks before the town, and discussed further measures. In the face of the concentration of ducal troops in Leipzig at the beginning of May, an open rebellion was threatened by the radical forces, but it was nipped in the bud. Its revolutionary core, to which the suburbanites belonged, had planned to open the gates to the peasants, in order together with them to expel the princes, lords and nobles, and to depose some council members so that a fair evangelical government could be established. Finally, bishops, prelates and monks were to be removed and deprived of their power. No wonder that the duke and the town council had the most steadfast of the revolutionaries, the ringsmith Michael Rumpfer, publicly decapitated (Gess, 1917: no. 1063). With some justification, we can assume that the suburban population was equally involved in the risings in the south Thuringian towns Salzungen and Schmalkalden, as in Plauen in the Vogtland and in Saxon Zwickau. But it was first fully involved in the mining towns of the Erzgebirge, where the capitalistically exploited miners played a special role (cf. Mittenzwei, 1968).

Let us sum up the results of our investigation.

(1) The suburbs were an important socio-economic component of the town. In them were concentrated, in the closest connection with developments within the city, both agricultural and commercial-artisan establishments of production which could not be located in the town because of local, technical or social reasons. The suburbs developed especially quickly in the fifteenth and sixteenth centuries through the growth of productive forces and the intensification of the money–goods relationship. Early forms of capitalist production also grew up here, such as the putting-out system and manufacture, since economic and social relations were especially favourable.

(2) The suburban population was composed of various social groups. The first consisted of independent producers of simple goods:

farmers and artisans, dominated by the master artisans whose trades were exiled into the suburbs, either on technical grounds or, as was more frequently the case, because they belonged to the socially less respectable trades. A second group was composed of the dependent productive artisans and the productively active plebeian forces, such as day-workers, labourers, journeymen, apprentices, couriers, etc., besides serfs and bondsmen. They were probably the most important group of the suburban residents socially and politically, for they were themselves a product of primitive accumulation and had the characteristics of an early proletariat. The third group contained non-productive plebeian elements: beggars, vagabonds, the poor and the sick.

(3) There was not just a social gap between the city bourgeoisie and the suburban population. Compared to the citizens, the suburbanites were politically and legally underprivileged, something often clearly expressed in a conceptual distinction between the two. Moreover, it was often the case that the entire population of a suburb, or some parts of it, stood in feudal dependence, that is, they had to supply corresponding dues and services. The suburbanites' underprivileged position, socially, politically and legally, had a levelling effect in which the differences between their individual groups receded and their common opposition to the city bourgeoisie became more prominent.

(4) On the basis of their socio-economic and constitutional position, the suburban population became politically susceptible to social conflicts and was often their driving force. That was seen during the struggles of the inner city bourgeois opposition during the fourteenth and fifteenth centuries, in which the suburbanites were often involved. In the early bourgeois revolution they now became a special socio-political driving force. Through the popular reformation movement and the Peasant War they hoped to realise their demands and aims of equality and improvement of their position. The results of this German early bourgeois revolution did not, however, fulfil their hopes and desires.

The development and significance of the suburb, as it has been investigated here in a certain cross-section of time and space, justifies intensive research, both backwards into the Middle Ages and forwards into the epoch of capitalism. During the Industrial Revolution the suburb again became largely a point of concentration of the factory industry, of the proletariat and also of the workers' movement.

SIEGFRIED HOYER

8 Arms and Military Organisation in the German Peasant War*

The course of the German Peasant War is characterised by the armed struggle of the popular masses for demands formulated in grievances, articles and programmes. This was the first time in German history that tens of thousands of peasants, plebeians, rural and urban day-workers, artisans and miners armed themselves and waged a revolutionary war against the armies of the feudal nobility. It was not only the issue of power that was decided here, but the success and failure of the entire revolution. In its scope the revolutionary war of 1524–6 is comparable to the medieval peasant rebellions in Italy (1304–7), Flanders (1323–8), France (1356), England (1381), Northern Spain (1437) and Hungary (1514), as well as to the revolutionary Hussite movement in Bohemia (1419–34). All these earlier revolts involved a highly developed but simplified commodity production within the framework of the feudal order. The German Peasant War was essentially different, for it depended on the development of manufacturing capitalism. This had begun to occur extensively in the Holy Roman Empire of the German nation since 1470. A significant centre of gravity in the rise of capitalist relations of production was mining. As a result of this qualitatively new social phenomenon, the German Peasant War became, together with the popular movement against the feudal church, a component of the early bourgeois revolution.

This historical situation determined the class basis: parts of the lower bourgeoisie stood on the side of the peasants, as they had during the peasant movements of the later Middle Ages, but so too did the pre-proletarian miners. The revolutionary situation challenged the bourgeoisie to achieve hegemony in the struggle against feudal domination. Neither subjectively, nor objectively, as a result of its stage of maturity, was it equal to this demand.

Features of warfare on the eve of the Peasant War
In the military system of the progressive countries of Europe during the fifteenth century, the dissolution of armies organised on the basis of

*Translated from Siegfried Hoyer, 'Bewaffnung und militärische Organisation im deutschen Bauernkrieg', Geschichtsunterricht und Staatsbürgerkunde 17 (1975), pp. 97–104. See also S. Hoyer, Das Militärwesen im deutschen Bauernkrieg, 1524–6, Berlin, 1975.

the feudal system was in full swing. The forerunners of this basic change reached back to the twelfth century, but there were considerable changes, especially in the fourteenth century, with the use of longbows and crossbows as auxiliary weapons, with the prominence of infantry in battle, and from the second half of that century the development of firearms. Guns and field pieces played only a limited role in battle for the time being, but castles forfeited their invincibility to wall-shattering cannons.

The economic basis of decisive change in warfare was increased commerce, and thus a more significant role for money in all areas of society. Here above all the extensive production of fine metals since the end of the fifteenth century had its effect. This enabled correspondingly greater expenditure and payment of larger military units. Yet the change from the feudal to the mercenary army did not occur simply through a further development of the older kind of paid footsoldier, who had appeared as an auxiliary alongside the armoured knight since the fifteenth century. There arose rather an infantry with new characteristics. Its model was the Swiss popular army, composed of free peasants and citizens, from the rural and urban communes which formed the Swiss Confederation. In the memorable victories at Morgarten (1315) and Sempach (1386), it had used the hilly country to force the heavily armoured knight to dismount and fight on foot, thus depriving him of the essential advantages of his armament. During the fifteenth century, the Swiss, seasoned by long struggles against the Habsburgs and other feudal powers, learned to assert themselves in open country. The mounted attacks of their opponents broke on the square-shaped phalanx of long pikes, which required discipline, courage and steadfastness. The Swiss sought to decide the battle in close fighting with short weapons, the axe and the short sword. Contemporaries called this kind of fighting, which sought to avoid a longer siege and to halt an opponent quickly, an 'ordinary war'. Yet it was dictated by the composition of the Swiss popular army, for it was difficult for those left behind in the towns and villages to dispense with the labour power of the warriors under arms, and simultaneously to support the army for any length of time.

The Landsknechte, who were being built up in the German feudal state from the end of the fifteenth century, and somewhat later in Spain, were founded on the Swiss model. In the beginning at least, they were a troop of free men of good repute who, despite the extensive disciplinary power of their superiors, possessed in certain matters an autonomous communal administration. The men elected a spokesman, and the 'commune' had the right to receive information on certain questions from the commander before battle, and to judge certain offences of individual mercenaries 'with the long pike'. Maximilian I, who is vastly over-rated in historical writing, at least performed the service of developing the first regiments of German Landsknechte as elite troops, by giving them special attention and by gaining nobles with military experience as officers.

The transition to the mercenary system as the basis of the army, in which incidentally the Swiss led the way by cashing in on their military fame and becoming the popular hired troops of neighbouring princes, began a new epoch of military organisation: entrepreneurial activity in warfare. Wealthy colonels equipped with an imperial patent usually recruited the mercenaries and paid their advances out of their own pockets. However, they usually sought to end a campaign profitably by cheating their employer on receipt of the pay for the recruits, and by extorting money from the population of the area under warfare by plundering and pillaging conquered villages.

Since the Landsknechte were recruited for limited periods from towns and villages, some of the men capable of bearing arms in this manner gained military experience which benefited the popular armies in the German Peasant War. Up to the first third of the sixteenth century the ties of many Landsknechte with their homes and with the class from which they came were not severed, as was to be the case half a century later, when the Landsknecht armies represented an exclusive troop of professional soldiers, for the most part declassed and morally degenerate. Once the mercenary army had become the basis of warfare, money played a significant role in every war: if there was no pay, the men mutinied and the conduct of the war was put at risk.

Did the ordinary peasant have arms and military experience before the Peasant War? In general, the first part of this question can be answered in the affirmative. The rural population in all territories was obliged to defend the wider area about their villages and to supply military service to the feudal state apparatus in pursuit of disturbers of the peace. To this end a great part of the peasantry kept a weapon (pike, short sword) in the home, as well as simple protective dress, which consisted of a harness or a leather jerkin. In individual territories, the ability to use these weapons was tested from time to time by officials of the territorial ruler. Over and above this, a small number of physically suitable men were levied for military service outside the territory, although in this case for wages. The villages were further obliged during a muster to supply wagons, draft animals and labour for field works.

Certainly not all villages before 1525 would have known the exact regulations for their role in the territorial muster. One must also consider that, as a result of the rise of a money–goods relationship, there was a sharply differentiated social structure in the villages, with numbers of day-workers lodging with peasants but engaged in artisan activity as part of the putting-out system. This group of the population was probably not encompassed by such defence regulations, or else only insufficiently. Thus we have to take into account village inhabitants who had no weapon of their own, and who were not normally included in a muster.

As far as the use of weapons goes, this consisted of familiarity with a simple defensive weapon, and of occasional integration into the territorial muster. That is a lot in contrast to those with no knowledge of arms, but not much in comparison with the military experience possessed by a Landsknecht, already a seasoned veteran.

Since the foundation of the towns, or at least since the victory of the communal movements against their overlords, every citizen was obliged to do military service. The armed men of the towns were organised in quarters. Since the fourteenth century the towns had recruited more and more mercenaries for military service, in part, too, those who served as mounted cavalry. For this many local members of the lower and impoverished nobility offered their services. It did not remove a citizen's liability to service, but the practice of richer citizens sending a servant to replace them in the muster was more widespread than in the countryside. All reports confirm that crossbows, guns and cannons were above all concentrated in the towns. Urban shooting companies furthered the regular use of these weapons since the fifteenth century. In the muster for the territorial ruler the cities generally had to supply the guns. With this went the real specialists who could service them professionally, the master gunners. In peacetime the guns were stored in the arsenal. Every city arsenal had a number of such weapons, although by no means always of the latest type, since the acquisition or production of a single gun was extremely costly.

There was also in the towns a larger group of poorer inhabitants, who did not have citizenship and who were only partly, if at all, included in the muster, so that here too it was exactly among the poorer population that there was a lack of weapons and inexperience in their use. In armed risings, even before the early bourgeois revolution, the guild thus formed the nucleus of the rebels, for each guild master had a weapon and belonged to the civic levy.

Military organisation and tactics of the peasant rebels

After the peasants of the county of Stuhlingen, in the south-west of the German Empire, had risen against their lords on 23 June 1524, it soon became clear that the ruling class was no longer in a position to contain this rebellion as they had other local risings in the previous months. The German Peasant War began with the Stuhlingen rising. Certainly some weeks passed before the Stuhlingen peasants were organised militarily. It required a long and complicated formation of consciousness to bring the discontented peasant to the conviction that his demands could not be realised by a request to his lord, but had to be of necessity fought for in arms over time. The peasant was tied to the soil, and a small producer of his own and his family's needs. To bring him to armed struggle during harvest was extremely difficult. Centuries of subjection and recognition of authority, driven home by officials, from the pulpit and in the confessional, had first to be overcome.

It was only some weeks after the rising, at the end of June, that the Stuhlingen peasants 'hoisted the flag'. By this means they organised themselves into a military unit and elected officers. In the course of the Peasant War every military organisation was introduced by this 'hoisting of the flag' and the election of officers. That occurred in the shortest possible time after the rising, mostly some days later, and in the most acute situations only a day later. The election of officers meant the appointment of a field commander, lieutenants and other representatives. The commanders were often not identical with the political leaders of the 'Christian community', the 'Union' or whatever else the rebel organisation was called. For military functions, one looked in general to a man of military experience. In the case of the Stuhlingen peasants, it was the former Landsknecht Hans Muller from Bulgenbach, a man who also played a central role in the planning of a radical programme, namely the Black Forest Peasants' Letter of Articles (*Artikelbrief*). In the Allgau band, the political leadership lay in the hands of the convinced revolutionary Jorg Schmid or Knopf. The chief commander, on the other hand, was Walter Bach, who had served in the army of the Landsknecht leader Georg von Frundsberg, and who played an ambiguous role in the band's last stand at Leubas.

In many places the rebels had difficulties in finding a suitable commander with military experience. That was due in the first place to the fact that the peasants, artisans and day-workers had few of the necessary qualifications to fill this post. Here the political leadership differentiated itself from the military. That the rebels in their search for experienced commanders hit upon persons who left the band in the lurch at the decisive moment – the most significant example here is Gotz von Berlichingen, who acquired his knowledge of the trade of arms as a robber knight and highwayman before 1525 – was counterbalanced by the fact that significant military talent emerged from the people in the course of the struggle. Beside Hans Muller of Bulgenbach one must mention the miners Caspar Prassler and Michel Gruber from the bishopric of Speyer, who on 3 July 1525 surprised and defeated the Styrian territorial muster in Schladming.

The lieutenants deputised for the commander, but the role of the preacher in the peasant band should not be underestimated. On him depended whether the fighting spirit of the rebels was stirred up or not. The most significant example here is Thomas Muntzer, who first accompanied the united Thuringian and Muhlhausen bands and then joined the Frankenhausen band.

The other officers were elected according to the tasks faced by the band. The paymaster took care of pay, the victualer and forager saw respectively to the provisioning of men and beasts, the master of the spoils saw to the seizing of booty and the baggage master to the supply lines. The provosts carried out court-martial judgements and supervised the sale of foodstuffs which came into camp. The artillery master, or

master of the arsenal, and the wagon master had purely military functions. Every company had to elect a sergeant, who was responsible for
order on the march. Locally there were other offices: thus the united
Thuringian and Muhlhausen bands had a pillage-master, who had to
gather up the plunder from the abbeys, etc.

Almost the same offices are found in the Landsknecht armies. These
served the peasants largely as a model for their bands. But if there was
little difference in the specialised activity of the officers in both armies,
these were integrated in the army of the insurgent peasants into a
military order which displayed quite other basic characteristics. The
peasant band was subdivided into companies. However, these were not
of equal strength, for within the company format individual contingents
retained a special position which, without doubt, did not contribute to
the discipline of the total levy. On the whole, those who joined from
one town or one area each formed their own company, and their commander was determined by their place of origin. Also the size of the
band varied considerably. We know of small peasant bands of
2,000 to 3,000 men, but also of some comprising more than 15,000
rebels.

If one observes the activity of the bands during the course of the
Peasant War, it seems at first as though the peasants and plebeians who
were first organised militarily remained under arms until the defeat
of their units. A closer look shows this to be incorrect. Rather the
villages had to supply contingents which were changed about in a
definite period of two to four weeks. This system of rotation is not
difficult to discern in the sources, and was probably practised in all
areas of the German Peasant War, unless the armed struggle ended in
military defeat as it did in Thuringia, barely three weeks after the
beginning of the rebellion. In the archbishopric of Salzburg a few days
after the outbreak of rebellion, some of the miners were released back
into the mines to produce silver, from the sale of which Landsknechte
could be engaged. The Alsace peasants were divided into four groups at
the request of their leaders. By rotation, one group stood under arms,
while the remaining three groups returned to work in their villages and
farms. In this fashion, all farmers performed military service in the
course of a month. This system was dictated by the role of each peasant
in production, and so probably could not be avoided. There is no doubt
that individuals could gain little military experience by this short-term
rotation. This defect, grounded in the historical situation, was first
overcome during the later bourgeois revolutions, when the mass of the
popular armies were composed of the urban classes (petty bourgeoisie
and proletarians).

Both villages and individuals were summoned and, when necessary,
forced to join the insurgents. In the Black Forest Peasants' Letter of
Articles it states that those who refused to join the 'Christian Union'
had the secular ban laid upon them. No one was to have any kind of

dealings with them. The peasants implemented this measure in some areas of the south-west. A stake was affixed before the door of the boycotted person, and he was denied use of the common land and of the mills. He was to be treated as though a deceased member of the community. Revolutionary compulsion, in this or other forms, is a measure unconditionally necessary in an acute situation of class conflict. Neutrality or refusal of support for the revolutionary party means support for the opposition, and must be fought with all available means in the interests of the victory of the revolution.

As the example of the Salzburg peasants shows, a large number of bands sought to recruit Landsknechte, or else included these in their ranks. This was particularly the case in localities where such recruitment was traditional, around Lake Constance, in the Black Forest and in the Allgau. Although there were those in the bands who were in favour of dispensing with Landsknechte, and for whom the interests of the revolutionary struggle were not always uppermost, the military significance of these fellows is, apart from a few exceptions, to be rated highly. Before Weingarten the experienced military leaders of the Swabian League refrained from attack, not least because they knew that there were numerous Landsknechte in the united Lake Constance band, who would not yield at the first attack. In the closing stages of the rebellion in Franconia about 300 former mercenaries stubbornly defended Ingolstadt Castle, destroyed in the first weeks of the Peasant War, against the attacks of the Swabian League.

Peasants brought with them the simple weapons that they kept at home to the muster of the band, supplemented what they lacked with makeshift domestic tools, and fetched firearms from castles and fortresses of the nobility or else from the towns.

In a few cases the towns joined the peasant movement at once, but pressure from without was also necessary. Muhlhausen in Thuringia and Waldshut in the vicinity of the Swiss Confederation offer the best-known examples here. Other towns were forced to join during the course of the rebellion under pressure and influence of an urban popular movement, and had to send men, or supply cannon, firearms or provisions. Most peasant bands were therefore relatively well supplied with firearms. At Boblingen the peasants and their allies had eighteen field pieces, at Konigshofen no less than forty-seven, a number not exceeded even by the armies of the Swabian League. However, the insurgents often lacked experienced gunners for the deployment of the cannon. In besieging large castles, they lacked wall-shattering cannons, although these were generally in short supply, and even ruling princes borrowed them from one another. When peasants demanded arms and provisions from the towns, it is interesting that they always requested the long pikes with which Landsknechte were equipped. This weapon was essential for defence on open ground, and it was in short supply among the peasant bands. Its use also required a certain amount of training, which Landsknecht armies carried out before battle, but which the peasant bands lacked.

Not all towns in the area of rebellion supplied the weapons and provisions requested. Above all, the great south-west German imperial cities such as Strassburg, Nuremberg and Augsburg refused support at the height of the Peasant War. They sent men to the ruling princes' army instead, as in the cases of Nuremberg and Augsburg, or preachers into the peasant camps, hoping to turn them from rebellion as in the case of Strassburg. Smaller towns, which were completely surrounded by peasant bands, but which had a strong conservative party within their walls, such as the Upper Swabian town of Memmingen, vacillated for weeks between both camps. Memmingen sent men and money to the Swabian League, but permitted the peasants to meet within their walls and allowed the rebels to acquire arms and powder, where possible without the knowledge of the conservative city fathers. As the revolutionary centre of the Peasant War in Thuringia, Muhlhausen supplied a well-equipped urban levy at the beginning of the rising, but refused permission for their forces to be deployed against approaching armies of the ruling princes, retreating instead into an ambivalent position of wait and see. Rebels obtained precious firearms from towns and citizens only in a few cases, but even these were usually commandeered. In no case were they able to make use of the power of urban armament.

The bourgeoisie was divided as a class during the Peasant War. On the one hand, a large number of urban companies, composed mostly of guild artisans and members of the plebeian classes, joined the peasant bands and fought bravely to the end. Among the defeated on the battlefield at Frankenhausen was found almost the entire population of this small Thuringian town. The economically stronger classes of the towns, including the capitalist bourgeoisie, either remained 'neutral' or supported the party of the princes. At their head stood the great merchant families, such as the Fugger, Welser, Hochstetter and others who were closely tied to the interests of the princes. In March/April 1525, the most critical weeks of the rebellion for the ruling class, they supplied that precious stuff without which it could not defend its class position: money.

The provisioning of the peasant bands presented a difficult problem from the beginning. Since supplies could be stored only in limited quantity, and bread and meat were the items of mass consumption, it was difficult to supply several thousand men for weeks on end. Bad harvests in the years before 1525 added to the problem. The peasants followed the same methods in procuring foodstuffs as in procuring powder and firearms. They took what they needed from the strongholds of the ruling class: monasteries in particular kept large storehouses. The storming of monastic seats therefore had the further aim of ensuring the nourishment of the bands. Towns and villages also received continued requests to supply foodstuffs to the bands. This system was unreliable in some areas, but in many it worked well. Foodstuffs were supplied to the camps by traders, although quantities are difficult to determine. Peasants and citizens received pay from their villages or towns to supply their own needs. However, with a prolonged concentration of a large band in one place, local stocks of food were soon consumed, leading to dearth and hunger among the rebels. It is characteristic of the class nature of the rebels' behaviour that, although the stores of noble seats and monasteries were cleaned out, there was no known case of plundering of a peasant residence. In the chief localities of the uprising the problem of food supply of the bands was, on the whole, solved. That was a significant achievement.

In their attempts to create a military organisation corresponding to their class aims, the rebels attached great importance to the right of all to settle decisive issues within the band by discussion 'in a ring'. Despite all the problems that appeared in the course of putting it into practice, this early form of democracy became a school for the oppressed peasants, plebeians and miners, who had usually been excluded from the settlement of all essential political questions. The not dissimilar laws of the mercenaries, even if these were seldom set down in Landsknecht regulations, and the practice of the village community each provided rules for this form of decision making in an open circle. But while the well-to-do peasants were the spokesmen in the village community and the propertyless and the serf usually had no rights alongside them, in the ring all could speak. The nobles who were forced to go along with the rebels also had the same rights as the plebeians. This practice of the ring established the basic importance of the band as an anti-feudal military organisation.

The success of this type of early democracy none the less depended on the power relationships within each peasant band. Everywhere there was a struggle between a moderate and a committed group. Often the moderates were associated with a narrow localism, which wished to limit the rising to one territory and refused aid for other bands. Where moderates predominated, fateful decisions could be taken. This occurred, for example, during the campaign in the Eichsfeld. A decision taken against the will of Muntzer and his adherents, brought a temporary success, but proved to be a mistake considering that the princes' army was on the advance. It prevented the spread of rebellion in the north, in the mining areas of Mansfeld territory, where an alliance with the miners might have been formed.

The rebels set down the questions of order in the camp, the tasks of the officers and the order of the march in field regulations. Regulations of this kind also were sometimes incorporated into political programmes, as in the Articles of Molsheim and Alsace, and the constitution (*Landesordnung*) of the Upper Swabian peasants, among others. Besides numerous regulations about individual offices, these field regulations confirmed in writing both the need to elect commanders and their obligations to the peasant band. This was a creative contribution made by the peasant bands to the development of the early modern military system.

The military operations of peasant bands generally began with the storming and destruction of near-by noble residences, except where moderate leaders were able to hinder such actions throughout the Upper German area. Besides the more obvious purpose of securing supplies and arms, the rebels destroyed noble seats because they regarded them as military and administrative strongholds of the ruling class from which the peasants were constantly threatened. These operations were outwardly little different from the defensive levy against breakers of the peace, to which the peasants were liable in the years before the Peasant War. But this was only an outward difference in that it too had only limited military aims. While the peasants were often successful in such actions, and in skirmishes against smaller units of the nobility, the reverse was usually the case when the larger peasant bands encountered noble armies.

The experienced armies of the ruling class defeated the peasants mostly after a short fight because these lacked experience in battle, and were rarely in a position to fight off mounted attacks. Steadfastness against the gunfire of their opponents was seen only (as at Gaisbeuren and Leubas) when a larger number of militarily experienced warriors stood in the peasant ranks. The general inferiority indicates that, as a result of techniques of warfare at the beginning of the sixteenth century, the possession of weapons no longer sufficed, but had to be linked to training in their use. Another weakness of the rebels resided in their defensive conduct of the struggle. Often the bands faced their opponents in an advantageous position, but they seldom went on to the offensive. When they did so (for example, at Herrenberg, at Freiburg in Breisgau and above all at Schladming near the border of bishopric Salzburg and Styria) the attack often ended with success against the nobles' levies. With such large numbers of insurgents, a crucial point was discipline in battle, and given their minimal training, one can see the disastrous effects when it was lacking.

In the early bourgeois revolution in the Netherlands which followed that in Germany at the end of the sixteenth century, and in which the bourgeoisie first lived up to its hegemonic role, one central military concern was discipline among the newly formed rebel armies. They discovered what today we call drill, as the late nineteenth-century socialist Franz Mehring wrote: the diligent, tireless training of soldiers, the inviolable obedience which automatically obeyed the captains' commands amid the terror of battle just as had been instilled on the parade ground.

Friedrich Engels indicated one essential, objective cause of the military defeat of the insurgents. The rebellion was fragmented because of the activity of the peasants as small producers. This enabled noble armies, usually numerically inferior, to defeat the peasant bands one by one, and so to triumph. The defects of the peasant bands and their military defeat should not, however, push into the background their achievements in numerous areas of warfare, the achievements of the first popular army in German history. For the first time, masses of the people attempted to create their own military organisation by adapting the contemporary model of the mercenary army. In the areas of arms, muster, supply and the drafting of field regulations among others, the peasant bands accomplished much that was of significance. In several small and in some large battles and sieges, they emerged victorious. Through their work, military traditions were created which the workers' movement later took up and which it preserves as its heritage.

HORST BUSZELLO

9 The Common Man's View of the State in the German Peasant War*

It is generally thought that the German Peasant War of 1525–5 was a many-sided affair, in which religious, economic, social and political factors determined causes as much as effects. The complex nature of events can only be explained in the last resort by a variety of approaches, and not by a monocausal or teleological method. Hence it is important to stress that the following remarks only apply to those aspects of the 1524–5 movement which deal with partly or fully articulated political demands of the rebels themselves. These I have called 'the common man's view of the state'. What I want to examine are the *subjective* views of peasants and burghers towards achieving a better political system, and not any *objective* tendencies or directions of the movement (this is a distinction used in Marxist historiography – cf. Laube, 1974).

The German Peasant War has often been discussed as a political movement (cf. Angermeier, 1966; Vahle, 1972). Many studies suffer in that they either only partly examine the articulated demands or reduce the variety of expressed aims far too hurriedly into one overall basic and common conviction of the rebels. Establishing a chief aim or going back to general principles behind all the differences, confines rather than helps our understanding of the movement. Hence I will try to examine the political aims of the rebels in each specific and peculiar circumstance and then say something about these aims in general (cf. in more detail, Buszello, 1969).

To start with, we should be clear that the Peasant War presented no cohesive whole in its outward, organised form nor in its political aims. Status, social position, measure of political education, local tradition, the course which any uprising took as an internal territorial or supra-territorial movement affected the rebels' thinking just as decisively – and that means differently – as proximity to or distance from the Swiss Confederation. A variety of different political attitudes were produced.

In the second section we will look at the question of whether or how far individual, specific political demands add up to any consistent

*Translated from Horst Buszello, 'Die Staatsvorstellung des "Gemeinen Mannes" im Deutschen Bauernkrieg', *Revolte und Revolution in Europa* (ed. P. Blickle), *Historische Zeitschrift*, Neue Folge, Beiheft 4, 1975 (also in paperback, Oldenbourg Verlag, Munich, 1977), pp. 273–95.

'common man's view of the state'. The concept 'common man' will include rural population without nobles and clergy, inhabitants of towns within the jurisdiction of territorial states, people living in imperial cities who did not have the right to co-opt town councillors and, where they existed, the miners. Demands for reform were above all directed towards the direct, daily needs of the common man at a basic communal level of village and town politics. Of an actual 'view of the state' as such, one can only speak once demands were conceived in terms of larger territorial states and of the German Empire, whether as a conscious recognition of existing realities, or whether as a result of attempts to change or totally overthrow these realities.

I

1 Peasants' and burghers' demands for local autonomy within village and town ran like a red thread through all the petitions and proposals of the Peasant War, irrespective of origin and when they were composed. The proposals were formulated as local and specific instances so typical of the time in which they were produced. In them, local communities demanded the right to draw up their own by-laws; to elect their own parish priest and other officials of the local administration, including the bailiff, judge and village mayor; burghers' own supervision of town gates and keys; return of alienated common land to the village community, and so on (Walder, 1954: 22).

Peasants gave different reasons for their demands, but often referred to ancient rights which should be reinforced: 'Item, the community has always exercised this right . . . but the bailiff does not allow it' (Franz, 1935: 151). Cases were also justified on grounds of general equity: 'Since we have to pay wages to the bailiffs' (ibid.: 154). Other demands were based upon a fundamental, biblical standpoint: 'According to God's wish' (ibid.: 151). From this one can conclude that the peasants were not merely content with returning to a traditional way of doing things, but that they were also prepared to agitate for 'just reforms' ('*gerechte*' *Neuerungen*), which went beyond that which had always been thought customary practice.

The extent of peasant demands for internal communal autonomy, as well as for more far-reaching reforms which we will deal with later, does not, however, become clear until seen in the context of concomitant social and socio-political demands. The rebels consistently demanded that clergy be deprived of their economic and political powers. Clergy should only preach the Word of God: they are servants of their communities who pay them appropriately (Buszello, 1969: 23–40). In contrast, the nobility was usually recognised as landowners, renting lands to peasants at a just and fair price. Yet, like the clergy, the nobility were to be deprived of any independent jurisdiction. They could remain owners of the land but would no longer be lords over the land. They could control the land but no longer exercise power over peasants as lords or judges. Sole authority to do this would in future rest with the territorial ruler, who was to be invested with all existing noble and ecclesiastical jurisdictions. Nobles and clergy would become equal to the 'common man' at law, and they would contribute equally with peasants and burghers to communal taxes and duties (Franz, 1963: 275). Naturally, in this blueprint for the future there was no place for serfdom.

In their desire to abolish the autonomous jurisdictions of nobility and clergy, peasants followed the same path long since taken by territorial rulers with a policy of extending their own high jurisdictions. Peasants and territorial rulers, however, clashed when the latter demanded sole control over villages and local courts, from which the former attempted to free themselves in order to put the village community in as autonomous a position as possible (Walder, 1954: 21). Hence the demand to abolish noble and ecclesiastical jurisdictions as well as their transfer to the territorial ruler should not be seen as an actual increase in the ruler's power. Nor should it be interpreted as a conscious act of centralisation. The power of the territorial ruler, which was left untouched as such, was to have its counterpart in the autonomy of self-administered local communities. Village community and territorial ruler were to be two complementary but independent political units.

Franz (1975), Waas (1964) and other Western historians regard the struggle between village community and the growing power of territorial rulers for control of internal village affairs as the real cause of the Peasant War. The uprising was carried out by village elders, partly by quite well-off, self-aware and respected, albeit truculent, people (Waas, 1964: 24, 30). They wished to obtain a position in politics which was more consistent with their economic standing (Franz, 1975: 287). They fought against the increasing territorial power of their rulers, who in turn attempted to curtail peasant self-government in the interest of a modern state system. According to their view, the Peasant War developed predominantly from tension between the emergent territorial state and local autonomy (Walder, 1954: 20). It is a conflict between communal practice and customary law on the one hand, and the sovereign jurisdiction of territorial rulers on the other hand (Franz, 1975: 291). Since rulers attempted to extend their power by means of economic policies, the conflict also extended into the economic sphere (Waas, 1964: 35). In opposition to this view, Marxist historiography sees the increased demand for power on the part of the rulers solely as a means to increase the economic exploitation of the peasants, from which it is concluded that economic pressures on the peasantry were the real cause of the uprisings (Wohlfeil, 1972: *passim*; Laube, 1974: 8–34, 102–5). Sabean has recently added another interpretation based on studies of villages around the imperial city of Ravensburg in Upper Swabia, according to which the struggle for control of internal communal self-government took place not only against landlords and over-lords, but also primarily against the demands of an increased number of day-labourers in the community itself. Well-off tenant farmers saw in self-government of their own villages the best way of protecting their property rights against the demands of landless day-labourers, who made increasing efforts to parcel out the common and insisted on creation of new farms (Sabean, 1972: 100–13).

Peasants and their demands for internal village self-government have stood at the heart of the discussion so far. Yet it is important to note also that these peasant demands had their exact counterpart in griev-ances put forward by townsmen. Urban uprisings did not automatically link up with those of the peasants, but towns also attempted to curtail the powers of their overlords by expanding the competence of burgher self-government. Townsmen likewise wished to subordinate nobility and clergy totally to all urban duties and responsibilities. Ample evidence of this comes from the whole region of revolt stretching from Erfurt to Salzburg, and from Trier to Bamberg (Buszello, 1969: 127–33; Endres, 1971: 112–14).

2 The struggle for local autonomy and self-government can be seen among both peasants and burghers, and had these basic demands been successful they would have been of considerable importance to the further political development of Germany. However, it should not be forgotten that these demands were overwhelmingly defensive and inward-looking. They represent attempts to withdraw from the develop-ment of centralised state power as carried out by territorial rulers. The question therefore arises as to whether peasants and burghers in 1524–5 were content to leave their demands at that, or whether they were also making an attempt to influence politics and institutions above the level of local parish affairs.

This leads in the first place to an examination of persistent demands to set up government by territorial estates to run affairs of state along-side or even instead of territorial rulers. Such proposals were made in the bishopric of Bamberg (see the Plan to regulate the affairs of the bishopric, Endres, 1971), and in the Markgräflerland, the territories of the margraves of Baden: Rotteln-Sausenberg and Badenweiler (see the letter of margrave Ernst von Baden to the town of Basle, 7 May 1525); in the archbishopric of Salzburg (see the Complaints of the town of Salzburg, articles 46–59); in the County of Tyrol (see the twelfth of the Meran Articles); in the ecclesiastical territory of Waldsassen; in the duchy of Wurttemberg (see the so-called offer of arbitration made by the towns of Wurttemberg to Duke Ulrich); and in the bishopric of Wurzburg (see the Articles of the Wurzburg townsmen of 30 May 1525).

In the archbishopric of Salzburg, the duchy of Wurttemberg and the lands of the margrave of Baden, territorial rulers were to be deprived of all power and replaced by regency governments. In Wurzburg the rebels were content to demand an estates' control committee that was to meet four times a year with the bishop and discuss all outstanding problems. This would have left the bishop considerable freedom to take initiatives in day-to-day affairs of state.

The governments of Salzburg, Wurttemberg, Wurzburg and Bamberg were to be staffed by members of the three secular estates of nobles, burghers and peasants. Clergy were to be excluded. In Waldsassen the arrangements were 'four advisers appointed partly by the town of Tuschenreuth and partly by the common country [*Landschaft*]' who would run the administration of this ecclesiastical territory together with the ruler's bailiff. The Markgräflerland was to be run by an all-peasant government, and all administrative offices were to be held by peasants. There were probably two basic reasons for this. First, the countryside (*Landschaft*) of the Markgräflerland consisted almost exclusively of peasants, and secondly, the idea of exercising some control over the territorial ruler overlapped with the further thought that peasants might achieve imperial status (*Reichsunmittelbarkeit*) and eliminate all nobility (see below, I, 4). By way of contrast, Tyrolean rebels demanded no new government but instead tried to exercise influence over the existing Habsburg council, which in future was to be staffed only by native nobles, burghers and peasants. Foreigners, clergy and trained lawyers were to be excluded.

There is no doubt that the members of the governments in Salzburg, Wurttemberg, Wurzburg, Bamberg and in the Markgräflerland were to be elected by each respective countryside (*Landschaft*). Yet, in Tyrol, the ruling archduke was allowed to retain his personal right to select the members of his council, although the pool from which he would in future draw eligible candidates was restricted to native nobles, burghers and peasants who made up the community of the countryside (*Landschaft*) (cf. Blickle, 1973: 3–23, 139–43). By this restriction, as well as by the order to take the members from each of their estates, the countryside (*Landschaft*) would secure some influence.

The reason given for proscribing a territorial ruler's power was a desire to uphold peace and justice more effectively, combined with a hope also to protect 'the common man' from the ruler's arbitrary use of prerogative. If we examine these various attempts to limit or even take over the power of territorial rulers as a whole, then we find that attempts merely to impose limits on the existing system were more often characteristic of larger and compact territorial states than of their smaller and more fragmented counterparts. In these larger territories (but also in the Markgräflerland and in the ecclesiastical territory of Waldsassen) the Peasant War remained an internal movement, merely a conflict between the rebels of one territory and their ruler.

The main towns of a territorial state usually helped to lead any moves to curtail the power of the ruler. These towns were the seat of the ruler's court, and the burghers often had direct experience of the ruler and his style of politics. This applied above all to the main towns of three ecclesiastical territories (Salzburg, Wurzburg and Bamberg), where there were long traditions of conflict between burgher community and rulers' officials. Yet the small territorial towns of Wurttemberg and Tyrol followed similar policies to these three ecclesiastical main towns. Furthermore, in Tyrol and in the Markgräflerland peasants were very prominent in demanding limits to rulers' powers. It is this point which could supply us with a clue to understanding the whole phenomenon. For it was a demand only made by those peasants who already had sufficient status to be accepted as members of the territorial states (*Landstandschaft*) (Blickle, 1973: 54–156). These peasants, along with burghers from Salzburg, Wurttemberg, Wurzburg, Bamberg and Tyrol had already gained some political experience by attending territorial assemblies where they took part in the formulation of general policies, giving them opportunity to think in terms of state politics. Their views went beyond the confines of village or town community and looked towards the central institutions of the territorial state. Since the right of peasants to attend the territorial assembly was an exceptional one, most proposals to impose limits on the power of the territorial ruler came significantly from towns and burghers.

3 Plans to limit a ruler's power by setting up a regency government were only implemented during 1524–5 in those territories where conflict between peasants and burghers on the one hand and the territorial ruler on the other hand kept strictly within its own state frontiers. This was overwhelmingly, though not exclusively, the case in larger and more cohesive territorial states. In Upper Swabia this was not achieved. The region between the upper reaches of the Danube and the Allgau, between Lake Constance and the river Lech, was noted for its extreme territorial fragmentation. Rebellious subjects from these territories therefore formed themselves into three substantial supra-territorial leagues or bands during late February and early March 1525: the bands of Baltringen, Lake Constance and the Allgau. Furthermore, the bands of Lake Constance and Allgau reached agreement before 6 March, on which day all three bands also combined to form 'the Christian Union of Upper Swabia' (Franz, 1975: 127–34; Buszello, 1969: 53–7).

The Union created a new situation to which the famous Twelve Articles probably owe their existence. Between 27 February and 1 March 1525, a journeyman furrier from Memmingen, Sebastian Lotzer, probably made a precis of about 300 petitions from the region occupied by the band from Baltringen, and he recast the grievances in a more generalised and unified set of demands. Freed from local peculiarities, they were drafted on the basis of 'godly' law (Franz, 1975: 122–7). But the leaders of the Baltringen band were not content merely to support redress of generally formulated grievances. They went further in attempting to secure 'the common man' against any future move to oppress him. Within the Christian Union of Upper Swabia, they developed the concept of a general land-peace to be enforced collectively by a confederation (*Eidgenossenschaft*) of towns, markets and countrysides (*Landschaften*) throughout Upper Swabia to protect for all time peasant and burgher rights against encroachment by their overlords and rulers. In other words, the attempt was made to set up a supra-territorial league of peasants and burghers to prevent any territorial ruler from misusing his power (Franz, 1963, no. 50).

The aim of the Christian Union of Upper Swabia was not to alienate or disadvantage anyone. On the contrary, the ideal was to re-establish brotherly love among men on the basis of the Gospel and the Word of God. The union wished to protect, achieve and secure justice for everyone within the existing political system. It was to keep watch over and protect 'the common man' from falling foul of any attempts by rulers to behave in arbitrary and oppressive ways. That meant, however, that existing rulers were clearly recognised and accepted, as expressed in article one of all three versions of the agreement, namely that 'that which is owed to ecclesiastical and secular authorities through God's justice, shall always be carried out truly and obediently'. The general idea of paying taxes and dues was not refuted as such. Instead, the justification for each and every levy was to be proved on its own merits. The existing system of law and order was to continue, although former officials of rulers and lords would annul their oaths of loyalty and take new ones binding them to the Christian Union itself. If this had been successful, politics in Upper Swabia would have been altered significantly. Although existing rulers would have stayed in office, they would have lost effective power to leaders of a peasant and burgher confederation (Franz, 1975: 286; Angermeier, 1966: 335; Steinmetz in Laube, 1974: 260–62).

The aim of the Baltringen band to protect 'the common man' more effectively from arbitrary rulers was identical with the aims of rebels in Salzburg, Wurzburg and in the Markgräflerland (as already discussed above). Only the means varied for carrying this out in Upper Swabia. Different territorial structures accounted for the variety of actions taken, and in Upper Swabia the rebels formed supra-territorial organisations to take the initiative since existing territorial states were too small to provide a sound base for action. .

The leaders of the Baltringen band were not peasants but craftsmen, parish clergy and preachers, whose proposals presumably went beyond the immediate desires of their followings. But more important is the fact that their ideas for a perpetual confederation were opposed decisively by the bands of Allgau and Lake Constance. There were serious differences of opinion at the negotiations in Memmingen on 6–7 March 1525. As a result, the final agreement varied at crucial points from the two drafts on which it was based – no doubt due to the insistence of Allgau and Lake Constance peasants, as was reported by Kessler in his

Sabbata (cf. Buszello, 1969: 64–7). The final version of the Christian Union plays down the notion of a perpetual confederation of towns, markets and country communities.

We must assume that the Allgau and Lake Constance bands only wanted a military pact with the Baltringen band, though the latter wished to go further in making constitutional demands which were to include a permanent confederation of towns and villages confirmed by sealed documents and based on a long-lasting tax system. Yet the Baltringen leaders had to be satisfied with a compromise solution that offered them considerably less than this.

Similar demands to those made in Upper Swabia came from Franconia, where the Peasant War became supra-territorial, finally also producing general proposals for reforms on the basis of 'godly' law (Franz, 1975: 176–208; Buszello, 1969: 35–52).

In drawing up his agendum for the Heilbronn assembly scheduled for mid May 1525, Wendel Hipler, leader of the Neckartal–Odenwald band, was already trying to plan for the future when after a successful fight 'the common man' could be sent home to work (Franz, 1963: 371). Yet even then a small band of troops was to be kept on, being led by a few of the present leaders and advisers. Their task would be to watch out for any crimes and irregularities and ensure that order, peace and justice prevailed among the people themselves, especially as regards any extraordinary incidents; preserving law and order for 'the common man' and organising mutual aid against any excess of rulers and lords. However, Franconian rebel leaders also generally wished to keep existing rulers and their servants in office. Florian Geyer declared from Rothenburg that it was not the aim of Franconian peasants to abolish all the duties that subjects owed to their rulers, but rather that the authorities should discuss these duties with their subjects with a view to reaching mutual agreement on them (Franz, 1963: 367).

Hipler wanted rebel leaders and advisers to create a band that would form the core of a police force for the whole of Franconia. Arrangements for the up-keep of a common executive organisation made it necessary to keep some form of supra-territorial institution in being. In other words, it envisaged the continued existence of a supra-territorial union consisting of Franconian peasants and burghers (Steinmetz in Laube, 1974: 260–62).

4 The Baltringen leaders wished to use the Christian Union of Upper Swabia as an effective supra-territorial confederation to protect 'the common man' against violence and oppression. They were not proposing to abolish existing territorial rulers as such. Such demands did not come until the last stage of the German Peasant War of 1524–5, and then only from the southern part of the Upper Rhine, Upper Swabia and the alpine lands, where the rebels eventually threw off all superior authority except for that of the Emperor. They wanted peasants to

have the same status as enjoyed by territorial rulers in the German Empire (*Reichsunmittelbarkeit*). We have fifteen cases of such a demand being made during the whole of the Peasant War. Eight were from the Upper Rhine, three each from Upper Swabia and the alpine lands, and possibly one more from Franconia. Yet this concept of peasant equality with territorial rulers is older than the years 1524–5, and derives from earlier peasant revolts of the Upper Rhine such as the Bundschuh conspiracies of 1502, 1513 and 1517, as well as the Carinthian peasant uprising of 1478 in Austria (Baumann, 1876: 250).

Their demands show a desire for drastic reforms among some of the rebels, who were no longer content with limiting the power of existing territorial rulers by imposing supervision by the estates or through supra-territorial alliance. Instead they wanted to abolish all middle instances of government between 'the common man' and the Emperor. But how widespread were these radical demands? At least their occurrence over a wide area of south-west Germany shows that they were more than the mere mouthing of an unrepresentative few, though in at least one half of the known cases the proposals were made by specifically identifiable individuals. The last fact, together with the more moderate behaviour of the rebels in negotiation and decision making, lead us to the conclusion that the demand for peasant equality with territorial rulers was the maximum the peasants could possibly wish for, a dream rather than a necessity. These radical proposals occurred only on the southern fringes of the area covered by the uprising such as Upper Swabia and the alpine lands. In Tyrol and Salzburg such demands came in late 1526 and were the result of the failure of earlier and more moderate policies, after attempts to reach agreement with rulers at territorial assemblies had broken down.

It would be incorrect to assume that these extreme demands amounted to a struggle by peasants and their leaders to establish a new and more powerful German Empire by imposing national unity and centralisation. It was not in the service of any German imperial ideal but rather for their own sake that these rebel leaders demanded abolition and expulsion of existing territorial rulers and authorities. They were not interested in Emperor and German Empire but in their own freedom and independence. Although they may have been prepared to declare loyalty to the Emperor, they wanted to keep his authority weak and remote. The rebels in Alsace declared their support for Emperor and German Empire, but wanted to proscribe imperial officials' competence (Franz, 1935: nos. 73, 75). Black Forest peasants were prepared to pay the Emperor his due, but insisted that he should not be allowed to command anything from them (Mone, 1854: 90). Rebels only used the argument of loyalty to the Emperor to show that they were in favour of the existing system of law and order, despite a wish to depose their territorial rulers. Following a formulation of K. S. Bader (1950: 58f.) we should speak of a negative or passive view of the

German Empire (*negatives Reichsbewusstsein*).

Demands for peasant equality and independence combined with direct loyalty to Emperor and German Empire are limited to the south and south-west frontier regions of Germany. Furthermore, it is questionable as to how far these demands obtained the support of the local mass of rebels. No real appreciation of the German Empire emerges from the rebels' demands, and it prevents us from seeing in the German Peasant War any conscious attempt to use the strength of the peasantry to build a new German imperial system from the base upwards into a unified national state (cf. Franz, 1975: 287, and Steinmetz, Theses).

If the existing authorities had been overthrown, it would have necessitated the creation of a new political system, which was only clearly envisaged by the peasants in the Markgräflerland and by Michael Gaismair in Tyrol, who insisted that a peasant government should wield state power. The new system was seen either within existing territorial boundaries or as a supra-territorial alliance, as outlined in the Black Forest Peasants' Letter of Articles, which was used to coerce existing territorial rulers to join the Christian Union (Franz, 1963: no. 68).

5 Friedrich Weigandt, the regional bailiff of Mainz at Miltenberg, was the only one to demand a fundamental reorganisation of the German Empire during the Peasant War. Weigandt made several far-reaching proposals in response to uprisings in Franconia. He drafted a writ to nobles and imperial cities which included a number of articles; a formula for imperial reform; and a final letter with proposals from 18 May 1525 (Franz, 1963: nos. 123–4). Each proposal ended with a demand for imperial reform, which he justified on the grounds that it was necessary to innovate in order to coerce territorial rulers to obey the Emperor and stick to the overall well-being of the Holy Roman Empire. According to his letter of 18 May 1525, the new system would cover all people within the boundaries of the German Empire.

Weigandt's schemes have been interpreted by historians in different ways. Waas stresses his prescience and the bold, clear lines of his proposals, which went beyond the mundane problems of local peasants towards considering the needs of the German people as a whole (Waas 1964: 225f.). Franz's criticism of this view is that Weigandt was only interested in integrating the peasants into an overall legal system. He says nothing about a system of state administration, and his plans were worked out at his writing desk rather than in the peasants' camp (Franz, 1975: 200f.). Marxist historiography equally stresses Weigandt's failure to take the peasants' demands into account, although his plans for urban reform are seen as objective and sensible proposals for the period in which they were produced (Steinmetz in Laube, 1974: 257–60).

Friedrich Weigandt was no peasant leader and he only corresponded with the rebels in Franconia, above all with the leader of the Neckartal–Odenwald band, Wendel Hipler. It is not clear whether Hipler adopted Weigandt's proposals for imperial reform, or whether he developed similar views on the matter. However, in Hipler's own writings there is no mention of imperial reform; and after the deed of Weinsberg, 16 April, he took up Weigandt's writ to the nobility almost verbatim but ignored the appended proposals for imperial reform.

II

In the first section we examined some of the constitutional and political demands that were produced during the German Peasant War, and we looked into their content and meaning. In this section we will try to explain to what extent specific, individual aims and plans could be comprised into an overall view of politics. We will examine the question as to whether there ever was such a thing as a thoroughgoing 'common man's view of the state', and the following brief points are intended to stimulate further discussion.

We must try to establish what were the overall political attitudes that were held in common without thereby ignoring the real individual differences of opinion that undoubtedly existed. The contents of political demands cannot be separated from social and economic aspects, and to do so would be false. Only when the two areas are combined can one possibly reach balanced conclusions.

(1) A substantial part of the petitions and programmes produced in 1524–5 concerns demands to reform society and ease the economic burdens of 'the common man'.

(a) The existing estates of nobles and clergy should lose all their legal and economic privileges and be subordinated to peasant and burgher arrangements in both areas of law and economy. They should pay local taxes and shoulder local duties like peasants and burghers. The articles of the Franconian peasantry state 'Henceforth all nobles and non-nobles, ecclesiastical and lay, shall obey the common laws of burghers and peasants, and not presume to more than any other common man (*gemeiner Mann*)' (Franz, 1963 : no. 120). These demands did not aim at a radical levelling of all people to replace the existing social structure of ranks and orders. Total equality of all people was only very rarely an issue, as for example in Michael Gaismair's Tyrolean constitution (*Landesordnung*), where article five talks of total equality in the territory (*ain ganze Glaichait im Land*) (ibid.: no. 92). The great mass of rebels did not question the existing social system. They 'merely' accepted demands to place nobles and clergy on the same footing as burghers and peasants.

(b) Over and above this, the clergy were to lose their economic power. Their property was confiscated and all their rents and taxes abolished or reassigned for upkeep of the sick and needy with the exception of the large tithe, as expressed, for example, in article two of the famous Twelve Articles. By way of contrast, the nobility retained their economic status as landowners.

(c) Serfdom was universally abolished and personal ties, dues and services associated with it cancelled.

(d) Remaining dues and services were to be re-examined and new rates fixed. According to Florian Geyer's Rothenburg speech, 'It is not proposed to abolish all taxes and dues, but rather to make the authorities negotiate with their subjects about the level and fairness of these dues with the active help and advice of educated, god-fearing and loving people' (ibid.: no. 119).

(e) Alienated rights to the use of woodland, water and meadow were to be restored to 'the common man'.

(2) It seems that 'the common man' wanted to achieve political equality among all subjects (*Errichtung einer gleichmässigen (politischen) Untertänigkeit*). The special and independent powers of nobles and clergy were to be abolished, and all authority was to be exercised solely by territorial rulers, whether ecclesiastical or lay. Indeed, some ecclesiastical rulers tended to offer the rebels secularisation under their own continued leadership, ostensibly as ruling 'dukes' (Buszello, 1969: 28ff.). Article two of the Meran proposals demands that 'neither ecclesiastical nor lay noblemen shall have any kind of power to run towns, law courts or coerce anyone at law, but all these powers shall be in the hands of our territorial ruler' (Franz, 1963: no. 91). For the peasants this meant abolition of landlords' jurisdiction over them. Nobles and clergy would remain owners of the land but unable to coerce and judge anyone in their local law court. As the Salzburg *Landschaft* put it in their grievances, 'a judge is invested with authority by the territorial ruler to deal with such matters and landlords and landowners have no such authority. They have no right to grant or forbid anything' (ibid.: no. 94, art. 18). Abolition of noble and ecclesiastical jurisdiction found symbolic expression in the occasional destruction and defortification of castles, palaces and monasteries (Buszello, 1969: 28, 39).

(3) In the field of administration and politics rebel demands for more village and town autonomy was of crucial importance. Autocratic and communal government practices clashed. Peasants wanted to regulate their own affairs by majority decision in the village community and run their affairs through institutions of their own choice (Walder, 1954: 19). Similar conflicts occurred in the towns.

(4) Where the rebels went beyond local issues, they usually recognised that the authority of territorial rulers would have to be checked if peasant and burgher rights were to be protected. Differences of

opinion merely occurred when it came to deciding how to carry this out, above all in areas of rebellion within one territory as against regions of supra-territorial uprisings. The former situation usually applied to larger territorial states and the latter to the splinter territories (see above, p. 112–14).

In larger territories, the state provided the boundary for reform, usually with a regency council to supervise or even take over the existing internal government. In splinter territories, there was to be a collective supra-territorial confederation of burghers and peasants as protection and counterweight to existing internal government.

(5) On the Upper Rhine, and partly in Upper Swabia and the alpine lands of Tyrol and Salzburg, the rebels went a step further. They wanted to abolish all authority except that of the Emperor himself. This would have meant putting an end to the existing structure of society with its ranks and orders (cf. 1(a) above). The margrave Ernst von Baden was even asked to become a peasant himself after the rebels had recognised his authority over them as representative of the Emperor. Rebel demands for equal status with territorial rulers under the Emperor were made within movements that kept to territorial boundaries just as much as among supra-territorial confederations.

(6) Although several programmes mention Emperor and German Empire (cf. 5 above), it would be an exaggeration to say that the uprising of 'the common man' was a war for the Emperor and the German Empire, for a unified and centralised national state. Friedrich Weigandt's radical plans for reform of the German Empire were the work of one man sitting at his writing desk. They were not matched by declarations of any actual peasant leader (Franz, 1975: 201).

(7) The aims and plans of 'the common man' were not expressed on the basis of any underlying grand political and social concept or theory. Reform proposals were an attempt to overcome specifically felt shortcomings and to protect 'the common man' from further treachery, coercion and spoliation, which does not exclude the fact that the single, specific aims taken as a whole add up to a thorough-going view of state.

(8) In their attempt to limit or even abolish the power of territorial rulers (cf. 4 and 5 above), rebel leaders made use of earlier plans and views.

(a) Attempts to limit or even take over the power of territorial rulers by setting up a regency government consisting of territorial estates go back to the fourteenth century, and in the decades just before the Peasant War such attempts were very frequent in many parts of Germany (Buszello, 1969: 140). The novelty in 1525 was that the clergy were to be excluded and the peasantry were to be substituted instead.

(b) In seeking to protect peasant and burgher rights by forming a union or confederation, the leaders of the Baltringen band were making use of ideas that had long been current in south-west Germany. The Christian Union of Upper Swabia was modelled on older south-west German or even Swiss lines (ibid.: 59–63). Had it succeeded, it would not have been an unusual phenomenon in south-west Germany. The only novelty for the German-speaking lands outside the Swiss Confederation would have been the great importance given to the peasantry.

(c) Demands for peasant equality with territorial rulers (*bäuerliche Reichsunmittelbarkeit*) presumably originated in Switzerland, as brought out by the slogan that the German peasants wished to be as free as the Swiss (ibid.: 81–90, esp. 85).

(9) In 1524–5, demands by 'the common man' for reform affected all areas of social and political life, especially in two ways: first by being expressed at the local level of village and town life (see 1–3 above); and secondly by operating at higher and more abstract levels of state reorganisation – at the level of the territorial rulers and of the German Empire (see above, 4–6).

(10) Those demands which concerned the immediate life-style of 'the common man' were supported by the mass of the rebels, and they were much the same among all the uprisings that made up the Peasant War of 1525. More far-reaching plans and programmes only came from specific individuals among the leadership. In part they show considerable differences, not so much as regards basic ideals, but concerning practical ways and means of implementation.

We have tried to examine specific rebel demands with a view to understanding their overall relationship to one another. The question whether they all amounted to a reformation or a revolution of the existing system may now be left to further discussion.

SIEGFRIED HOYER

10 *The Rights and Duties of Resistance in the Pamphlet* To the Assembly of Common Peasantry *(1525)**

Among the many manifestos of the German Peasant War there are very few that can be ascribed to the left wing of the movement. Alongside the writings of Thomas Muntzer and Michael Gaismair's Tyrolean Constitution, the only other left-wing manifesto usually mentioned is the Black Forest Peasants' Letter of Articles. Yet there is another vital document to which Hesselbarth (1953) and Smirin (1956) called attention. It is entitled 'To the assembly of common peasantry who have angrily and defiantly risen up in Upper Germany and many other places', and its importance lies, among other things, in the fact that it was one of the few peasant pamphlets to be printed immediately (Stern, 1929: 186f.). The pamphlet has now been reprinted by Buszello (1969), who ascribes it to Upper Germany near the border with the Swiss Confederation, and in a critical edition by Hoyer and Rüdiger (1975). However, its ideological influences have not been fully explained, nor indeed its relationship to other peasant manifestos. Its authorship remains uncertain.

Smirin (1956) pointed out that the pamphlet was a political tract and not like Muntzer's sermons and writings which were more specifically concerned with social equality. It set out to justify the peasants' struggle, and it distinguished between human and divine authority. Peasants were to obey only authorities whom they had elected and not the existing corrupt human order. In the clarity of its propagandistic style and passionate tone, the pamphlet resembled Muntzer's work, and it could be ascribed to radical ideologues among the bourgeoisie, who welcomed the Peasant War in anticipation that the organised union and firm action of the rebels would lead to the abolition of feudalism and the system of princes and estates. However, Smirin (1956) saw the pamphlet as a local product of the radical wing of the Bildhauser band in south Thuringia, and like Hesselbarth (1953) he ascribed possible authorship to Muntzer's friend Hans Hut.

*Edited translation of Siegfried Hoyer, 'Widerstandsrecht und Widerstandspflicht in der Flugschrift, "An die versamlung gemayner pawerschafft" ', *Der Bauer im Klassenkampf* (ed. G. Heitz, *et al.*), Berlin, 1975, pp. 129–55.

According to Buszello (1969: 108ff.), the pamphlet gives the impression of being a scholarly dispute concerning the cardinal question of the Peasant War, whether rebellion was just or unjust. It sought to establish whether the peasants had a general right to resist the authorities. It centred on the question of uniting to protect their own rights in the 'Christian Union of Upper Swabia', i.e. the union of the three Upper Swabian peasant bands of Allgau, Baltringen and Lake Constance. Buszello also stressed the differences from Muntzer's ideas, yet indicated parallels with Zwingli's views on authority which the Reformer had formulated, especially in his tract (*Auslegungen und Gründe der Schlussreden*, 1523). But the pamphlet did not quote Zwingli, and in view of the differences of opinion, it is important to examine the new situation after the outbreak of hostilities in the Peasant War. The views of the author of the pamphlet coincided with the republicanism of Zurich. From a social point of view, he supported a limited rejection of the authorities' arbitrary actions. Buszello finally noted that the author seems to have had a view of politics similar to that held in the imperial cities.

There are thus considerable differences of opinion as regards where the pamphlet came from, what ideological influences it came under, and about its character. If one leaves aside its references to the urban order and the bourgeoisie, then the historians only agree that the pamphlet defended the justice of the peasant cause and that it sought to interpret anew the concept of authority. Although Muntzer and the pamphlet had the same aim to abolish godless authority, yet the differences between the two were similar to those that gradually developed between Muntzer and his followers and friends. In May 1524, Simon Haferitz proposed active participation of the community, but only with the help of the right to elect. 'Dear people, you should renounce your lords. Born princes will never do you any good. Therefore, elect your own prince and turn away from the princes of Saxony, your inherited lords. Elect a lord of your own' (Hinrichs, 1952: 13f.). Haferitz wrote this before the peasants rebelled and before he had to adapt to the new situation created by the outbreak of violence. Yet these remarks show the various ways in which obedience was withdrawn from an evil authority and the great variety of radical consequences. Possibly Haferitz was influenced by Carlstadt, who approved such communal activity in the context of the Wittenberg iconoclasm of 1521-2 and in subsequent years (ibid.: 151).

The author of the pamphlet stands very close to the views of Zwingli, as Buszello showed (1969: 117, 120). In chapters 34-43 of Zwingli's 1523 tract (*Schlussreden*), the principle of subjects' obedience to authority is discussed in relationship to the right and duty to resist an evil, unchristian ruler, as well as the refusal to condone attacks on property. There is an important distinction between the two as regards the way in which an evil ruler is to be replaced. 'Not with murder, wars and rebellions, but by many other means for God has called upon us to live in peace,' is the way the Swiss Reformer put it. 'Now if a ruler be a tyrant, not anyone is to overthrow him since that will lead to rebellion, whereas the Kingdom of God is in righteousness, peace and joy in the holy ghost . . . but if the whole people in agreement overthrows the tyrant who has offended against God, then that is with God' (Zwingli, 1908: 344f.; Schmid, 1959: 245). In this way Zwingli was saying in 1523 similar things to Muntzer's follower Simon Haferitz and Carlstadt before him, whereas the pamphlet and Thomas Muntzer agree in the use of force, although Muntzer also sought to alter property relations, and saw the fight against tyrants as a historically developed problem that was part of an eschatological view of the world. The differences of opinion as to the use of force do not alter the fact that there is a great similarity between the views of authority held by Zwingli and by the author of the pamphlet. The author of the pamphlet is likely to have been a close follower of the Swiss Reformer who had been radicalised under the influence of the Peasant War.

Despite holding views of authority formed from the position of the propertied bourgeoisie in the towns, Zwingli offered the peasants material to build a revolutionary ideology. His indignation with the tyrants who were the neighbours of the Swiss had 'led him to think about the heady doctrine of equality among men (Macek, 1960: 117ff.). His genuine understanding for the life and struggle of the peasant not only gave Zwingli's doctrine a radical and popular flavour, but also came close to the demands of the people's reformation (*Volksreformation*) in a number of questions. The political model that the author of the pamphlet uses is the community of states of which Zwingli was also a part, namely the Swiss Confederation, for whose republicanism he also cited examples from the past. It is 'the earliest origin and custom of the whole confederation of Swiss to have their own power from the nobility and other authorities' (165, 8/12: all references are to page and line of the text of the pamphlet according to Buszello's edition, 1969). The Swiss Confederation had earlier arisen from a similar conflict against tyranny to the one the German peasants fought against in 1525. The Swiss had also had to root out the tyranny of their lords 'by great wars, bloodletting and violence' (165, 18/20). He tells his readers, 'how often have not the poor peasant bands of your neighbours, the Swiss, been beaten down by those who considered themselves well-armed and well-consecrated', but in the last resort these were 'always put to flight, making a mockery of king, emperor, princes and lords' (190, 28/37). 'He who refuses to recognise the victories and defeats of the Swiss as God's work is blind although he sees and deaf with open ears' (191, 30/34). 'What benefits the Swiss but the greed of princes' (*Wer meret Schweitz/dann der herren geytz*) not only sums up the above quotations, but it was also the motto on the title-page of the pamphlet.

The places named in the pamphlet came from the region near Switzerland (Buszello, 1969: 94ff.). The unusual fable in chapter 11 which has caused much confusion refers in its peculiar way to the Swiss: 'the prophecy and ancient saying that a cow on Swan mountain which lies in Franconia shall stand, look about and break wind that it can be heard in the middle of Switzerland' (*dass eyn kuw auff dem Schwanberg imm land zu Franken gelegen solle stan/und da lugen oder plarren dass mans mitten in der Schweytz hore*, 191, 11/16). In his modern German edition of the pamphlet, Brandt thought that this fable pointed to authorship from the circle of radical peasant leaders in Franconia, and he named Rothenburg as the likely place of origin (1925: 315). Hesselbarth and Smirin followed him in placing the pamphlet in north Franconia among the Bildhauser band, although that meant disregarding almost all the rest of the place names mentioned. As well as Buszello, they missed Alfred Stern's interpretation in the opposite sense that the idea of Swiss freedom had reached all the way to Franconia (1926: 22). Contemporary versions of the fable with other regional cases have now been collected, and in all of them the meaning is that the political system of the Swiss should penetrate into neighbouring territories (Englert-Faye, 1940: 799). As is also shown by the fable, the pamphlet is one of the few examples of the Swiss Confederation being used as a paragon in the struggle of the Upper German peasants (Lötscher, 1943: 43f.). There was presumably no other programme in the German peasant war in which Swiss Confederate and Zwinglian influences are mirrored so directly. The extensive excursus into Roman history given in chapter 5 of the pamphlet, pointing out that the decline of the state started when the Romans ceased to support their Republic and 'began to throw up kings as their lords' (167, 39/40) accords with Zwingli's view of the state, who saw republicanism as an ideal form and who refused to accept the principle of hereditary monarchy (Kreutzer, 1909: 38ff.; Wendorf, 1928: 103ff.).

The geographical location of the pamphlet in the south-west German regions near the Swiss border is also the place of origin of the most important and widely circulated peasant programmes, the Twelve Articles of the Upper Swabian peasants, the radical Letter of Articles from the Black Forest, and finally the largest of the peasant organisations, the Christian Union of the Upper Swabian peasants. Were there relations or links between them and the pamphlet as well as with the Christian Union? Buszello pointed to the extensive similarity between the social and economic demands of the Twelve Articles and those made in the pamphlet (1969: 115ff.). However, unlike the Twelve Articles, rejection of unjust rents, dues and serfdom are not the main concern of the pamphlet. Except for the demand for free hunting, a separate chapter is not devoted to social and economic questions. Presumably the author of the pamphlet knew the Twelve Articles and supported their implementation without adding more extensive demands

of his own. He was probably far more concerned to see them being
carried out, and hence it is particularly important to draw parallels
between the pamphlet and the introductory section of the Twelve
Articles in particular.

The latter turns against 'the great number of anti-Christians, who
now . . . have cause to say, are these the fruits of the new Gospel? To
be obedient to no one, to rise and rear up in all districts, to band
together with great force and form into troops . . .' In other words,
the point at issue is that the peasants are concerned to reject the reproach that they are disobedient and do not want to be subject to any
kind of authority. 'Anti-Christians' (*Widerchristen*) and 'enemy of the
Gospel' (*Feind der Evangely*) are the peasants' opponents, and when
such people oppose the demands of the peasants, i.e. 'rise up and rear
up', then they are being led through infidelity by the devil. In the
pamphlet we recognise the same definition of the peasants' enemies,
since in their role as exploiters of justice they have forfeited their right
to be treated justly. 'They are all false, not worthy to hold the lowest
office among Christians' (162, 21/23). They are tyrants and madmen
(163, 33), the devil's mercenaries and Satan's captain (164, 5/6). Both
programmes give the same judgement of the enemies of the peasants.
Against these enemies the peasants protect the Gospel, whereby they are
historically in the right, as much as in their demands as in their fight
against the tyrants who oppress them.

After 1517, Luther also spoke of his personal enemies as heathens
and 'anti-Christians'. But in the pamphlet and in the Twelve Articles
this judgement is taken over by the peasants in their social-revolutionary
struggle and is thereby given a new dimension. Since Luther and his
supporters had sharply distanced themselves from such an interpretation already in 1524 (Müller-Streisand, 1964: 80ff.), and since the
Zwinglian followers, the lay-preacher Sebastian Lotzer and Christoph
Schappeler, are known as the authors respectively of the Twelve
Articles and their introduction, this is confirmation that the author of
the pamphlet was in the group of Zwinglians who were in direct contact with the rebellious peasants.

A few weeks before the actual outbreak of the peasant uprisings,
Lotzer had already argued along similar lines as Schappeler did in the
introduction to the Twelve Articles, at that time to relieve pressure on
Schappeler. His 'Excuse of a devout Christian community at Memmingen with its bishop . . . concerning the uprising which took place
among us' was written after there had been riots in the main church of
the imperial city against the Catholic preacher, and Schappeler and his
followers were accused of starting the tumult (Rohling, 1864: 113f.).
The tenor of Lotzer's defence, which was printed at the beginning of
1525, is strikingly similar to the concerns of our pamphlet. Lotzer
begins by defending himself against the reproach 'we do not want to
give anything any more to any authority on earth, nor do we want to

obey any such authority any longer', with the words, 'he, who like this accuses a Christian community that they do not want to obey the authorities in all fair and seemly matters, spares the truth and talks with a false unchristian heart only to arouse animosity against an honest community' (Lotzer, 1902: 82). Thereby Lotzer polemicised, as pointed out by the editor of his writings, against a letter of the Lutheran preacher, Urbanus Rhegius, who already in February 1525 was one of the first to accuse the peasants of rebellion and disregard of the Gospel. After Lotzer had refuted the charges against Schappeler, he continued 'if one is going to take such an event as an uprising, then Christ also created rebellion', 'but rather it is those who refuse to allow the poor sheep of Christ to hear the Word of God and who do not do what is godly and Christian, that fear that their power and wealth are waning' (ibid.: 84–5). Rebellion is thus made by the opponents of the Reformation in Memmingen, who fear that they will lose their wordly power and influence; in the pamphlet they are the opponents of the peasants. In their argument here, both use the same quotation from the Bible (Matthew 21: 12f.) about driving the money-changers from the Temple. The pamphlet even suggests 'then surely Christ must also be a rebel' (184, 25).

On a further important question, raised later in the pamphlet, Lotzer shared the same view as Zwingli concerning the property of opponents. St Paul warns us in 1 Timothy 6 'that when we have food and shelter we should be content: for those who wish to enrich themselves, will fall into temptation and many harmful lusts, which sink men into ruin and damnation' (Lotzer, 1902: 82). Again we have the warning not to alter property relations. Lotzer's defence of the Memmingen riot of December 1524 is much more substantial than the brief introduction to the Twelve Articles in stating the arguments that are now known to us concerning Christian government and the right to rebel against tyrannous authority, which the pamphlet also reiterates. This further confirms our ascribing the pamphlet to this leading circle of preachers, spokesmen of the Upper Swabian peasants. However, a number of differences must not be forgotten. Schappeler and Lotzer used strong arguments, but not so aggressively against lords and rulers as the pamphlet spoke against those who 'hit and run, the gamblers and guzzlers [*Banketierer*], who are there more satiated than puking dogs' (163, 21/24); 'May God protect us from these ravening wolves and not allow harmful and damned vermin to breed among themselves' (166, 2/7).

After the Baltringen, Allgau and Lake Constance bands had agreed to act in unison in February 1525, the Christian Union of the Upper Swabian peasants had been formed. The Baltringen band had brought with them the draft of a league constitution (*Bundesordnung*) which may possibly have come from Sebastian Lotzer, who was the military secretary of the Union (*Feldschreiber des Bundes*). From this draft a compromise with the harsher demands of the Lake Constance and

Allgau bands was produced on 7 March 1525, and it was shortly thereafter put into print (Franz, 1956: 127f.; Radlkofer, 1887: 253ff.). Like the final league constitution, Lotzer's draft began with a declaration of loyalty towards the authorities, which was also like the introduction to the pamphlet (Franz, 1963: 193ff.). The second article of the league constitution denounced 'unseemly games, blasphemy and heavy drinking', just as the pamphlet did which ordered 'suffer in no way the heavy drinkers, and in no manner allow blasphemers with their damned tongues come among you' (183, 30/34). Long before they were written into the league constitution at Memmingen, these demands had been a part of Reformation pamphlet literature, as, for example, among the *Fifteen Confederates* of Eberlin von Gunzburg (Radlkofer, 1887: 33). The author of our pamphlet could have known these and used them as a model, which once more shows his closeness to many of the general demands of the early bourgeois revolution. He also used the Memmingen league constitution as shown in article sixteen about tolerance to strangers, which is repeated in the pamphlet as 'let the one tolerate the other in all modesty and kindness' (183, 28/30). A look at the Black Forest Peasants' Letter of Articles shows the great difference between it and our pamphlet. The latter knows neither the concept of secular ban (*weltlicher Bann*), nor does it demand destruction of centres of feudal power, so we must be careful not to link our pamphlet with the radical programme of the Black Forest peasants.

Since our pamphlet can, because of its many points of agreement, be placed in the region around the Christian Union, we must not only look for its author in this circle, but also examine the history of this peasant league more closely, to see whether we cannot perhaps here find the main reason why our pamphlet was produced. The author was well acquainted with the Bible, just as he was with ancient history, and he concerned himself with legal questions despite his doggerel against 'text-learned plodders with their Clements and Codes, Dements and Lodes' (156, 2/3). As this colourful expression shows, the author must have possessed powerful talent of expression, and he may well have been a really experienced preacher. Hence the journeyman furrier and lay-preacher Sebastian Lotzer is hardly a likely candidate, though he often shared similar opinions in his writings.

Buszello considered Balthasar Hubmaier and Christoph Schappeler as possible authors, but rejected both on the basis of secondary literature (Buszello, 1969: 121–2). His patchy use of sources makes it necessary to examine the possibility for and against authorship by the two most well-known Zwinglians among the south-west German peasant leaders. Balthasar Hubmaier's constitutional draft (Franz, 1963: 232f.) is in extensive agreement with the basic ideas of our pamphlet. In Hubmaier's draft there is talk of creating a communal organisation (*Landschaft*) of the people, which should then order the authorities to join the Christian

Union. If the authorities stay away, they are to be deprived of the power of the sword and deposed. Should the deposed rulers plan revenge, Hubmaier's draft proposed that they be placed under the secular ban (a concept which does not appear in our pamphlet), and subsequently the use of weapons against them.

However, Hubmaier's draft of a constitution has only come down to us from a hostile source, since the bishop of Vienna, Johann Fabri, published it in order to justify Hubmaier's burning as a heretic in 1528, and whether we thus have an original, edited or even invented text, we have as yet not been able to establish (Bergsten, 1961: 282ff., 295ff.). No records seem to have survived of the role of Hubmaier in Waldshut concerning the revolutionary peasant bands, and the new edition of his works concentrates on his religious writings (Hubmaier, 1962). He preached about the free use of village common land (*Allmende*) to the Klettgau peasants in Waldshut at the end of January 1525 (Schulze, 1957: 233). The text of this sermon is presumably lost. His statement that he had presented the peasants with several articles led to the mis- understanding that he was the author of the Twelve Articles or of the Black Forest Peasants' Letter of Articles (cf. Bergsten, 1961: 282ff.). In 1527, two years after the peasant war, Hubmaier in the tract 'Con- cerning the Sword' took up again the question of authority and the use of force, this time as an anabaptist leader, polemicising against the pacifistic tendencies among the anabaptists under Hans Hut, who totally refused to accept the right of the sword. The basic views in this tract 'Concerning the Sword' are Zwinglian. The question often posed in the tract, how is a Christian subject to behave when faced with an evil authority or ruler, he answered in a clearly hesitant way. If 'the ruler cannot be deposed in a seemly and peaceful way without great damage and rebellion, then he is to be tolerated' (Hubmaier, 1962: 455). He claims to have preached this view 'in the public pulpit at Waldshut and elsewhere' (ibid.: 435). But this does not give sufficient evidence to suppose that Hubmaier only supported the Peasant War as a Reformer and anabaptist (ibid.: 301). By the year 1527, the socio-political situ- ation had changed fundamentally in favour of the ruling circles. Anyone who had been spared the first ragings of the reactionaries was not slow to deny any involvement on the side of the peasants. The failure of the revolutionary situation caused many of the participants in the Peasant War to reverse their former revolutionary convictions. The tract 'Con- cerning the Sword', despite its reference to events in Waldshut, cannot be wholly accepted as a reliable source for claiming that Hubmaier was denying the peasants the right to use force in 1525 (i.e. political involve- ment between 1525–7 made him change his tactics). The views in the tract are diametrically opposed to those held in the constitutional draft, and the contradiction between the two cannot be resolved by use of the printed sources. If Hubmaier is an unlikely author of our pamphlet, then it is above all because of the orientation of Waldshut towards the

Black Forest peasants, whose radical wing formulated the Letter of Articles as a programme that takes a quite different approach from the one in our pamphlet.

Opinions about Christoph Schappeler's involvement during the decisive months of early summer 1525 vary, not least because he was one of the few peasant leaders who escaped persecution and who ended his life at a ripe age in 1551 as preacher in St Gallen, Switzerland. The Chronicle of St Gallen produced by his associate, Johannes Kessler, suppressed all mention of the close relations between Schappeler and the rebellious peasants and avoided mention of his part in the Twelve Articles. Even Schappeler himself in 1531 denied that he had thought up the Articles (Kessler, 1866: 326ff.; Franz, 1939: 209). The ascription of the only possible anonymous tract that may have come from Schappeler, namely the 'Responsible reply dissolving several so-called arguments', is very controversial (Clemen, 1908: 341ff.; Scheible, 1974: 111, n. 17). If one takes a friend of Zwingli as its author, then one sees that the views expressed in it are generally re-formatory: 'He who takes on the Word of God, pays no particular attention to the person who promulgates it, whether it be Peter, Paul, a tailor or a cobbler'. Luther also used this image in the sense of a general Christian equality of all classes and estates (*Werke*, 11: 258, 50). In Schappeler's 'Responsible reply' this has become a general right to preach and in our pamphlet the group 'whether you are now like tailors, cobblers or peasants who are cast up as rulers' (161, 8) stands for a Christian authority – i.e. political power in the hands of the people. It was more important to obey God than men, but at the same time he agreed that in matters temporal everyone was under some authority which would have to be obeyed. That is still almost word for word Luther (*Werke*, 11: 262f.). The question 'whether the present doctrine of the Holy Gospel awakens much riot, rebellion and offense of subjects and also disobedience against their rulers' is the same as the one posed in the introduction to the Twelve Articles. It is clear that there the author also answers in the negative. 'For this very discord is brought about not by the Word of God . . . but by the godless, who are enemies against the true Word' (Clemen, 1908: 374, 381). How to act against a godless ruler who goes against his subjects with force and tyranny did concern Schappeler. But at this time he favoured moral condemnation: 'not only will such a ruler have a troubled wretched conscience all his life but in his reign he will experience all manner of disobedience and opposition' (ibid.: 376f.). After the statement 'it is still the opinion, as well as the time, that ecclesiastical and secular rulers and authorities . . . fear that their power might vanish' (ibid.: 378), is not followed by saying how this might come about. He does not exonerate those 'who outwardly rage and act with much clumsiness', but does consider that the Word of God would eventually get through to such people. This rejection of the people's right to take up arms he also phrases with the words that 'the Holy Gospel forbids all physical opposition or prosecution' (ibid.: 381). However, in this tract of Schappeler's there are a number of thoughts which also reappear in the introduction to the Twelve Articles (Götze and Schmitt, 1953: 212f.).). That Schappeler, just like his friend Zwingli, rejected the use of weapons by the people in 1523, is no proof for a similar attitude after the Peasant War had broken out. The latter confronted reformatory preachers, who were closely tied to the people, with the question anew, and forced them to reconsider their position. There is evidence that Schappeler gave advice to the peasants in the months of the Peasant War and that this was highly valued by them. Lotzer, as his associate and spiritual pupil, had gone a step further after the Memmingen tumult of December 1524 in that he had justified an actual tumult by saying that the disturbance was caused by the godless.

Certainly between this attitude and the appeal in our pamphlet to the peasants to armed struggle there is still a sharp gap. Schappeler's authorship could only be demonstrated if a change in his attitude to the use of force can be shown to have taken place in the months of the German Peasant War. The few witnesses seem to say the opposite. According to Johannes Kessler, during the consultations over a league constitution at the first Memmingen assembly he is supposed to have influenced the peasants 'with manifold examples out of the Old and New Testament', 'in order that they should undertake nothing rebellious with the sword, but instead act in love and friendship to their lords' (Kessler, 1866: 327). Yet Kessler is not altogether trustworthy. As was seen over the question of the Twelve Articles, he was concerned to separate Schappeler as much as possible from the revolutionary peasants in order that his account of the Memmingen preacher's moderating role, which was nowhere else confirmed, should not awaken any scepticism. Against the sweeping judgement that he rejected the uprising (Franz, 1961: col. 1388), we have at least the intervention of the Swabian League from 11 March to the Memmingen town council that they should forbid Schappeler's political activity (Dobel, 1877: 75f.; Radlkofer, 1887: 305). Since Schappeler enjoyed great popularity in the town, and even had supporters among the councillors, the town council did not act, so that the preacher remained in the town until 22 May, when, warned by friends, he fled, escaping only three hours before a contingent of Swabian League mercenaries moved into the town (Baumann, 1876: 370; Kinter, 1971: 6). Unfortunately, there is no known statement of his own views at this time, and we cannot therefore prove that Schappeler was the author of our pamphlet, though there is a certain closeness of ideas that accords with his views.

A contemporary voice even speaks in favour of Schappeler. The copy of our pamphlet in the Dresden Library has the following notes in a sixteenth-century hand on the title-page and after the last line: 'one called Schapplerus had fooled the peasants with these Twelve Articles'.

Presumably the writer of these words confused our pamphlet with the Twelve Articles, and this also occurred on the copy in the Senckenberg Library in Frankfurt-am-Main, which is annotated 'the 12 Articles of the Peasants'. This mistake gave the reference to Schappeler, for based on Jacob Holtzwart's *Rustica seditio totius fere Germanica*, Johannes Carion had maintained in his chronicle of 1532 that Schappeler had been the author of the Twelve Articles (Baumann, 1876: 639ff.; Franz, 1939: 208f.; Steinmetz, 1971: 54ff., 114). And presumably both annotations on our pamphlet know of Carion's chronicle. Yet did they by chance confuse our pamphlet with the well-known programme, the Twelve Articles, or did they have a certain proximity to both tracts which were already unknown a short time after the peasant war? That this was really the case we have seen by examining aspects of contents as well as of location. That is why the author of our pamphlet can be identified only as a trained humanist supporter of the peasants, whose name we do not yet know, of which there were a substantial number in the towns of Upper Swabia and neighbouring regions. About their appearance and journalistic activity we know nothing apart from a few casual remarks. In searching for the author there is a further difficulty in that up to now no reference to our pamphlet has been found among contemporaries, although further finds are possible.

From the understanding gained so far, we can also allude to the likely date of its completion and to its purpose. The Twelve Articles appeared in mid March 1525, before our pamphlet. Since negotiations between the Swabian League and the peasant bands of the Christian Union took place until early April, and since alongside the margrave Philip of Baden the pamphlet names as still alive Frederick the Wise, who died on 5 May 1525, we may surmise that it was produced in the weeks between early April and about 10 May, for news of the Saxon Elector's death would have taken some time to reach south Germany.

More precise possible dating comes from evidence about its aims, given in the last two chapters (10 and 11) of the pamphlet itself. Chapter 10 opens, 'Listen, dear brothers, you have embittered the hearts of your lords so mightily that their gall has spilled over, and it will never again sweeten, for all such hopes are unrealistic. The lords do not want to quarrel, they want to be lords, yes even their own gods' (185, 38–186, 1). Reconciliation between peasants and nobles is therefore hopeless. Who would have wished to achieve such a thing?

It was in the general interest of the rebels to set up a common land-peace (*Landfrieden*) and not let mercenaries immediately devastate the countryside (Bensing and Hoyer, 1970: 6ff.). To achieve this through negotiations and not by destroying enemy strongpoints was the task of the moderate leaders of the Christian Union since early March 1525, above all Ulrich Schmid. The author of our pamphlet could hardly have condemned this policy before it had been given a chance, when it was eventually shown that the Swabian League had no intention of carrying out the peasants' demands. The Swabian League's military attack on the Leipheim band and the official failure of negotiations in early April 1525 are hence possible starting points for our inquiry.

A dark note over the raging feudal reaction after the victory of the lords is stressed by an appeal to the peasants not to become faithless and dishonourable to each other, and not to desert each other but rather to stick together bravely and fraternally (187, 12–15). These commands are repeated several times (cf. 187, 32ff.), and it is unlikely that they were written without very real justification.

The development of the Christian Union after it was attacked by the Swabian League until about the beginning of May evoked the danger of a disintegration of the peasants' common army through two events: the consequences of the defeat of the Leipheim band and the Weingarten agreement. The first military confrontation with the nobility took place between 5 and 14 April, and was a moral shock above all to the Baltringen band. Some of the peasants wanted to surrender without a fight and give up their common agreement with the other two bands comprising the Christian Union. After the swift and catastrophic defeat of the Leipheim band, the suspicion of treachery was also rife (Franz, 1933: 213, n. 1). The author of our pamphlet warned 'and if there is among you in the band someone who with much ado gives himself out to be a cheerful fellow, he is the one who is likely to be the first to flee' (187/8, 42–4). This warning is repeated, 'for there is no rhyme in slipping wolves' hair among sheep's wool, nature will never allow the hawk to unite with the dove' (188, 25–30). The passionate call to arms in the face of this inner crisis of the Christian Union therefore could have been produced at the earliest in the days after 5 April. But a more likely background of events for the pamphlet was the military and political situation after the Weingarten agreement of 17 April between Truchsess of Waldburg (General of the Swabian League) and the Lake Constance band, according to which the peasants agreed to disperse, dissolve their union, swear a new oath of loyalty to their lords and take their complaints to a court of arbitration, headed by Archduke Frederick of Austria (the brother of the Emperor Charles V). Again the reproach of corruption and treachery was voiced above all against the leader of the Rappersweiler peasants, a patrician from Lindau, called Dietrich Hurlewagen, who according to the Swabian League official, Ulrich Artzt, begged General Truchsess on his knees not to make a direct attack. He would find ways in which to get the peasants to disperse (Franz, H., 1924: 36ff.; Franz, G., 1963: 214).

'Do not trust the princes of men, or the children of the world in whom there is no safety' (185, 30/33). The peasants of Lake Constance, however, did trust them with the Weingarten agreement, and only the Allgau peasants refused, thanks to the efforts of Jorg Knopf (Bensing and Hoyer, 1970: 106). 'Your enemies rave and rant complaining about justice; offer you impartial judges and lovers of God, above all evangelical preachers' (183, 10/13). As 'impartial judges' over peasant complaints, the lords offered themselves according to the agreement. More than a month previously the peasants at the second Memmingen assembly had drawn up their own list of arbitrators, including the names of Luther, Zwingli and Schappeler, who were to examine the basis of the peasant demands according to godly law (Cornelius, 1862: 186ff.). Yet the Weingarten agreement gave no reference to evangelical preachers. Since the author gives special emphasis to them, presumably it was because such attempts at deception on the part of the lords affected him personally, i.e. he came from this circle of preachers. In this critical situation, he advised not only unity and warned against false leaders, but above all gave specific advice to give effective organisation to the peasants' military forces. 'Verily necessity demands [*die not erhaischets*] that over ten men there be a corporal [*Rottmayster*], that ten corporals have a centurion over them, that ten centurions have a captain or commander, that ten commanders have a prince, and thus onwards' (188, 17/22).

The Memmingen agreement mentions the corporal (*Rottmeister*) as the lowest military officer, but offers no parallel to the military organisation outlined in our pamphlet, which seems to have been influenced more by examples from ancient history than by actual practice (cf. Hoyer, 1975: 82, chs. 2, 3). But neither from this nor from other of his comments can it be affirmed that the author was conducting a learned dispute over this cardinal question of the Peasant War, i.e. military effectiveness, as Buszello suggests (1969: 108). For that, the references are too precise and urgent. He insists on discipline 'like other devout imperial cities to the Emperor in the name of Christian order' (188, 42/3). Did the author write these rousing words to the peasants from one of the many imperial cities in south-west Germany? The quotation is presumably to be understood in this way, and *not* as a desire to introduce a political system like the imperial cities had among the peasants, since he does not go into any further detail. Once more he refers to Swiss models in the military sphere: 'And since the oft-mentioned Swiss must fight for themselves, their community [*landschaft*], women and children, and must protect themselves against arrogant power, they have for the most part always been victorious, and acquired great honour' (190–91, 40–42). Therefore, 'fight for your houses, and also women and children' (192, 4/5).

The way in which the pamphlet is drawn up and the number of lines used shows that for it the central problem was that a community (*Gemeinde*) had the right and duty to depose its unchristian authorities as well as call to arms if it was being hindered from carrying this out. Its polemics against Lutheran preachers who demanded obedience to the authorities is only a prelude to this. The author was not writing for them. He wanted to draw the peasants' attention to the very real danger that they had not understood that the lords opposing them were 'unchristian', i.e. their fundamental class-enemies, and that instead they would quarrel among themselves, hence neglecting their necessary preparations for the inevitable military conflict that was to come.

As Smirin pointed out (1956: 85), the pamphlet argues in a political and not social-revolutionary way, though its aim is very close to that of the people's reformation (*Volksreformation*). The pamphlet is the only known tract from the peasant side which took up the crucial question of the political aim of the revolution and how to accomplish it by military means. What was its desired political aim? Without doubt it was a sworn confederation along Swiss lines made up of rural and urban communities who would carry out strictly limited services to feudal lords. Its view of society is thereby burdened with all the contradictions which the Swiss confederation carried within itself at the beginning of the sixteenth century: the continued existence of feudal lordships alongside free communities (*Landgemeinden*), and political independence from ruling princes, but with recognition of the imperial feudal overlord, i.e. the Emperor. In the economic situation of the opening of the sixteenth century, a change in the feudal relations of production created more favourable conditions for development of the forces of production in the towns, increasing their primitive accumulation of capital more than had previously been possible in south-west Germany. Yet the author of our pamphlet was no ideologist for the bourgeoisie, but much rather for the peasant community made up of the dominant upper layer of property-holding but still feudally dependent peasants.

Nowhere in the pamphlet is there discussion of the view held in the moderate Twelve Articles that feudal services should continue to be performed. Our author only polemicised against a fundamental overthrow of feudal property. Yet in this question, his rigorous political demands alone place him close to the representatives of the people's reformation (*Volksreformation*), even if in his flight of thought he did not rise to those bold visions of a people's republic dominated by peasants and miners which the friend and follower of Zwingli, Michael Gaismair, formulated in his Tyrol Constitution.

PETER BLICKLE

11 Biblicism versus Feudalism *

The crisis of feudalism which appeared in Germany at the beginning
of the sixteenth century could not be settled by traditional means, for
example, on the model of common legal settlements between lord and
peasant. Why? To answer this, the points of contact, superimposition
and mutual dependence of the fields of conflict should be indicated,
and an attempt made to determine the value of critical factors in a way
that covers both general relations and regional peculiarities.

It is difficult to estimate correctly the situation of central European
agriculture around 1500. However, in the last five decades before 1525
the situation of the peasants deteriorated to this extent: the area of
agriculture now became recognisably scarce, rights of usufruct were
energetically reduced and taxes were perceptibly raised. How far this
process went on against the background of a recession or an economic
revival in the agrarian economy cannot be determined. However, it is
relevant as a causal factor – though without giving it priority of place –
because the deterioration fell within the range of experience of only two
generations, and so was felt to be a change for the worse.

Here one might object that it is mistaken to stress the economic
position of agriculture as a causal factor of the revolt, in view of a not
exactly stormy development in the agrarian area both before and after
1500. Such a statement is correct, but it overlooks the fact that additional economic burdens actually were sufficient to provoke revolts even
before 1525. The rebellion of the Salzburg peasants was the reply to
the doubling of the *pallium* (tax to Rome for the investiture of a new
bishop). Disturbances in the monastic lordships of Weissenau, Schussen-
ried and St Blasien were a reaction to the increase in serfdom dues,
and the Poor Conrad rebellion in Wurttemberg reflected opposition to
the territorial lord's forest protection policy. It may be incontestable
that the causes of such revolts can be sought in deeper levels of peasant
consciousness, for example, in an injured sense of justice. But in no
single case can one overlook the fact that the conflicts were provoked
by measures from the lords which always penetrated directly to the
peasant economy. When the revolts broke out at ever shorter intervals
after the middle of the fifteenth century, then that points to the sharpen-

*Translated from Peter Blickle, *Die Revolution von 1525*, Munich, Oldenbourg Verlag, 1975, pp. 135–43.

ing of the crisis before 1525. And not only that. The numerical increase in the risings can be co-ordinated with the growing economic burdens. The Elector of Mainz even wanted to have this viewpoint considered in the imperial election of 1519, and canvassed for Charles V because of the economic power of the Habsburgs 'so that the poor common man would not be burdened with impositions and levies without notable need and cause, for no good would come of it, but only a Bundschuh' (*Deutsche Reichstagsakten*, 1963 : 843f.).

Two things are noteworthy in these revolts. They were conducted with the argument that this or that duty had not been usual at the time of their 'parents and grandparents', and they were conducted with the aim of removing a concrete grievance. Argument and aim fused one with another. There was no demand without legitimation, and the legitimation given was old custom – plainly and simply, the key concept of all medieval legal thought. It is thus self-evident that nothing was demanded in the late-medieval revolts and rebellions within the Empire that could not be legitimated. Put another way, the revolts could only strive to remove a definite innovation. This answers the question why the revolts remained territorially limited, why there was no revolution in the fifteenth century comparable to that of 1525.

The additional economic burdens encountered an already tense social situation in the family and the village. Since flight from the country had been effectively prevented, a growing population struggled to share an area of cultivation which could hardly be extended. In areas with partible inheritance of property, society levelled itself downwards; in those with impartible inheritance, the opposition between rich and poor was sharpened by a growth of the rural lower class. At first sight it seems absurd when the lords further hindered freedom of movement in the face of such difficulties within villages. They did this not with an eye on the cottagers and small peasants, but in order to be able to increase the tax-value of the large farms. The same motive, complemented by the interests of the territorial state, lay behind the prohibition of extra-tenurial marriage (*Ungenossame Ehe*).

The socio-economic development stands in noticeable contrast to political development, which can be summed up in a phrase as the political emancipation of the peasants. If extensive village self-government furthered the peasants' capacity for political decision making, then their success in disputes with their lords must also have raised their political expectations.

The call for more regional differentiation is appropriate at this point. Gradated differences in economic burdens, in social tension and in political expectations cannot be disputed. They also forbid declaring these to be a generally binding hierarchy of causes. On the contrary, it is necessary to evaluate them as variables of regionally differentiated importance. In Tyrol, the higher political expectations outweighed the lesser economic burdens; step by step, subjects had come closer to their aim of a territorial constitution (*Landesordnung*). In Franconia, the economic burdens had more weight than the political expectations. The manorial and territorial load exceeded the limits of tolerance when half of one's income was eaten up by duties. Such examples, which could be multiplied at will, show that the combination of the variables in the long run always had the same effect: the load capacity of the relationship of lord to peasant had reached its limit. Where this was not yet the case, possibly in Thuringia, which did not know the forms of serfdom or communal autonomy prevalent in upper Germany, a revolutionary figure such as Thomas Muntzer could fill up that narrow ditch without difficulty.

But the revolutionary breakthrough did not take place. Such lethargy among the peasants seems incomprehensible only if one excludes loyalty from the structural relationship of lord and serf, for this was the ethical element which bound the peasant to his lord. Certainly, loyalty, the bond of the medieval social and political order, was depreciated by the growth of economic dependence which the peasant perceived very clearly, although he was not yet in a position to overspring these older ethical barriers. These expressed themselves in his legal thought, which certainly stood on a high moral plane, but which in its ties to old custom was none the less unfitted to master problems of a rapidly changing order of society and government. For example, old custom offered no solution to the population problem. Where the lord could produce 'old law', 'old custom' was powerless. The sibylline proposition said that written law, forgeries included, was superior in argumentative power to old custom. Old custom could only act as a defence against innovation where it could prove itself as 'documented'. In cases of doubt, the presumption lay with the stronger party. As this was not always so, and had not been so for a long time, the peasant placed his hope in the power of old law. To become aware that this hope was illusory understandably took a certain period of time. This could be expressed in the following formula:

$$\text{willingness to rebel} = \frac{\text{economic burden} + \text{social tension} + \text{political expectations}}{\text{force of legitimation}}$$

The smaller the force of legitimation, the greater the willingness to rebel.

When it finally became clear that conflicts could not be resolved in the traditional form of a legal settlement, the only remaining alternatives were: to refuse any legitimation of their demands, or to turn to a 'new' law. An ethical, by which we understand a legally based, demand was obviously superior to a naked demand. If a 'new' law was congenial to peasant legal understanding, and if it was capable of transforming their needs, tensions, hopes and expectations into ethically justified demands, it would work as a downright deliverance. The 'new' law was found – in 'godly' law.

The Peasant War really began in January/February 1525 in Upper Swabia. In the Allgau, on Lake Constance and around Baltringen the peasants rose and organised themselves into the Allgau, Lake Constance and Baltringen bands, at first independently of any mutual influence. Given the homogeneity of agrarian and feudal relations, the increase in economic burdens, social tensions and political expectations had all obviously reached the same level, especially since nobles and clergy had consulted one another in their attempts at intensification and territorial-isation. Numerous legal proceedings in the fifteenth century must have furthered communication among the lords, for they sat on the arbitra-tion commissions, and so knew the problems in the upper Swabian lordships far beyond their own territorial borders. An institution such as the Swabian League which brought together at its assemblies nobility, prelates and town councillors must have facilitated the exchange of experiences which finally led to the levelling downward of society referred to above. This is sufficiently proved by the remarkably frequent arguments from the lords' side for restrictive measures based on customs of neighbouring lordships.

A feature of the rising in January/February 1525 is its supra-territorial character. Peasants of various lords banded together; villages rebelled, no longer the subjects of one lord. That was something new, in that the previous revolts had never broken through the narrow frame of reference to the individual lordship. A supra-territorial union pre-supposed overcoming the previous force of legitimation. That is under-standable, for old custom could be injured by the local lord and by no one else, and consequently demands cloaked in old custom could be addressed to him alone. Surmounting the traditional force of legitima-tion and isolation was possible in two ways: through a 'new' law which abolished the narrow legal community of peasant and lord, or through a renunciation of the law. The former occurred in the Allgau, the latter in Baltringen.

The serfs and tenants of the Allgau monastery of Kempten had pressed with increasing vehemence since the middle of the fifteenth century for a loosening of personal dependence. The revolt of 1491–2 was the first, the only conditionally given allegiance (*Huldigung*) of 1523 the second highpoint in a wider dramatic campaign conducted by the peasants with the weapon of old custom. In January 1525 arbitra-tion between abbot, convent and countryside (*Landschaft*) collapsed. The countryside, i.e. the organised peasantry of a territory similar to the parliaments, then discussed on 23 January in Leubas, the judicial seat of the imperial territorial court for Kempten, how to proceed further: war or legal procedure. The majority voted for legal proce-dure (Blickle, 1973: 326). At this point of time the common com-munity's composition was restricted to the subjects of the abbey of

Kempten. The complaint of the abbot that peasants of outside lords
had joined their union, by which he wished to blame his own peasants
for the outbreak of the Peasant War, was repudiated energetically by
the community, who claimed that they had forbidden all strangers to
join their alliance (Franz, 1963: 131). This documents very clearly
the connection between old law and personally, regionally limited
activity.

The community's representative Jorg Schmid (or Knopf) of Leubas
went to Tubingen to consult a jurist. He was first recalled by the
community on 20 February, after the whole Allgau was in uproar, and
the peasants had found a new legitimation for their demands: 'the holy
Gospel and the godly law' (Franz, 1933: 184). The local limitations
were overcome and feudal subjection no longer formed an insuperable
barrier to collective alliances. By the end of the month, peasants of the
count of Montfort, rural citizens (*Ausbürger*) of the town of Wangen,
serfs of the abbot of Kempten and subjects of the bishop of Augsburg
all found an institutional framework for their enterprise in the 'Christian
Union of the Community [*Landart*] of Allgau'. The Kempten peasants
had never rejected legitimation, but had exchanged old, worn-out legal
presuppositions for new, firmer ones – old custom for godly law.

The second alternative to old custom accompanied the rising around
Baltringen. Within a month, up till the middle of February, 7,000 to
10,000 peasants found themselves in the Baltringen camp from the
most varied lordships south of the Danube, from the Black Forest to
the Bavarian frontier. On 16 February, in response to a request from
the Swabian League, the peasants presented their grievances. Only a
few of these had been sent directly to their lords beforehand. If one
evaluates them according to their form of legitimation (Blickle, 1975:
31), it becomes apparent that only 5 per cent were based on godly law,
11 per cent on old custom, while 84 per cent were not justified by
anything at all. It is natural that a justification based on the older
customs has crept in only here and there. The most careful analysis
seems to confirm the suspicion that certain demands were left unfounded
because no proven injury to old law was present. Thus, in the grievances against serfdom and manorial lordship, a bare 1.5 and 8 per cent
respectively were argued on the basis of old custom; this rose to 14.8
and 20.7 per cent respectively in administration of justice and claims
to usufructs.

The search for legitimation or legal approval only lasted ten days.
On 27 February the Baltringen band, which now called itself 'Christian
assembly', decided to elevate the divine Word to a programme. 'What
this same divine Word then takes from or gives us we will obey, whatever thereby befalls us, be it good or bad' (Vogt, 1879ff.: no. 83). To
seek legal grounds for grievances seemed superfluous, and even raising
them could be dispensed with, since it was no longer necessary to strive
for a settlement with each individual lord. Whereas the rebellion sought

legitimation or legal approval, the revolution had a definite aim, which remained to be specified more precisely and to harmonise economic, social and political demands with the divine Word. The revolution needed its manifesto and found it in the Twelve Articles.

To implement 'godly' law, whatever the peasants may have understood by it in detail, became the aim of the revolution. The Twelve Articles were successful because they formulated godly law as a new legal principle, because it could be used to overcome the structural problems of feudalism, and finally feudalism itself. Even where they could not serve as a basic argument because feudalism was too stable, or where feudalism had already been eroded by the new doctrine of the early modern state, the superstructure of godly law could be adapted independently to put forward demands of quite different content.

As a mirror of peasant aims in the first phase of the revolution, the Twelve Articles at first only sought to prove the legitimacy of demands by quoting the Bible, consequently stigmatising as unchristian the evil measures of lords and rulers which had provoked such demands. The divine Word as a legal principle worked redemptively for the peasants: the lords bore the blame for the rising which was justified through the Bible. What means could and should be seized upon to implement the divine Word still remained open. 'First, the Gospel is not a cause of the disturbance or risings'; the revolution itself was justified by the divine Word. 'Second, the disobedience, indeed the rebellion of all peasants is Christianly excusable' (cf. Götze, 1902: 8).

Godly law was potentially dynamic in a threefold sense. Now any kind of demands which were deducible from the Bible could be put forward. The social barriers which had previously separated the peasants and townsmen were now removed. In principle the future social and political order now stood open.

Where deeper insights into the lords' reactions to peasant demands are possible, it becomes again clear that old custom was of little use to the peasants as a defence against innovations. In all their replies to the articles of their subjects, which had been sent to the Swabian League, the nobility contested the view that they had introduced any innovations. They argued that their actions had corresponded to ancient custom and local usage. Any compromise was thereby made impossible. The peasant remained in a defensive situation from which only godly law could liberate him. Certainly, the argumentative force of ancient custom paralysed the peasant only where exclusively feudal structures of rule existed. On the other hand, the towns replied to the complaints of their peasants far more pragmatically; in fact, they even modified them with a touch of irony. Thus the city of Memmingen parried the demand for abolition of tax for transfer of possessions (*Ehrschatz*) with the reply that they would in future confer the farms 'just as their subjects desired that they might henceforth deal with their parsons'. To acknowledge various interests and handle them as did the imperial city of Memmingen clearly made an agreement easier, while ancient custom became a refuge for noble and clerical lords against godly law. Throughout a conference in Basel all the attorneys of knights and prelates from Alsace and the Sundgau used ancient custom to argue against the peasants. Labour service was 'used from of old'; heriots were 'not thought up of late, but were used by many'; carnival chickens were still demanded 'because they and their elders had given these for such a long time'; goods of murderers were confiscated 'because it had been in use longer than human memory' (Schreiber, 1866, no. 382). Whether in Tyrol, Salzburg or Franconia, the lords became more and more insistent on old custom the longer the uprising lasted. A complete exception was the elector Frederick the Wise when he conceded to his brother, Duke John, 'that the poor have been burdened in many ways by us secular and clerical authorities', and that 'perhaps one . . . has given the poor folk cause for such a disturbance' (Franz and Fuchs, 1942: 91).

Without godly law the revolution would not have been possible in this form. The power of godly law in argument was also displayed in the towns. Regardless of the fact that the peasants had obtained the argument of godly law from the towns, as was quite clearly attested for the Twelve Articles, yet godly law as a principle to shape the social and political order was first carried into the towns by the peasants. In general, the slogan of godly law first arrived in the towns after the peasants had taken it up generally (Franz, 1972: 227ff.). The Twelve Articles had already clearly put forward the claim that the political order should fundamentally be held open with a saving clause: if it should be proved that the articles they proposed 'were unjust, they would be null and void from that hour and of no value. Similarly if more articles are truthfully found in the Scripture that are against God and a burden on neighbours, we will reserve these and include them' (Götze, 1902: 15). Peasants wanted not just to hear the Gospel, but also to live according to it. The individual grievances formulated in the Twelve Articles were not the last word. Their belief in the power of proof and of conviction in the divine Word was likewise unshaken. Yet for all its liberation, this entailed a new servitude since it was the preserve of theologians to question the Bible for its applicability to everyday life, and furthermore since the peasants trusted the lords to subject themselves to such an interpretation. Where would the revolution go when the theologians rejected the peasants' arguments, and the lords closed their minds against it?

HEIDE WUNDER

12 The Mentality of Rebellious Peasants – the Samland Peasant Rebellion of 1525*

I

Social history, understood as the history of society, combines the history of structures and the history of events. It attempts to recognise the connections between 'dominant relationships', individual and collective action, and historical events and developments. Since the structural components are as important as the history of events, it is possible through 'social history as a research strategy' (Wunder, 1975: 146–50) to encompass such social areas and groups which hardly ever find a place in traditional political history. That is especially true for peasants, who have mostly been discussed as a 'part' of economic relations in agricultural and economic history, and who only turn up in political history when they attempt rebellions or peasant wars.

A new possibility of social history illuminating the connections between structure and event resides in the construction of social processes as social interaction between individuals and groups, between various social, political, economic groups, strata, classes (Moore, 1966). This method of interpretation, applied to periods with a scarcity of sources, or to groups who have no written tradition of their own, allows the historian to offset the fragmentary nature of his material, to gain an insight into the structure of social relations and into the framework of action of individuals and groups. The interaction model cannot content itself with fitting the object of investigation into the institutionalised structures of power and dominance within a given hierarchical system. Nor can it proceed from the results of political action, which form the chain of historical 'facts' and connections. Social interplay admits of ever more possibilities of action and decision which must be investigated in order to recognise the contemporary levels of action. Within the framework of the interaction model, politically relevant behaviour is seen not only in the deeds of individuals, but also in solidary actions in

*Translated with abbreviated text and notes from Heide Wunder, 'Zur Mentalität aufständischer Bauern', Der Deutsche Bauernkrieg 1524–6 (ed. H. U. Wehler), Sonderheft 1, Geschichte und Gesellschaft, Göttingen, 1975, pp. 9–37.

various social sectors and historical situations. Exactly how the co-operation of individuals, and the groups which are dependent on, or independent of them, is formed in a given situation must be investigated in each individual case.

The interaction model thus permits the detection of politically relevant action for social groups such as the peasants, which hitherto have had no part in political history. In this way both the entire social structure, and its given structure of action, can be more completely comprehended. The consistent application of the interaction model further requires research into the motives and mental orientation of these groups which hitherto have not been included in the political process. This is especially the case with the investigation of violent social conflicts.

Progress in this direction is attributable above all to English and French historiography, which much more than German historiography has been concerned with revolutions and mentalities. In England this has been in connection with the Industrial Revolution and the history of the working class (Thompson, 1963), in France with research into the French Revolution and popular culture in the early modern period (Furet, 1965, 1970). If the social and political role of the peasant in Germany is to be investigated, then this cultural aspect, in its widest sense, must be illuminated. This work has been hampered to date by lack of documentary material. Above all, we lack personal testimonies from the peasants which would give a direct and first-hand view of their pre-suppositions. It has been no less hampered by lack of the necessary historical investigation. Even folklore, which sees its area of interest as popular culture, and especially 'peasant culture', has proved to be of little use. It has investigated largely the *material* survivals of peasant culture, but hardly at all the peasants as thinking and acting persons.

In the present state of research into the history of the peasants, both in traditional agrarian history, as well as in the GDR, one can refer to a considerable number of regional and local studies on the basis of the socio-historical direction already mentioned. International academic exchange, above all that with western European countries, has brought new aspects for the investigation of peasants and workers, especially the concept of 'moral economy' (Thompson, 1971), which has recently been taken up for the analysis of peasant uprisings in the early modern period (Le Roy Ladurie, 1974). The interdisciplinary exchange between history and folklore has provided excellent opportunities for further research (Braun, 1960; Wiegelmann, 1972: 223–400). But these new approaches are more single 'building bricks' than the necessary architect's plans.

In this situation the way is open to seek suitable concepts in those neighbouring disciplines to whose field belongs research into peasant societies and peasant cultures, that is, ethnology (Nipperdey, 1973). In what follows I shall adopt American usage of the term anthropology in the sense of 'social anthropology' and 'cultural anthropology' (Honigman, 1973), since I shall base my observations largely on results produced under their premises. It cannot be the task of this essay to give a descriptive definition of social and cultural anthropology, which has already given trouble enough to their own specialists. Rather we shall explain briefly what stimulus the historian who wishes to investigate the social and political role of the peasant in German history can receive from predominantly anthropological investigations. Here we shall distinguish between, first, general and, secondly, particular stimuli.

1 The anthropological categories of personality structure, modal personality and social character are suited to modify and correct existing presuppositions about the primitiveness and timelessness of the peasant character. These categories have been developed by drawing social psychology into ethnographical field work, where it is a matter of finding out the determining elements of culture through participatory observation of the given human group, whether tribal associations or village societies (Honigman, 1973: 2f.). Here the ethnographer relies basically on information from individuals, who provide him with knowledge about the functions of their society as well as information about their values and presuppositions. The presupposition that the individual in these so-called primitive cultures has little or no individuality has long since been given up by anthropologists. Rather, an essential finding of their work is the multiplicity of possibilities for the organisation of human corporate life, and the multiplicity of individual behaviour within the framework of simple societies. The possibility of an overview of their 'population' and their regional extension, as well as the purposive catalogue of researchers' questions, can easily deceive one about the complexity of social relations.

The historian who wishes to explain the mediation between individual behaviour and social process should therefore be on the lookout for suitable anthropological examples and ask himself whether and how far these results can be tested and used. For further progress in the investigation, one must hold firmly to the following: the question of the mentality of a definite social group in a definite historical situation is separate from the unscientific, colloquial concept of 'mentality' which, similar to the concept 'character', fixes observable, 'typical' behaviour as a firm and unchangeable attribute. As a technical term, mentality describes acquired and changeable presuppositions, attitudes and outlooks of social groups. Group behaviour and individual behaviour which shapes for itself socially mediated attitudes and outlooks are both observable and discoverable in the sources. These individual 'refractions' give information about the areas of applicability of mentalities and at the same time information about changes in them.

2 In the case study under discussion, the peasant rising in Samland in 1525, the absence of peasant self-testimony in the sources leads us to examine other peasant wars and risings which are better documented with the self-understanding of the peasants. Especially productive is the work of the American anthropologist Eric Wolf (Wolf, 1967, 1971). On the one hand, he sets out theses on peasant revolutions (Wolf, 1973), on the other he tests models of peasant society as a part-culture (Wolf, 1966), and works out its individual elements, such as peasant typologies in relation to 'open' and 'closed' communities, through South American examples. The usefulness of these anthropological works for relations in early modern Europe springs immediately to mind, but must appear dubious to someone outside this discipline. It can be justified on two grounds. The anthropologist Wolf concerns himself, as does the historian, with complex societies. By contrast with many of his colleagues, his writings reflect concern with the effects of political power, an eminently historical category, even if he has not overcome the predominant 'cultural' orientation in anthropology. This explains why Wolf's work can provide a general stimulus to the historian, which he can then test for its specific usefulness (cf. Hilton, 1974).

In the specific task of ascertaining the mentality of a definite social group such as the peasants, it is necessary

(1) To describe this social group as exactly as possible, and where possible to delineate it in terms of other groups.
(2) To discover the most important areas in which attitudes, views, experiences and expectations can be observed.
(3) To weigh up and assess the relation of the various views and attitudes one with another. In this, attention must be paid to synchronisms, contradictions and displacements.

One must investigate individually the attitudes of the peasants to their work, to the narrower and wider areas of family, to neighbours and village comrades, to the village elite (mayor, parson, innkeeper, miller), to the non-peasant village inhabitants, to landlords, to the church (as an institution), to the territorial lord, to justice and injustice, to religion, politics, and to society overall. This enumeration shows that peasant attitudes can be worked out systematically, corresponding to various historical approaches and neighbouring sciences, and arranged beside one another or separately in space and time. Only when the multiplicity of peasant attitudes has been investigated, can we clarify the question whether and how far the traditional characterisation of their behaviour, itself determined by attitudes and expectations, can be designated as 'traditional' or 'conservative'.

Such a programme aims at a structural analysis which includes the categories of social time and social space. This cannot be claimed with regard to the preliminary studies on the example chosen here, the

Samland peasant rising, but we shall attempt to show the fruitfulness of this approach. In this essay only the mentality of rebellious peasants will be in question, that is, the clarification of their traditional behaviour, actions and reactions. That will be done neither with the aid of 'anthropological constants', nor through analogies with individual psychology, nor by means of popular and mass psychology, but with reference to two of Eric Wolf's theses on the role of the 'middle peasantry' and of 'middle men' in peasant rebellions, as well as to the theory of collective behaviour (cf. Smelser, 1971).

When the mentality of rebellious peasants is to be ascertained, one must clarify:

(1) What kind of peasants are concerned (Wolf, 1967: 503f.).
(2) What historical experiences and contemporary expectations influence the peasants.
(3) How the behaviour of rebellious peasants differs from their previous behaviour.
(4) What models were available in the spectrum of the time for the mastery of conflict and what possibilities could be seized on by the peasants.

The initial question as to the mentality of rebellious peasants, apparently very specific, involves therefore a complicated methodological procedure, not least because of the poor state of the sources. We will commence with structural conditions and relationships, which will be worked out with the model of a peasant society (Wolf, 1966). The next question considered will be the relationship between definite events and actions, in order to direct particular attention to the role of attitudes and opinions in the group of acting persons.

II

The course of events of the Samland peasant rising has been ascertained by local history on the basis of the existing sources – chronicles, letters from the insurgent peasants, and the ducal government and administration – even if not all details have been investigated (Wunder, 1975: 151–8; Zins, 1959). It will be described in terms of the usual list of factors in Peasant War research: occasion, cause, supporters, leaders, organisation, duration, outcome, consequences.

After the peasant rebellions in the Empire had been almost everywhere repressed, German and Prussian peasants and Prussian freemen rose against the arbitrariness and arrogance of the junkers. The rebellion began on 2 September 1525 and ended with an armistice agreement, the Treaty of Quednau, on 8 September. The peasants declared their loyalty to the absent territorial lord, Duke Albrecht, but still rejected the claims of the nobility to lordship. They wanted a 'godly government' set up on the basis of the Gospel. Since the nobility was not mentioned in the Gospel, the peasants felt justified in disputing noble claims to lordship and privileges of usufruct of wood and water. Against this the peasants set a community of brothers and sisters, in which all earned their living by the work of their own hands. The Gospel was to be preached in future without human additions. The disturbed ducal government and the terrified ruling oligarchy of Konigsberg were assured of respect for life and property.

The peasants formed a military commune in the manner of Landsknechte and elected captains who were also their political spokesmen. As a political community they appeared as the 'Samland common community' (*Landschaft*). The size of the peasant army can be estimated at 2,500 men. Their activities were limited to capturing the nobility, seeing to provisions and providing a war-chest. The captains tried to win the support of the Konigsberg commons and to organise peasant resistance in other parts of the country. The commons did not dare to support the peasant undertaking, while the town council was concerned to mediate between the conflicting parties. Thus the Treaty of Quednau was negotiated after seven days, by which the settlement of the dispute between peasantry and nobility was put off until the duke's return. This treaty interrupted the spread of the movement and the union of peasant bands which had already gathered in Natangen, Insterburg and Memel. On his return the duke did not uphold the treaty but took the side of the nobility and disarmed the peasants. About fifty peasant leaders were executed.

Even this short description shows that it is necessary to distinguish between various groups of rebels, namely German peasants, Prussian peasants and Prussian freemen. It also shows possible differences between the peasants as bearers of the movement, and the leaders. One can surmise that, at least at the beginning of the rising, these different groups also had different attitudes and that one cannot speak of a unified peasant mentality. The question as to what changes in outlook were effected by the transition from 'peaceful' behaviour to active self-help must therefore be posed separately for each peasant group. Only then can the wider question of the characteristic behaviour and outlook of the peasants and freemen during the rebellion be treated. In accordance with the procedure outlined at the beginning, this requires some notion of Prussian rural society, in which attention must be paid to variations in Samland.

All propertied groups of the rural population of Samland provided participants in the rising: the German peasants, the Prussian peasants and the Prussian freemen. The relative size of the various groups can only be crudely established; roughly 300 Prussian freemen who were all said to have taken part. The number of German peasants cannot have been too great as there were relatively few settlements in Samland. As the largest population group, the Prussian peasants presumably supplied the greatest number of participants. The rural poor (agricultural labourers) and the landless seem to have played no part, since their numbers in Samland would not have been very great (Wunder, 1968: 234). The fishermen and journeymen participating from Konigsberg can be regarded as peripheral.

German peasants and Prussian freemen based their position on charters (for the peasants, collective village charters; for the freemen, individual assignments of their goods), in which were laid down their rights and their moderate obligations to the landlord, the Church and the territorial lord. The property structure of the German villages was characterised by a uniform farm size, while the property of the freemen had a great variation of area. Each group certainly had a written guarantee of its position, but the material content of the current inheritance law and the social status of peasants and freemen were still basically different. Prussian freemen did military service for the German Order, and thus stood above German peasants, although village mayors (*Schulzen*) who were freed from peasant services but provided a special service (*Schulzendienst*) were placed equal to the freemen. The German peasants were organised into communes with self-administration. Prussian freemen stood directly under the jurisdiction of the German Order, and freemen with larger properties also had legal jurisdiction over their peasants.

However, Prussian peasants were basically worse off. Their landed property was smaller than that of the German peasants. Their economic obligations were certainly regulated by custom, but not fixed in writing, so that they were in a legally worse position. Inhabitants of Prussian villages were also organised as communes, but without the privileges of German villages, so that they had more the character of a dependent community. On the basis of these economic, social and legal facts the various rural population groups were arranged in a hierarchy. At the very bottom was the broad stratum of Prussian peasants, above them the German peasants, and at the top the Prussian freemen and the privileged stratum of the German villages: mayor (*Schulze*), parson, innkeeper and miller. There was no nobility in the proper sense, so it formed no constituent element of the rural society in the territory of the German Order from the thirteenth to the fifteenth century. Ethnic differences, in this view, had little discriminatory effect.

The concept of 'peasant society' allows us to comprehend recognised economic and ethnic differences among the rural population more sharply in their social significance and to use them to characterise the state of the German Order. It poses explicitly the question of the relations between the various peasant groups and between these and their environment and, in particular, the relations with the town as an economic, cultural, administrative and religious centre.

Since the German peasants supplied the greatest part of their dues to their landlords as money rents, they depended on selling part of their harvest in the city market. The village artisans also expected payment in cash. The city court was also the appeal court for the village courts of the vicinity, so that the German peasants were closely tied, economically and legally, to their district town. There were probably also family connections between the artisan stratum and at least the village elite (mayor (*Schulze*), innkeeper, miller). The drawing power of the city for the countryside is often attested, but the differing possibilities of migration for menials, artisans and peasants have as yet been little investigated.

The Prussian peasants had to supply predominantly natural dues to their landlords, so that a great part of their harvest went direct to the German Order, the greatest landlord in the country. The town thus had no economic function for the Prussian peasant, since in view of their heavier burden compared to the German peasant, he would have had little left for sale. Significantly, hardly any artisans lived in Prussian villages. The chief link between the Prussian villages and the wider world was through the economic and administrative centres of the German Order, which also drew the majority of its servants from the Prussian population. The dependence of Prussian peasants on the German Order was strengthened by them being subject to the direct jurisdiction of the Order's local and regional officials, in whom were also vested powers to alter the legal status of a peasant to a freeman in individual cases. The German Order thus held the Prussian peasants in personal, economic and legal dependence, which the German peasants had left behind as they settled in Prussia under the conditions of a developing market and money economy.

The varying economic and legal positions contributed to keeping the ethnic groups separated. They lived in separate settlements, had different economic forms and relations, varying rights and notions of right; a marriage of the two was not possible. This economic and social order was reinforced by religious and cultural differences. The Prussians had certainly been baptised after the final conquest of the land, but the Christian faith was only a thin veneer over continuing pagan customs and attitudes. The Prussians still spoke their own language, and neither the Order nor the bishops made efforts to instruct them in it.

Following this interpretation, the various peasant groups can be arranged not just in the traditional manner into a hierarchical system of social strata, but horizontal social divisions were of equal significance. These horizontal divisions I designate as segments (cf. Wolf, 1967: 502–5). Decisive for the self-awareness of the peasant groups was not only their conception of 'above' and 'below' within the given order, but also their conception of 'beside one another', which was asserted on the one hand in the spatial division of the settlements. On the other, it had a wholly social dimension through inter-ethnic relationships, which were determined by the different social levels of the participants. To round this off, the peasants conceived of the town–country relationship as one of mutual dependence.

A consequence for the question of the mentality of the peasants is that the peasants of the various segments had different 'world views'. The segment of German peasants can rightly be designed as a part-culture, while the segment of Prussian peasants can be characterised rather as a sub-culture. The German peasants belonged to a market-oriented economy. The Prussian peasants were tied to a social relationship which was determined by the personal links between landlord and peasant.

This 'ideal structure' of German part-culture and Prussian sub-culture has a different heuristic value for the individual parts of the Order's territory. In an area with a predominantly Prussian population, such as Samland, one can establish a mixture of German and Prussian legal and economic forms even in the fourteenth century, without the 'cultural' boundaries between both peasant segments falling away (cf. Barth, 1970: 9–38). In areas with stronger German settlement, the beginnings of an assimilation process can be observed at the end of the fourteenth century. Individual Prussians are traceable as hidage rent farmers (*Hufenzinsbauer*) in German villages, and this 'rise' also signifies a socio-cultural assimilation to the German part-culture (cf. Wunder, 1968: 168). At the same time there are numerous reports of many Prussians leaving their villages to engage themselves as menials in German villages and in the towns, and they must have seen this as an improvement of their position. This regional mobility of the Prussian population, however, corresponds only in a limited way with a vertical mobility. In the new environment, too, the difference between part-culture and sub-culture remained for a long time, and was here already tied in fact to a social structure in town and village, in which the difference between 'above' and 'below' was always marked by oppositions resulting from economic developments in the fifteenth century. In general, however, it can be asserted and documented that at the beginning of the sixteenth century, the 'ideal structure' of German part-culture and Prussian sub-culture has claims to validity. An assimilation, whose character in the economic and social area will be depicted, was effected first by the 'Christianisation' of the Reformation, which directed itself equally at Germans and Prussians and finally expelled pagan customs among both.

It only remains to determine the position of the Prussian freemen in the framework of rural society. They cannot be described as a peasant segment, since they regarded military service as their 'profession' until well into the sixteenth century. Besides, they were by no means a homogeneous social stratum, as is expressed in description of them as 'the great and the small freemen', involving differences of privilege, property and quality of estate. The size of the landed property of a Prussian freeman could make him the economic equal of a German peasant, of a Prussian peasant, or of an immigrant German noble. According to the size of the 'estate', the freeman worked his land with his own family, with the aid of menials and agricultural labourers, or as landlord over dependent peasants (Wunder, 1968: 192). Although little is known about the economy of the freemen, it can be surmised that they appeared in the town market either with their own produce, or with the natural dues of their peasants, since they required money to procure and maintain their military equipment. The freemen belonged to the military and administrative organisation of the Order's state, but also participated in the market process of the towns. This double system of communication with the wider world was broadened by the freemen acquiring experience outside the Order's territories on their military campaigns.

The Prussian freemen were more closely tied to Christianity than the Prussian peasants, since part of them had already been linguistically assimilated in the fourteenth century. However, one can surmise that the majority of the small freemen behaved in this regard more like the Prussian peasants, with whom they often lived in a village association. None the less the Prussian freemen of Samland preserved and developed a special consciousness: the conception of knightly honour and loyalty, which was binding on the knight of the Order, continued old Prussian traditions and served to strengthen the social self-consciousness of the Prussian freemen. This pretension was reinforced by the German Order, which conferred fishing and forest rights on the 'possessed Prussian peasants' of Samland as reward for their past and present loyalty, and in this regard placed them in the fifteenth century equal to immigrant nobles.

The cultural uniqueness of the Prussian freemen found its outlet, last but not least, in special forms of settlement. Undisturbed by the encroachments of the German Order, which arranged the settlement and property structure of the subject Prussian peasants according to its own interests as a landlord, the freemen preserved their traditional settlement and inheritance customs. Larger complexes of land were not occupied by subject peasants, but were farmed by several members of one family or its relatives. This type of settlement is described as a 'family community'. Equally, the manorial system of the freemen does not seem to have been organised as uniformly as that of the Order, and it preserved traditional structures. The group of 'great and small freemen' formed, despite its strong internal differentiation, a unique segment of rural society with a unique value-orientation, elevated above the peasant segments of Prussians and Germans.

The complexity and multiple stratification of the rural society of Prussia was regulated and integrated through the territorial power, the German Order, since it understood how to bind individual groups of its state to itself, each with a special means, to hold them on different social levels, and so to limit the possibilities of conflict. The great social and cultural differences between the individual segments of rural society represented from the viewpoint of the territorial power a stabilising element, because they impaired, if not hindered, communication between the existent groups on the basis of their varied levels of life, experience and expectation.

This raises the question as to what new social constellations at the beginning of the sixteenth century could produce the basis for a community of all rural segments, through which common action and the presentation of common demands was made possible. It can be asserted, with Eric Wolf, that it is not sufficient to refer to general social upheavals in order to explain a peasant rebellion. This thesis is negatively attested by the great civil war of the fifteenth century, which provoked no peasant war. How general political and economic crises influenced the life of the 'common man' and how the 'common man' reacted, or could react, to political, economic and social pressures must be determined for each individual case, and cannot be deduced.

Despite this reservation, a further general aspect must be added to the description of the crisis of the Order's state, which provides a link to the above social description. Since the Thirteen Years War (1454–66), the Order had lost the power to regulate the economic and administrative system that it had created in the thirteenth and fourteenth centuries. The social system thereby lost its centre and its equilibrium. In place of the territorial lord as the greatest landowner came a stratum of immigrant German mercenary leaders, who frequently occupied government and administrative posts and in part administered the territorial lord's property. For the first time in Prussian history, a nobility had established itself as a political, economic and social partner of the territorial lord and had interrupted the relations between subject and lord.

This new nobility, whether as private landlords or as administrative officials in territorial offices, were the common opponents of German and Prussian peasants, and of Prussian freemen. The sources contain plentiful evidence that the nobility sought to increase the services of the Prussian peasants, to introduce an obligation to ploughing service (*Scharwerk*) for the German peasants in general, and to change the now useless military service obligation of the small Prussian freemen into economically remunerative services. The sources contain just as much evidence that the Prussian freemen and German peasants, under the leadership of their village mayors (*Schulzen*), innkeepers and millers, complained about these injustices to the last grand master, and later first duke, Albrecht of Brandenburg. The path of petitioning was the legal method which had sufficed in past centuries to guarantee and uphold the rights and privileges of the charters and assignations, which is proven even by the peasant 'disturbance' in Mehlsack (Ermland). But the last grand master was no longer in the position to guarantee this legal process, since he possessed no means of force to ensure the implementation of his decisions. Doubtless he was also not prepared in many cases to support the cause of the peasants and freemen. The freemen were especially concerned here, for their social position depended on the attitude of their military overlord.

While the Prussian peasants had to suffer the unrestricted exploitation of their labour power, and the Prussian freemen were humiliated
by forcing them to do ploughing service and had to accept in fact
economic disadvantages, the small increase in ploughing service signified
a social degradation for the German peasants, which would soon be
followed by an economic degradation (manorial farming – hereditary
subjection). All groups saw themselves confronted by a social levelling
of the previous rural social order, which brought with it social insecurity. The tendency of this social levelling was downwards, the reverse
therefore of the upward levelling tendency since the fourteenth century,
which aimed at an assimilation to the better personal and economic
level of the German peasant. The peasants and freemen sought by
means of their rebellion to reverse this levelling process, which established the nobility as an idle, unproductive ruling class. This concern,
expressly taken up in the peasants' programme, is characteristic of many
peasant rebellions; for the peasants in Prussia, however, these demands
represented the reaction against a relatively new constellation of social
forces.

The common experience of noble repression, arbitrariness and, not
least of all, noble arrogance formed the unifying element for the various
segments of rural society. The discontent was general and was fully and
openly discussed in inns and mills. Active opposition is documented
above all for the German peasants and Prussian freemen. The traditional interpretation that it was not absolute misery, but rather the
threat to their previous, relatively good situation that caused their
opposition, fits both groups. Eric Wolf's thesis that the 'middle
peasantry' is the driving force of a peasant rebellion can be used in the
Prussian case, both with reference to the socio-economic position, as
well as to the 'traditional' direction of freemen and peasants. They
struggled for the continuance of the previous social and economic order.
Eric Wolf's attribution of traditional attitudes with political implications
as limited to a specific peasant stratum is essential, since traditionality
is thereby excluded as a characteristic of all peasants. In the present
case the Prussian peasants do not belong to the 'middle peasantry', and
the demands of the peasant rebellion represent no assurance of their
former position, but a clear qualitative improvement.

The development of the confrontation between nobility and peasants
and freemen can be followed back over some decades on the basis of the
petitions. The question remains, what occasioned the peasants to give
up the 'peaceful' path of individual opposition and to turn to active,
solidary self-help. One must also explain how the attitudes and expectations involved in upholding legal claims by legal methods were
replaced by a new attitude, which regarded as legitimate arbitrary action
to secure ancient rights.

In the rebels' letters, noble arbitrariness was touched only generally as the cause of the rising, and they contain no information about the actual process of mobilisation. However, the chronicler of the peasant rising, the Konigsberg mayor Nikolaus Richau, reports in detail about the immediate pre-history and the beginnings of the rebellion. Richau places the miller Caspar von Kaymen at the centre as initiator and first organiser of the rebellion. The miller learned from the peasants who visited his mill of the arbitrariness of the nobility. This so depressed him that he sought ways and means to aid the peasants. After six weeks of secret preparations (meetings with German peasants and freemen), he called the peasants of the surrounding places together at midnight on 2 September and held a speech to move them to rebellion. The secret preparations of the uprising recall the conspiratorial forms of the struggle for 'godly law' (Franz, 1975 : 42, 81). The argument presented by the chronicler Richau as his verbatim speech was founded on the Gospel and its popular interpretation. He thus mediated to the peasants the impression that their undertaking had divine legitimation. At the same time he linked this to the suggestion that the territorial lord, who had introduced the Lutheran Reformation into Prussia some months before, stood on the side of the peasants. The peasants thus came to the conviction that their concerns were also the concerns of the territorial lord and were legitimated by the words of the Gospel. The Prussians, who had no mastery of the German language and so could not follow the miller's speech, were convinced by a display of ducal letters. The behaviour of the Germans and Prussians thus confirms the concepts of German part-culture and Prussian sub-culture. The concrete aims of the rising were the struggle for 'freedom' and 'property', in which one must note that each signified something different for German peasants, Prussian peasants and Prussian freemen. In any case, the miller succeeded in bringing together the heterogeneous segments of rural society into a community of action. The tenor of his speech, which contained unambiguous notions of redemption, may also have appealed to the peasants' expectations of a new and better world. These were linked to the change of political rule and the introduction of the Reformation, the more so as the first months of the duke's government and his failure to keep his promise of a territorial assembly had disappointed them.

The beginning of the rebellion and the process of mobilisation thus stand in close connection with the problem of the peasants and their leaders. The choice of these leaders contains as much testimony about the leaders as about those who chose them.

Particular attention is due to the first leader as the initiator. The chronicler explains the process of mobilisation by the miller Caspar von Kaymen, a puzzle to him, as the work of the devil. The historian Gunther Franz, on the other hand, characterises the miller as 'a thoughtful, sensitive man' (Franz, 1975 : 277). One can take as reliable information from Richau's chronicle that the miller was deeply impressed by Luther's teaching, which had been disseminated in Konigsberg for years and had decisively altered the life of the citizens. It is reported that citizens gathered in their houses to read the Gospel together. One can recognise in the words of the miller the 'individual appropriation' of the Gospel and its direct application to the area of his own life. One can see the miller, with Max Weber, as a self-appointed charismatic leader. At the same time the miller is an example for the traditional thesis that the village elite were particularly suited for the task of leadership. But Eric Wolf can also claim the miller for his functional interpretation: the miller belonged to the group of 'middle men' who exercised mediating functions between the world of the peasants and their environment and the wider world. His regional mobility is depicted in detail in Richau's report; his spiritual participation in the Reformation movement emanating from the city of Konigsberg is documented by his speech. In this speech, in which he depicted for the peasants that individual and apparently unalterable problems were a problem of the entire society, including the territorial lord, he dissolved the peasants' fixation on definite persons and the related feeling of absolute dependence.

The 'poor man', a part of the traditional conception of society and a self-description used as a devotional formula, was changed by means of the 'fleshly' interpretation of the Gospel into the 'Christian man', the 'confessor of the holy Gospel', who had a right to 'self-determination'. Here the disputed role of 'old law' and 'godly law' can be quite clearly determined in the Samland peasant rebellion. Peasants and freemen had protested for years against the innovations introduced by the nobility, relying on the contents of their charters and assignations and in fact on prescribed and formerly successful legal methods. Yet with the appeal to the old law they could certainly uphold legal claims, but could change little in actual relations, since, as 'poor folk', it was not legitimate for them to counter the power of the nobility with the same means. It was the newly interpreted message of the Gospel, which first allowed the nobility to appear as 'godless', that gave the peasants' concerns divine legitimation. This made possible the step from written petitions from individual freemen and communes to common deeds. The appeal to old law legitimated the peasants' demands, the appeal to the Gospel legitimated their rising.

During the course of the rebellion the self-appointed leaders were replaced by elected leaders; those known by name belonged to the village elite and to the freemen. They had military training, and in part administrative experience, such as the leader of the Schaaken band, Hans Gericke, a former official of the district of Pobeten. They had already been spokesmen in numerous previous complaint proceedings, and had not recoiled in the course of these proceedings from being arrested when they refused to accept decisions of the territorial lord which seemed to them unjust. This social selection of the leaders is often cited as evidence that economic grounds were not the real cause of peasant rebellions. Noteworthy, however, is that these middle men took the side of the peasants and regarded themselves as a part of the peasantry in their struggle against the nobility. Herein resides an essential difference from the middle men in peasant societies of the twentieth century, which Rodney Hilton also found in investigating the English peasant rebellion of 1381.

The leaders' letters to Konigsberg citizens give authentic information about the aims of the peasants. Here one must take account of the fact that the leaders, as authors of the letters, were not only the spokesmen of the peasants, but must also be regarded as the inspirers of the movement. In order to trace their role in the opinion-forming process among the peasants, further research into their biographies is required.

The rebellion ended without a battle, and fifty leaders were executed. Only ten of these can be identified; the majority remained anonymous and probably belonged to the wider peasantry. This ratio gives the rough proportion of elected leaders to the wider group of 'mutineers'. There is even less information about the actual peasant army. The alleged size (2,500) is credible, but the proportion of German peasants, Prussian peasants and Prussian freemen is not reported. Quantitative information can first be traced when the state of settlement and population in Samland around 1520 is investigated. Richau speaks of different behaviour of Prussians and Germans only at the beginning of the rebellion. Possibly he noticed no difference in behaviour. It is also possible that no greater difference in the behaviour of German and Prussian peasants was visible in the special circumstances of the rebellion.

The beginning of the rebellion shows how new possibilities of action were opened to the peasants, in that they acquired a new 'outlook' towards their concerns. To this extent the mentality of the peasants before the rebellion can be distinguished from that during the rebellion. But can one speak of a 'mentality of rebellious peasants', that is, can one observe specific attitudes and modes of behaviour? A striking difference is doubtless an increased readiness to take risks: the leaving of house, home and family for an uncertain, inconstant, if not un-organised, warlike life. But their points of reference remained the same: the territorial lord and the traditional leaders of the narrower sphere of life. When the danger of excesses arose, these elected leaders inter-vened and were obeyed. In opposition to this, they did allow free rein to spontaneous actions in the first days of the rebellion, when the peasants played 'the world turned upside-down' with the first noble prisoners, something which has parallels in carnival customs, as well as being a frequent phenomenon of peasant rebellions in general.

The chronicler Richau spoke contemptuously of the peasant army as the 'poor, mad, senseless mob', but his depiction contains few points of reference for this characterisation. The peasants stood in a tradition of corporative self-organisation of their communes and attempted to organise the rebellion too on this model. But they were not militarily trained mercenaries and were unaccustomed to military discipline. The shortness of the rebellion did not allow them to accumulate their own experience. It corresponded completely to their trusting outlook that they gave up their armed resistance with the hope of arbitration through the territorial lord. On this point, the distrust of their leaders was proved to be more realistic.

The shortness of the Samland rebellion, which actually passed through only the first, localised phase of the Peasant War, also explains why no radicalisation can be recognised, nor any consolidation of the experience during the rebellion into a lasting new self-understanding. The step to defensive self-organisation effected no lasting change of peasant attitudes. It remains to ask whether a latent readiness to put up resistance does not belong to the constituent elements of peasant mentality: their forefathers had shown a readiness to take risks in participating in the settlement movement, and their own experiences were shaped by long periods of political and social upheavals. In any case, the prehistory and the history after the rebellion show that the oft-cited 'East Elbian peasant', with his subservience and lack of political development, whom many historians deduce from the relations of the German Order's state, cannot be found in the sixteenth century. It remains for other investigations to analyse Prussian history in the early modern period with the instrument of 'peasant society' and to seek the reality and the myth of the 'East Elbian' peasant type.

JÜRGEN BÜCKING

13 The Peasant War in the Habsburg Lands as a Social Systems-Conflict *

In 1969 the sociologist and historian Barrington Moore put forward a theory which deals not just with the German Peasant War, but with pre-industrial peasant revolts in general (Moore, 1966: 469ff.). According to Moore's theory, a highly segmented feudal hierarchy uses very disparate measures to relieve their peasant subjects of agrarian surplus and to maintain their own upkeep. However, peasant resistance to this exhausts itself through further segmentation. Secondly, an agrarian bureaucracy under a centrally directed absolutist government is highly susceptible to peasant rebellions. Between these two poles there is a third type of society in which the actual power is divided into several centres, but all of which stands under the nominal overlordship of a monarch. This intermediate type, which includes the south German area, is susceptible to a peasant revolt under three conditions:

(1) When the feudal upper strata do not succeed in bringing about a technical-commercial 'revolution', i.e. an early capitalist stage of development, and in preventing peasant self-organisation.
(2) When the weakness of the institutional links which normally tie the peasantry to the upper class becomes obvious.
(3) When the exploitative character of this relationship becomes clear.

Moore's historical theory can be tested on the basis of research into the Peasant War in the Habsburg lands.

I THE WEB OF CAUSES

Macro-economic changes

Three structural elements can be counted among the grave socio-economic changes of the period 1440–1510, which took root above all in the Habsburg Austrian territories:

*After the sudden death of Dr Jürgen Bücking in 1975, Dr Hans-Christoph Rublack of the University of Tübingen prepared the German text of this essay for publication by adding the annotations from Dr Bücking's notes. For full references, see J. Bücking, 'Der Bauernkrieg in den habsburgischen Ländern als sozialer Systemkonflikt, 1524–6', Der Deutsche Bauernkrieg, 1524–6 (ed. H. U. Wehler), Sonderheft 1, Geschichte und Gesellschaft, Göttingen, 1975, pp. 168–92.

(1) Population increase of 0.5–1.0 per cent per annum.
(2) Intensification of long-distance trade with flourishing commerce in cloth and so on.
(3) Stronger demand for money as an accepted medium of exchange between buyer and seller.

The last point especially necessitated a stronger circulation of money from newly discovered silver mines in the alpine area, which was predominantly a private business, increasingly involving great merchants, the nobility or the higher clergy. This mining boom received further stimulation through injections of finance supported by territorial princes. The territorial bureaucratic apparatus was continually in need of money as a result of the extension and increase of its tasks, and it continually drew this in from *Fron und Wechsel* – dues to the territorial prince either as percentage (10 per cent) from raw silver (*Fron*) or silver smelted below the market-price (*Wechsel*) (Bauer, 1956). Because of the rising demand for cash, other territorial rulers who were not blessed with the gift of silver mines turned to inflationary measures by mixing metals of inferior value into the minting process. So did the great merchant companies. In this period, production in the commercial and agrarian sectors did not increase considerably, while the rate of minting and coinage debasement increased greatly. This economic development led to inflation – put concretely, to price increases in basic foodstuffs and in the textile industry.

In what way did these developments influence the Peasant War? The chief sufferers from this economic crisis, besides the urban bourgeoisie, were the landowning noble families and the monasteries, because they had their property leased out predominantly on limited or hereditary tenure. The rents and natural dues accruing from these were fixed in size, and so could not be adjusted to the rate of inflation. Added to this were the growing demands of the nobility and the prelates for food and clothing, which widened the gap between the elitist pretensions of the upper classes and their real impoverishment. The formation of monopolies by Augsburg and Nuremberg merchants and by merchant societies increased the dependence of the nobility on supra-regional markets, and doubly weakened their purses. In the foreground of the 1525 Peasant War one must therefore place a far-reaching agrarian or feudal crisis, and in this regard it was no matter of pure chance that the Knights' Revolt of 1523 and the Peasant War coincided.

Why did this crisis of the noble rentier spill over on to the peasant tenant? The nominal landholders could no longer master inflation with their traditional ground rents. They thus sought to compensate for rising costs by means of new duties or by illegal extension of old natural dues. These multiple burdens must have hit the peasants the harder since they had largely attained an improved legal position (Blickle, 1972: 115). Almost everywhere in the Habsburg lands they had either won recognition of the right of hereditary tenure against all forms of limited leasehold, or else the status of serfdom was waning. Since around 1470/80 this legal improvement had been halted by economic deterioration – inflation. In the alpine valleys the dependence of peasants, artisans and miners on local markets rose specifically. Moreover, excessive prices in the isolated markets could also be asked. A continual chain of natural disasters or wars in the period 1500–20 only aggravated this trend. South Tyrol was hit by the following natural catastrophes: 1512, flooding of the Eisack, and again in September 1520, and following a thaw in 1521/22; severe winters in 1513–15 and 1519–20, with consequent price rises and hunger; harvest failure in 1513–15; epidemics in 1512 and 1521/22; and by the following wars: 1509–16, following the Venetian war, a special tax of *c.* 2 mil. florins for all Tyrol; 1523, a special tax of 150,000 florins; 1499, devastation of the Vintschgau in the Swiss War; 1513–17, damage by mercenaries.

The winners in this creeping inflation were less the producing classes than the merchants, for the peasants and artisans were largely excluded from the market in the course of the exchange of goods. They had to cede the distributive role to merchants who specialised in it. Great merchants, then, were the first who brought money-hungry artisans to depend on them for credit in the putting-out system, and so changed human labour-power into a commodity. The beginning of early capitalism can, by and large, be pinpointed with this separation of capital and labour. In this manner the former upper Swabian weaver family, the Fuggers, rose to become the financiers of the Augsburg artisans, and later the creditors of the house of Habsburg for the double marriage of 1515, the election of Charles V in 1518 and the payment of the Swabian League's army in the Peasant War during 1525–6. It was at this time that the Fuggers acquired mining works in the alpine lands.

The ossification of the feudal order

The structural changes described above also had effects on Habsburg feudal society, just as the noble-clerical changes in their turn influenced the economic structure, e.g. the desire for luxuries, town dwellings or tournaments. The same applied to peasant lifestyle and consumption (demand for fish, meat). The main body of the Habsburg higher nobility had forfeited their functions in the exercise of justice and defence. The excessive dues and labour services through which the noble landlords were compensated for supplying protection and defence appeared the more irksome to the peasants. In the feudal conception of the world there existed a balance between rights and obligations, which was ideally reflected in the concept of ranks and orders. By analogy, the monasteries performed spiritual and charitable functions (e.g. mediation and care of salvation) for peasant tenants, for which the monastic landlords had the right to collect peasant dues. The reciprocity in this system between the burdens of the peasant tenants and the spiritual cure of souls was disturbed; in other words, a functional defect had entered the feudal order.

The relation of the peasantry to the bourgeoisie in the various towns was affected in the same manner. An added complication here in the relationship of the upper urban classes to their archbishop or bishop and to the higher clergy was the struggle for urban autonomy. In general, the politically disfranchised magistracy in the episcopal cities sympathised with the rebellious peasants in the short term because the clerical privy council still held power in local politics. The broad technical-mercantile stratum of the towns other than those affected by spiritual lordship must also be kept in view. Generalising, the following hypothesis is proposed: the more socially differentiated and technically progressive the large towns were (such as Constance, Salzburg or Freiburg in Breisgau), the more brusquely and aggressively they turned against the peasants. The experience of the Bundschuh (1492–1512) also played a great part.

Besides the clergy and the nobility, a third group faced the hostility of the lower classes: the Jews. That was a general indication that a socio-economic crisis was spreading. The Jews, forced to engage in finance, largely profited from the changed pattern of demand and from creeping inflation, and were among those creditors regarded with hostility. That they also faced religious enmity and were ethnically alien only added to the hostility shown to them as outsiders. A result of the rebellion was the plundering of Jews for their money, the destruction of written records and often enough pogroms (Wiegerstein, 1856: 347; Stern, 1959: 71).

Regarded as a whole, the pyramid structure of orders had lost its validity as a divine reflection of the functional division of labour in society, at least in the eyes of the peasants. They criticised the absence of obligations and the excess of privileges on the part of the upper classes, for whom they had to supply a surfeit of dues and services. The firmly interlinked upper classes (including the great burghers) were alienated from the loosely linked peasants and bourgeois occupations susceptible to crisis (miners, artisans, mercenaries). This is clear in the disparaging comments of many humanist burghers.

Up to 1515 the peasant/bourgeois leaders of the forerunner rebellions (such as Joss Fritz) turned to Hussite ideas of equality in order to demonstrate that their political, social and economic inferiority was against old law. Here we come to the complicated question as to how far Reformation thought provided motivation for peasant rebellion and played a role in drawing up their programmes. The example of the Bundschuh movement, and the first articles directed against socio-economic abuses in Austria in 1524–6 show most clearly that economic and legal abuses, evoked by the secular nobility and the prelates, were the cause of the peasant risings. But it was the Hussite axiom of the divinely intended equality of all men, taken up again by the Reformation (e.g. Luther's *Freedom of the Christian Man*) which awoke the peasant will to resistance (if not, indeed, the claim to a right to resistance) against the ungodly social order, and so against the illegal repression of the peasants. For as the peasant sense of justice was still religiously founded, the authors of the articles legitimated the peasant rebellion with the newly discovered free Gospel. Secretaries or preachers with knowledge of Scripture were especially called to attend peasant committees and formulate preambles to the peasants' written demands. This merging of the original socio-economic abuses with a biblical argument produced an ideological consensus for the peasant rebellion.

Miners and artisans joined the peasants in loose association. The miners were experiencing a phase of recession around 1520, and many artisans were in a similar situation. Most local guilds failed to compete effectively against superior competition from the supra-regional merchant companies and they suffered a loss of turnover. In these years there arose the loose connection of the peasants with bourgeois occupations susceptible to crisis. But it would be mistaken to speak of a bourgeois revolution. First, the Peasant War or systems-conflict was no revolution, because it intended no elevation of bourgeois strata to the top of feudal society, though Gaismair's second Tyrolean Constitution may prove an exception to this. On the other hand, no bourgeois, that is technical-progressive, stratum participated on the peasant side; rather it was exactly those who resisted the peasants most vehemently.

One factor has now been dealt with: alienation within the social structure. A second factor that was discussed concerned an ideological consensus between religious norms and social reality (among others, Bavaria was an exception here). A basic reason is to be found in the clerical landlords' idea of using the weakness of the territorial princes to install themselves as a strict court of appeal, an intermediate jurisdiction. In other words, the rebellious peasants sought to defend themselves against refeudalisation.

The fragmentation of clerical landlords in the south-west German territories (e.g. St Blasien, St Peter, St Trudpert) and the legal subordination in these regions accelerated the growth of opposition energies fed on religious beliefs. Also the increased registering of dues had long since been criticised by the peasants – one more reason why the peasants vented their aggression on the registers and why they fell next upon the well-stocked larders and cellars of their landlords. The great landed property of the upper nobility, intensified by official and military power, kept pace with that of the spiritual landlords. However, it must be mentioned that a number of knightly noble lordships in the south-west were concentrated in a single village (*condominium* or part-lordships). Here abuse or exploitation was openly visible. In Austrian Attergau, or in the monastic economy of the Muhl valley and the forest area of the Enns, the strength or weakness of the peasant rising was ultimately dependent on the degree of peasant autonomy or assimilation to economic rule. The latter (the assimilation) was weakly developed in Upper and Lower Austria, and was a reflection of the Salzburg rising rather than an original armed rebellion in itself (Hoffmann, 1952: 98).

We now turn to a comparison with Moore's theory, to which we reached similar conclusions here, but with one modification. The exploitative character of the system does not become apparent *per se*, but requires a common platform, an ideological consensus through which an entrenched manorial system is recognised as exploitative by comparison with an (alleged) divine purpose. What is lacking in Moore's theory is a point of comparison with the real peasant position. Only an ideological consensus could unleash that explosive force through which a movement of rebellion could extend from the south-west to the south-east. This religious and communitarian programme is also the connecting link to the Hussite religious ideology of equality, as it had been disseminated in south Germany through the merchant and lay-bishop, Friedrich Reiser (Waas, 1964: 89; Haupt, 1888: 245f., 285; Kurze, 1974: 467–71).

Social stratification

A tiny minority of the secular nobility concentrated in their persons a high official, or military function with a considerable share of land and property. These petty absolutist lords amassed a great amount of power for themselves, which could also become a threat to Habsburg territorial power when grave differences arose. The distribution of mortgages in the face of the notorious lack of money was both reward and payment for services rendered (the bureaucratic nobility had to raise the full amount of the mortgage, though under favourable conditions). This arrangement had the advantage that the mortgaged local jurisdiction was given to a dependent official, and he could not attempt to remove subjects of this court from the sovereignty of the territorial ruler. Since the time of the Emperor Maximilian I (d. 1519), the territorial bureaucracy had been a ladder to ennoblement and enfeoffment with landed property for skilled bourgeois-humanist scholars, although as a rule their children rose no further socially (cf. Bücking, 1970: 239ff.). Those on the lower rungs of the Tyrolean agrarian bureaucracy stayed on their own social level, and it was all they could do to pick up, for example, a pension of 317 gulden from castle Sigmundskron.

The overwhelming majority of the Habsburg nobility, whether from ignorance or pride, did not jump on the bandwagon of an expanding administrative bureaucracy, but persevered in a stubborn subsistence mentality, resting on their high position of pre-eminence (as they regarded it), and on their contempt for peasants and burghers. Largely deprived of their local political power, the privatised nobility in the Austrian territories sought and found a field of activity appropriate to their estate mainly in tournaments, in the hunt, and as bailiffs in court sessions. The outspoken Bavarian chancellor, Leonhard von Eck, scolded this section of the nobility as 'old women already dead, afraid for their houses, who will treat of nothing with no one (Franz, 1963: 151, 19f.). A double pressure was thus exerted on the small noble landlords: on the one hand they were levelled under pressure from expanding territorial rule, on the other distressed by the feudal crisis, and in its wake by the peasant rebellions of 1492–1502.

Prime targets were monasteries and foundations, as well as the property-owning cathedral chapters and parsonages. These spiritual institutions clearly showed their difference from secular landlords by having more severe courts and levying heavier dues and labour services. The clerical subjects of the monastery of Ochsenhausen defended themselves in 1525 with the claim that they 'were sold like cows and calves, although we have only one lord' (i.e. Christ) (Götze, 1901: 8, 11). Without doubt, immoderate burdens and legal humiliations from clerical landlords were a major cause of the Peasant War.

There are three further elements. First, the legal position and independence of the peasants in the Black Forest and alpine valleys were relatively advanced, while the great number of clerical landlords and their capacity to expand their rights was most marked in this region. Two such contrary tendencies brought friction and conflict in their wake. Secondly, it was the position of the regular clergy, supported by the old belief and by a privileged economy, which first aroused the combativeness of their peasant tenants, for these saw their oppressed existence being prolonged by suppression of the Bible. Thirdly, the secular nobility and the regular clergy merged as a target, in that a great number of noble sons and daughters found that by joining the latter they could obtain a peaceful living and an education becoming to their born status. Residence and education in distinguished religious foundations were taken for granted by the nobility, as was seen in 1518 when the Tyrolean nobility claimed these foundations to be the hospitals of the nobility, and reserved to themselves scholarships which were tied to residence in a foundation. This is also an index of the impoverishment of great part of the nobility.

As a rule, burghers and peasants favoured territorial power. True, the tightening tax screw set the peasant above all under pressure, but this taxation was offset by advantages. Territorial state officials, as the equivalents of manorial and legal lords, could issue tenants with lucrative letters of privilege or protection against the incursions of secular or spiritual landlords. Of course, there were also gentle patriarchal rulers among the spiritual and noble landlords, but these were rare (Bezold, 1878: 54f.). The nobility and the regular clergy were drawn together through the opposition, indeed after 1500 through the hostility, of the peasants; here their identity of interest as landlords may have played a part.

The links between the peasantry and the burghers was both looser and sensitive to a higher degree. If one takes 'burghers' here to mean inhabitants of towns who had citizenship, then their relationship with the peasants was extraordinarily cool (if there was no identity of interest against the town's bishop). The political attitude of the magistrates who came from these burghers was a neutral stalling tactic, or at least mediation between peasantry and landlords. But those townsfolk who held occupations in the guild hierarchy susceptible to crisis or held seasonal occupations in areas of contact between town and country can be classified as clearly friendly to the peasants.

Political and legal developments

During the confused feuding and warfare of the fifteenth century, the peasant population in the Habsburg lands had placed their hopes on imperial reform, which they understood (falsely) as the restoration of the Emperor's power. However, the Habsburg Emperors squandered this reserve of peasant sympathy, and even the religious enthusiasm for an imperial extension of power (Pferschy, 1963: 50f.). This level of expectation may have been the fruit of the humanist, nationalist guild of secretaries on the Upper Rhine, who prepared for and accompanied Maximilian's expansionist policies with a German nationalist ideology (Bücking, 1973: 181). Much of it may have been born of an inferiority complex, in envy and wonder at the superior and socially appropriate humanism of Italy and France. The gulf between nationalist pretensions and the real fragmentation and impotence of the Empire appeared in the Nuremberg regency (legally active from 1521 to 1530), which lacked an executive, sickened and finally expired at the Diet of Speyer in 1526.

While hope of a restoration of the Empire collapsed around 1500, particularly in the minds of the peasants, and made room for the religiously tinged mysticism of the 'Black Forest Emperor' (ibid.), or vented itself from 1502 in new Bundschuh risings, Maximilian I concentrated all his energies on building up a territorial bureaucracy with the reception of Roman Law into the administration. Both measures can be evaluated as a sign of the territorial and legal fragmentation of the Habsburg regions. Although the levelling brought about under the norms of Roman Law created in the long term a 'judicial state' and thus procured the desired land peace for the burgher–peasant population, it also found its strongest opposition among them. First, the administration and justice established according to Roman Law, along with other matters (e.g. defence against the Turks), over-burdened the capacity to pay taxes of the burghers and peasants who had become subjects (*Untertanen*). Secondly, the long-term change from religiously based customary law to formally structured Roman Law produced extraordinary bitterness, as did especially the arbitrariness and corruption of territorial or clerical officials. The great distance to court (from Alsace to Rottweil in Swabia, for example), the complicated process of appeals and other imponderables were added´ expenses for the peasants and were all signals which drove the majority of them into opposition.

Linked to the long-term development of Roman Law was also the fact that the councillors in the government, schooled in Roman Law, but predominantly foreign, carried out their activities not only according to a foreign legal code, but they also paid extensive care to filling their own pockets, as did Gabriel Salamanca in Tyrol (Hollaender, 1968: 10ff.). Thus the Augsburg chronicler Wilhelm Rem complained that Maximilian 'had councillors who were rogues . . . who all became very rich and the Emperor became poor' (cf. Bauer, 1956). The loss of functions and the weakness of the Habsburg rulers of the interregnum 1519–22 was both a point of burgher–peasant criticism and an encouraging signal for a rebellion which sought a new ordering of society.

II   THE DEVELOPMENT OF PROGRAMMES

Programmes written down by peasant leaders are seldom found, or else they are offshoots of the Twelve Articles of Memmingen. Max Weber explained this by the dependence of the peasant on the traditional rhythm of the seasons of the year, which made systematic and rational training impossible (Weber, 1956: 301). This also resulted in peasant inability to propose their own rational proposals for systematic social alternatives. Weber's hypothesis seems to be proved correct, for the authors of peasant programmes as a rule were clerics, city secretaries and episcopal secretaries.

A further reason for the poor state of remaining peasant programmes is connected with the outcome of the Peasant War itself. Neither the conquered peasants nor the victorious upper class wanted to conserve the peasants' social ideas for posterity. For the peasant leaders and their fellow travellers, such well-planned programmes were incriminating evidence, and so something to destroy. The ruling landlords were concerned to suppress the bourgeois-peasant programmes as quickly as possible (Waas, 1964: 42f.). Reforming or revolutionary views were strongly dependent on the state and stage of development of the struggles between the peasants and the upper classes. Concretely stated, the initial stage of the Peasant War was characterised as a rule partly by demands for cessation of abuses, partly by a desire for settlement. Hence it is understandable that these programmes presented very few clear alternatives from the outset. However, the election into the Peasant War committees of clerics or secretaries who had to supply the peasant assemblies with questions and answers about the future could also be decisive for the 'maturity' or otherwise of alternative proposals. In the first phase, rebellious peasants took the agreement of articles of settlement very seriously, as for example the Treaty of Weingarten in early

April 1525 and the treaty of Salzburg in early September 1525.

The behaviour of governments and ruling classes was two-faced as long as they were forced to compromise through military weakness and inner dissension. In this the archduke Ferdinand I was a model for his councillors and captains. In the first phase he pretended to be a stern father of the people, but one willing to compromise; in secret he collected money to hire mercenaries and for the Swabian League and sought openly to split the rebel elite from 'the common mob' (Landes-archiv Innsbruck, Cod. 1874, fol. 51v; Nationalbibliothek Vienna, Hs-slg 14365/1, fol. 11). Diplomatically and tactically inexperienced, the peasant leaders in most cases fell for the double-tongued strategy of stalling, and concluded an armistice with him or his vice-regents, or even a settlement. Ferdinand and his three governments only thought of upholding these compromise formulas until they were militarily strong enough to attack the neutralised peasant bands under some pretext or other. Then they would hold a terror court and thus make all formulas mere scraps of paper. The time of this radical alteration of strategy naturally varied from region to region but occurred between July and September 1525.

This period was the decisive moment when bourgeois 'ghost writers' of the peasant bands became radicalised, advocating a revolutionary overthrow of social hierarchy in their location. This ideological change can be observed in Tyrol and Salzburg. Doubly deceived by the forked-tongued Innsbruck government (*Hofrat*), Michael Gaismair changed at the end of September 1525 into a social rebel and revolutionary. In the second Tyrol Constitution, written in the spring, relying on the three peasant unions in Graubunden, he sought by every means to implement an evangelical peasant union in Tyrol. In general one must note that the peasant leaders went through a learning process, which influenced their programme considerably within a month. For example, the common community (*Landschaft*) of Salzburg wanted to replace Cardinal Lang with a secular Bavarian prince on 4 June 1525 and thereby secularise the archbishopric. Barely fourteen days later, on 17 June, they were leaning towards a representative constitution, in which they would provide two thirds of all the deputies and Cardinal Lang one third.

As a rule, the programmes disseminated in Austria began with a religious motivation, or more precisely, a Reformation one. There was a feedback process between the new-found understanding of the Bible, its interpretation and application to real situations. Hence, each com-mune was to elect its own pastor. There was to be little or no payment of tithes. Here the connection between Reformation and Peasant War was clearest. The original economic impoverishment of the peasants, and the ossification of the social order was fought out in the pre-Reformation period predominantly with the argument of old law. In the Reformation period a 'new Gospel' directed against 'obscurantists and pettifoggers of biblical freedom' took over the function of legitimating peasant rebellion (Bücking, 1971: 127–42, esp. 133f.). Thence came the contemporary legend, in which Luther was said to have stirred up the peasants to rebellion (e.g. Franz, 1963: 151).

Despite wide variations, all the peasant programmes stemming from Habsburg territories attest in their individual articles the correctness of our theory: that a great economic-agrarian crisis encompassed both landlord and tenant and led to a segmentation of the social structure. The rigorous rejection of Roman Law or, as the peasants felt, of legal arbitrariness, found its reflection in the articles. Since the legal levelling of the emergent modern state could hardly be repudiated out of the Bible, the rebellious peasants turned to customary law as it was laid down in statutes as the fruit of other conflicts. Here too it is clear that the spongy concept 'Reformation influence' (for 1525) played a religiously legitimating, but still secondary, role in the Peasant War. At this point articles written by clerics inclined to the Reformation could be adduced as clear counter arguments. However, these articles have the characteristic quality that they take a stand only against abuses (with anabaptist perspectives), but offer no social alternatives.

On these lines, the four phases of the peasant programmes could be diagrammatically represented as in Figure 13.1. The demands of the Wurttemberg common community (*Landschaft*) to the Habsburg sequestration government in May 1525, that the expelled Duke Ulrich of Wurttemberg be given his territory back, played a marginal role. As it recognised Duke Ulrich's disturbed behaviour and unsoundness of mind, the rebellious community argued as follows: 'according to godly and imperial law', no one may be deprived of his rights, 'be he Turk, heathen, Jew, murderer, thief or whatever his name'. So the duke must also be allowed this right, and his return permitted. This did not prevent the community from laying down stringent controls against Ulrich's arbitrariness (Franz, 1963: 426–8, 429). Events soon overtook them, because on 12 May 1525 Duke Ulrich was defeated at Boblingen and had to return to Hohentwiel. Besides the bold equation of Duke Ulrich with heathens, Turks and murderers, the argument contains new and interesting aspects. Hitherto all legal systems had automatically deprived racial or confessional outsiders of their rights, and punished criminal lawbreakers severely. One can assume therefore that the community turned to this tactical move to get out of the fire back into the frying pan.

Finally, let us attempt to sum up the peasant programme. The peasant alliances with individual towns or noble landlords in the south German area provide proof that the peasants, or their bourgeois 'ghost writers', wanted to keep the lower classes within the feudal order, but to assure them a share of local autonomy and political co-operation within the region. The peasant aim of removing the privileges of the secular nobility and the higher clergy, and elevating themselves to the same

PRELIMINARY STAGE
Stand against abuses

FIRST PHASE
Functional hierarchy

territ prince	territorial sovereignty
secular nobility	defence and protection
clergy	cure of souls
burghers	trade and crafts
peasantry	nourishment

———— labour service

———— multiple dues

———— legal arbitrariness

———— exclusion from common land etc.

REFORM

SECOND PHASE

Equality of all strata

THIRD PHASE

Peasant union (with economically necessary exceptions) ──→ "closed society" (Weber)

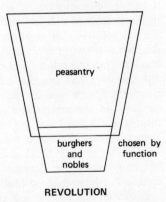

nobility prelates

territ prince

burghers peasants

peasantry

burghers and nobles — chosen by function

REVOLUTION

Figure 13.1

political and legal plane under the influence of the alleged Reformation claim to equality, is indicative of a movement of socio-political emancipation. It is an index of rising expectations. In fact, the great part of the peasant bands had an ideal in mind, that of giving all four estates or strata the same rights and obligations. The Emperor alone was to be politically and legally superior to all four strata. The diagram, however, calls attention to the fact that there were also immature visions of the future, that is, those still at the first stage, which added only godly law to the existing hierarchy of rule and wished to see it realigned from there. Mature programmes in the second stage, however, deliberately traced out a system of equal rights and obligations in the order of rule. Only exceptions, such as Gaismair in the later stages of his thought, after which he was driven underground as a rebel, could conceive such radical revolutionary programmes, but they failed in 1532 when the double-dealing Habsburg government outmanoeuvred them.

III   SOCIO-POLITICAL EFFECTS

In this area we can make only approximate estimates. That is shown in the enormous toll of blood paid by peasant rebels (according to sixteenth-century estimates, between 50,000 and 130,000 dead), as well as in material and non-material damage to the peasant population. Over and above this, the peasants had largely lost their right to bear arms and to use their banners, an important part of their social ritual. Prohibitions against gatherings and assemblies even of a non-political nature such as church fairs, marriages and wakes indicate the efforts of territorial lords not to allow the defeated unions and agreements to become new points of reference for peasant autonomy. If that was not everywhere or for long successful (e.g. Tyrol, Salzburg), the intention of the upper classes to cut the peasants out of self-government, and thus out of their share in the process of political decision making, was on the whole successful. This depoliticisation of 80 to 90 per cent of the population (including the farm towns) smoothed the path of the territorial state and of bureaucratic centralism and absolutism. Naturally, the Peasant War did not start this process, but it accelerated it greatly. On this point Friedrich Engels was correct when he stated that the openly displayed weakness of the secular and spiritual nobility encouraged the territorial princes in the legal and political levelling of all strata (MEW 7: 411). But Archduke Ferdinand was similarly defenceless and had himself to seek or beg money for Landsknecht hosts from the spiritual nobility. In other words, the Peasant War and the Counter-Reformation enormously accelerated the consolidation of an Austrian territorial state.

Secondly, the thorny and complex road of the Counter-Reformation denoted an important path through the feudal jungle of a system of personal associations towards a levelled and centrally governed territorial state. With Luther's angry call to slaughter the fractious peasants (*Werke*, Weimar edn, 18; 361), the peasants' initial enthusiasm for a new free Gospel was succeeded by a disillusioned attitude towards Protestantism. On the one hand, many peasants turned to the lay-religion of anabaptism and so towards the 'promised land' of Moravia. On the other, the original pluralist structure of Protestantism de-generated after 1526 into a princes' Reformation, that is, into a confessionalisation from above and into an ossifying territorial church hierarchy.

Thirdly, the defeat of the peasants and execution of their leaders induced a stronger turning away from humanist education and the liberal arts, and so cut the peasants off completely from the possibility of social rise, with the possible exception of Tyrol (Bücking, 1968: 78f.). On the whole, one can state that peasant sons were cut off from the path of education, rather than that they declined it. Humanist education counted as part of public life for the peasants, and since the majority, partly through force, partly voluntarily, retreated back into their traditional work rhythm, the theoretical possibility of gaining education evaded their consciousness and their pockets.

Fourthly, a further element can be introduced, in that the alienation between the majority of the peasants and the noble landlords deepened. On one side, the majority of landlords did not intensify dues and labour services, in the consciousness that only healthy cows give milk (excep-tions: Upper Austria, 1595, 1626; St Blasien against the Salpeterer or Hauensteiner in the seventeenth and eighteenth centuries (Hansjakob, 1867)). On the other hand, many of the peasants had no religious, legal or ethical legitimation which revealed the landlords as opposed to biblical principles. In other words, one can say that, with exceptions, the ossification of the south German manorial system was prolonged. The increase in peasant population actually strengthened the pressure on already parcelled-out land, and while the number of noble and monastic landlords increased, the peasant 'kettle' by no means exploded under the pressure. The younger brothers emigrated in droves. Some in the nineteenth century went with their families to North America, or else to the south-eastern borders of Europe, where as defensive border farmers they gained more land, more independence and better rights than ever before.

DAVID SABEAN

14   Family and Land Tenure:
A Case Study of Conflict in the
German Peasant War 1525*

In examining the structure of society and sources of conflict on the eve of the German Peasant War, we are in need of a series of local studies based on patterns of village organisation. In a recent book published in German, I examined in some detail the rebellion in the southern part of Upper Swabia (Sabean, 1972). In this essay I would like to open up several lines of inquiry by suggesting an approach to a reassessment of the whole war. I want to examine in the light of several kinship models a number of points I have already raised, an approach which might be especially fruitful because the amount of data available for the historical reconstruction of the society under consideration is small and disparate. By constructing models based on fixed points of reference, we can establish the bounds in which activity must have taken place; similarly we can demonstrate the relevance of other information.

The area which we shall consider is Upper Swabia, the centre of the first great movement in the war. The rebels organised themselves into three troops (*Haufen*) which allied together to form a league in order to press their demands. It was for this league that the famous Twelve Articles, an effective summary of the political goals of the peasants, were written. The peasants sought to extend the political control of the community (*Gemeinde*) over common land and forest, fishing and hunting rights, the election and deposition of priests, the collection and distribution of tithes, and the administration of local justice. A closer examination of the rebellion reveals a sometimes latent, sometimes expressed conflict between day-labourers and tenant farmers, which also involved a conflict within extended kin groups. However, the conflict was not always clear to either group, their conscious statements masking the real situation which was succinctly put by one lord:

> It was strange that the subjects in the Seigneurie of Messkirch rebelled from their lord, Gottfrid Werner, because they could show no substantial nor pressing reason. They maintained only that they were overburdened in the villages by too many cottagers and day-

*Adapted from *Peasant Studies Newsletter*, January 1974.

labourers who wanted to use the pastureland, and that they no longer could get the same living from their farms that they used to do. In reality the majority of the day-labourers were the farmers' sons, sons-in-law or closest kin. (Barack, 1869, vol. II: 197ff.)

I want to investigate the basis of the division of interest between these two groups. First, I shall deal with the evidence of rising population and its effects on land tenure and usage. Secondly, I shall deal with the status of personal bondage known as *Leibeigenschaft* and its implications for rights in land.

Population and land tenure

There is a good deal of literary evidence to show that by 1525 the pressure of population was being keenly felt in Upper Swabia. Sebastian Franck wrote in his *Germania* of 1539 that overpopulation was a serious problem for Swabia and Bavaria, advocating that steps be taken to colonise Transylvania. In the *Zimmerische Chronicle* a new movement of internal colonisation was described, with people leaving the overpopulated Allgau to clear land in the Baar (Barack, 1869, vol. IV: 303f.). It is difficult, however, to provide statistical evidence on the rise of population. There are no good series of hearth-tax records for Upper Swabia, but those for the region around Zurich just to the south of Lake Constance suggest that in the seventy years prior to the Peasant War the population may have risen by 50 to 100 per cent (Schnyder, 1925: 108).

Further evidence regarding the pressure of population, gathered from the Twelve Articles, underlines the fact that resources important to the peasant economy were becoming scarcer. Wood was in short supply and rising in price; as a result, lords were taking the administration of common forest land into their own hands. The same thing was happening to hunting and fishing rights. More important, the articles complain about the increasing number of cottages that were being built in the villages; often the lords took common land away from a village in order to provide farms for landless day-labourers.

To best understand the effects of a rising population on village social structure, we must examine the changing forms of land tenure prior to 1525. There is, to begin with, one set of documents from 1383–1569, relating to a freehold, preserved in the archival collection from the city of Ravensburg (Württembergisches Hauptstaatsarchiv, Stuttgart, abbrev.: WHSA, B198, docs. 445–61). Evidently all the legitimate children had a right to an equal share in the inheritance of the farm. In 1385 a woman sold the farm to six of her relatives, and in 1391 one of this group sold his rights to the other five. Not all the sale documents survive, but the next one in 1429 involved the sale of one of the remaining five parts by a group of four heirs. From this one might conclude that the process of inheritance would lead to severe fragmentation of a farm after a few generations. But there was a natural check on the process which is revealed in a court case in 1438 relating to the farm. The current owners of the farm brought suit to exclude from ownership two brothers who, while heirs to the farm, had taken up residence in another village. From this case, then, we may infer the rule that in order to take part in the ownership of a farm, the heir had to be resident on the farm. Otherwise the heirs had a right to buy him out, in this way keeping the farm unified.

Between 1463 and 1464, the current heirs to the property sold their parcels to a single buyer who in 1473 sold the farm to the city of Ravensburg, which leased the farm back to him for his lifetime. There are two contracts from 1532 and 1569 where the same farm was leased for the period of a lifetime.

Most of the farms surrounding Ravensburg were leaseholds, each *seigneurie* having a different customary form of tenancy. In the fifteenth century, the city of Ravensburg leased many of its farms as inheritable tenures, with the policy at the beginning of the century of allowing the farm to go to the eldest son (WHSA, B198, doc. 514). However, primogeniture does not seem to have remained the rule throughout the century, for a court case in 1492 reveals that all siblings had a right to inherit equally, and if they remained on the farm they had a right to continue to share in ownership. But no children of the third generation could inherit until all of the second generation were dead. These rules would act as a safety valve, for in the normal course of the development cycle of a family some members would leave the farm as they reached a certain age. The process would be regulated by the age structure of the family and the number of people dependent on the farm for support.

The conditions under which such a system as outlined above operates can easily be inferred. The farm has limited resources which regulate the size of the domestic group. Under a pattern of equal inheritance, those who can make a suitable living from the farm will choose to remain. However, there must be adequate opportunity for the excess numbers to find a position elsewhere; they might take over another farm, emigrate to a city, or become day-labourers. If the resources of the society become restricted, more members of the family will attempt to exercise the right to remain on the farm.

In the later part of the fifteenth century, the region under consideration was faced with a greater restriction of resources. With a rising population more competition developed for existing farms, for positions as domestic servants on the larger farms and for jobs as farm labourers. As a result, the children of farm tenants tended to delay leaving the farm, or perhaps claimed the right to remain permanently, bringing the possibility of permanent fission. Such a process did take place to the north in Wurttemberg, where better soil allowed smaller units to suffice for the provision of a family. The larger city population also provided the basis for intensive agriculture. In Upper Swabia, soil conditions at the contemporary level of technology and an existing demand made an extensive form of agricultural production necessary. Both lords and many tenant farmers pursued a course of adopting forms of tenure which would ensure the continuing unity of the farms. In the case of the last farm considered above, the city bought up the various parts inherited by different heirs. By 1510 the whole farm was leased to a single man for six years and later leased for a lifetime. There are many similar cases of the city buying up inheritable tenures (*Erblehen*) in this fashion, unifying the farms and leasing them for the period of a life (*Fallehen*). This last farm had split up into parts as small as a tenth, before the city purchased them all.

To the east of the city of Ravensburg, the farms belonging to the Truchsess of Waldburg were leased for a period of time, varying normally between ten and twenty years. However, the farms were leased in each generation to a member of the same family (Wolfegger Archiv, docs. 2123–33). Interesting changes occurred in the form of tenure for the farms belonging to the cloister of Weingarten. Until 1446 the farms were leased for the period of one man's life. From 1446 to 1485 they were leased to a married couple and all of their children. From 1485 to 1540 they were leased for the lifetime of a married couple and their youngest son, or if no son, their youngest daughter. After 1540 they were leased for the lifetime of a married couple only.

If the change in 1485 to contractual ultimogeniture is a response to the pressure of population, then the cloister may well have been trying to clarify the line of succession, insuring that only one son had the right to succeed to the possession of the farm. The change in 1540 to a contract involving only one generation was associated with the introduction of an entrance fee. From that date, whenever succession took place the new tenant paid an entry fee. But this did not necessarily change the form of inheritance. With regards to the contract specifying ultimogeniture, it may well be that the siblings had a *de facto* right to remain on the farm. However, the rules stated in the contracts of the neighbouring cloister of Weissenau suggest the contrary (WHSA, B523, docs. 2677–8, 2664, 2669). There the contracts throughout the same period all specify tenancy for the lifetime of a married couple, although, like Waldburg, the farms appear to have stayed in the same families in succeeding generations. The tenants, however, are often barred from having more than one relative living on the farm with them, thus making provision for a widowed or aged parent, but denying to siblings the right to remain.

From the information we have given I think we can infer a few things about the way the system of inheritance in the region worked. Probably some form of modified ultimogeniture was the rule. For one thing it would not make much sense for Weingarten to adopt ultimogeniture by contractual obligation unless the rule already tended to work in practice. As Goody (1962: 324) points out, such a form of inheritance implies the existence of land or jobs for non-heirs. As the older children reach adulthood, they take up residence elsewhere, for example, by taking over another farm or moving to a city. The youngest son gets the farm as payment for taking care of the parents. Similar conditions normally are in operation where the siblings are allowed to choose among themselves which one will inherit, as was, for example, the practice for the cloister of Ochsenhausen (Franz, 1963: 28–35).

We do not know a great deal about the possible opportunities for non-heirs in this region. The amount of immigration into the cities was not very large. As population increased, many men of the region went into service as Landsknechte. At the beginning of the fifteenth century, with no great pressure of population, there was probably a good deal of opportunity to take over an empty farm. In addition, a young man could marry into a family where there was no male heir. As the population rose, these opportunities still existed but the competition was so much greater. One set of social arrangements suggests itself from the pattern of settlement and from a practice prevalent in the eighteenth century. At that time, small-holders from Vorarlberg used to bring their young children (aged 8–16) to the market at Ravensburg early in the spring. Farmers from the area would take them on as household servants, bringing them back to the market late in the autumn, at which time their parents would return to meet them. Probably some such system worked in the fifteenth and sixteenth centuries for the farm families from the area. Larger or underpopulated farms would take into the domestic group young children as household servants and older children as labourers.

We can get an idea of the distribution of farm sizes from a sample of 195 farms belonging to the cloister of Weingarten in 1531 (Sabean, 1972: ch. 4). The largest farm was about 60 hectares, with 31 per cent under 10 hectares, 30 per cent between 11 and 20, and 39 per cent over 20. The mean size farm was 20 hectares, the median, 16. Calculations I made regarding crop production and consumption suggests that a farm of 14 hectares was sufficient to provide a living for a family of five people. The farms around Ravensburg were scattered, standing alone or grouped in small hamlets. Only further north around Memmingen and Biberach was the village the normal form of settlement. In these conditions it was natural for a family on a small farm to expect its children to leave early. In many instances, they would at first become members of the households of larger farms or of smaller farms with small families. If, by the time a servant reached adulthood, he had no expectation to property, he would take over a cottage and live as a day-labourer, although if he remained unmarried he would in some cases remain in the household of a farm family.

From the description of tenure changes adopted in the face of a swiftly expanding population, we can infer some of the accompanying social dislocation. There was dissatisfaction with and unease over what was taking place, but the peasants themselves were divided as to what policy to follow. Following old practices led in many instances to the uneconomical fractionalisation of farms. At the beginning of the fifteenth century, while still in the period of late medieval population decline, there was enough room to allow members of a family to find positions equal to their status somewhere else. Through marrying, assuming tenancy of an empty farm or taking a position as a domestic labourer on an underpopulated farm, a family member did not face under normal conditions a severe change of status. Under the conditions of the new forms of tenure, however, more members in each generation of a tenant family were forced into the position of becoming landless day-labourers. Often they no longer had claim in the inheritance nor claim to live off the family farm. Sometimes conflict developed over the right to succession. Undoubtedly kinship ties remained important, but they worked in a different pattern. Where day-labourers and farm tenants came into conflict as self-conscious groups, kinship lines would be crossed. The problem was a growing one, for with the number of farms remaining stable, an increased population meant an increase in the number of landless day-labourers.

This puts the goals of the peasant articles into perspective. They demanded an increase in the rights of the *Gemeinde*. They complained about the alienation of common land to provide dwelling places for cottagers. The common land was to remain and was to be administered by the *Gemeinde*. Similarly, woods, hunting and fishing rights were to come under *Gemeinde* regulation. It was to elect and depose the village priest, as well as to collect and distribute the tithe. The whole movement for *Gemeinde* self-regulation in this area involved the control of all village officials and the administration of justice. Since the *Gemeinde* was composed only of enfranchised members of a village, i.e. those who owned or leased a farm, this meant control of the resources of a village by farm tenants. Even the priest, among other things an important arbiter of disputes, would be their man.

In the area surrounding Ravensburg, the conflict between day-labourer and tenant farmer was unlikely to be very articulate because of the pattern of dispersed settlement. In the large villages in the north of the region, there were larger agglomerations of day-labourers, which, after a few generations, contributed to the weakening of kinship ties with farm tenants. However, to my knowledge there is in this area only one clear self-conscious movement on the part of day-labourers at this time. The articles of grievance composed by the subjects of the cloister of Ochsenhausen were in their interest, as can be seen by a comparison of the revolt at Ochsenhausen in 1502 with that of 1525 (Franz, 1963: 28–35; Vogt, 1885: no. 891).

Throughout the fifteenth century, the peasants of the cloister had sought to establish their right to hereditary tenure. On the other hand, the cloister sought to make all tenures revert upon the death of the tenant. After a rebellion and adjudication of the dispute, a treaty between the cloister and the rebels settled the matter in 1512. From that date all farms were to be leased on a hereditary basis, with farmers having the right to sell their hereditary tenancies as long as they were sold as a whole. Similarly, when farms changed hands through inheritance, they were to be kept unified, and within a short period all the heirs had to sell their shares to one among them. All these clauses of the treaty were sought for by the peasants themselves, for they were in agreement that farms should not be fragmented. A further point in the treaty was also in their interest. The abbot had alienated some common land and parcelled it out among landless cottagers in the form of leaseholds. The treaty specified that no further alienations should take place.

In contrast to the treaty of 1502, the complaints by the cloister's subjects in 1525 reflect the interests of the cottagers. One article demanded that all land be capable of being sold in block or piecemeal. Another article demanded the extension of the right to use common land to all inhabitants of the village. At one point the document condemned the treaty of 1502: 'The old treaty which was made between Abbot Hieronymous and the cloister subjects shall be done away with, because it is unbearable and destructive and caused pernicious harm.'

Having shown that an increasing population coupled with forms of land tenure which allowed only one heir to hold a farm helped bring about an increased differentiation within rural society; and that the continued expansion of population exacerbated the tensions generated thereby, we shall take another look at the implications of these forms of tenure for kinship structure. To show how the system probably worked we need to have a demographic model (Table 14.1). Lacking any for this particular region I will use the data from eighteenth-century

Table 14.1   *Number and age of children related to years of marriage –*
a model

	Years of Marriage															
	1	2	3	4	5	6	7	8	9	10	11	12	13	14	15	16
Husband	27	28		30		32		34		36		38		40		42
Wife	24	25		27		29		31		33		35		37		39
Age of																
Child 1		B		2		4		6		8		10		12		14
Child 2				B		2		4		6		8		10		12
Child 3						B		2		4		6		8		10
Child 4								B		2		4		6		8
Child 5										B		2		4		6
Child 6												B		2		4
Child 7														B		2
Child 8																B

Crulai given by Gautier and Henry (1958: 71ff., 91ff., 176ff.). The rate of age-specific fertility ought to be the same, and perhaps the mortality rate would not differ greatly; as for age at marriage, I can only guess. The implications for any marriage age can of course be worked out. For the moment I will use the mean ages at marriage for Crulai. We assume that a man marries at 27 years of age, that his wife is 24, and that neither dies young so that no second marriage is involved. They will have their first child by the end of the first year, and a child every two years thereafter until the wife is 39.

In this model, the difference in age between the first born and the last born is fourteen years. If we assume that the first and last are boys and that the father dies at 50, then when succession should take place the eldest is 22 and the youngest is 8. However, it would not often happen that all the children would survive. In Crulai only 60 per cent survived to 15, leaving in this model five surviving children. If an equal number of boys and girls are born and boys have a higher mortality rate, there will probably be three surviving girls and two surviving boys.

If we use this demographic model and assume the more optimistic mortality rates for adults given for Crulai, we have the following: the father dies at age 50, the mother at 60; when the father dies the eldest and youngest boys are respectively 25 and 17. If at this point a decision has to be made about succession, it would be natural for the eldest to lay claim to it. He is in a good position to assume control because of his age. However, in this case the mother is only 52 and would be able to exercise headship. At her death the boys would be 33 and 25. Here the youngest is in a favourable position to claim whatever rights he can. It is apparent that all sorts of combinations of ages are possible within the broad limits established so far. If a family must call upon one of the sons to assume headship, it would be unlikely to let it pass to one clearly not old enough to assume it. Where a modified ultimogeniture is the practice, headship would pass to the youngest son who is old enough to assume it. Depending on how the ages are distributed, the succession would be accompanied by varying degrees of conflict.

Let us examine the model a little more closely in terms of the development cycle of the family (cf. Goody, 1962: Introduction). During the first three years the family has some chance of saving. The wife can contribute more to the economy of the farm than she ever will be able to again. At the same time, there are not many children to feed. After that, dissaving is likely to begin, with the hardest period being between the tenth and eighteenth years of the marriage (between the father's ages of 36 and 44). In the tenth year there are three children, the oldest being six. In the eighteenth year, there are five children with the eldest 14. Under the conditions we have described, it would be normal from this point on to seek to place the oldest remaining child in another family as a servant or to find work for him outside the home farm, with the expectation that he would leave home completely after four or five years. The oldest is likely to leave when the next oldest is capable of assuming major tasks at home. With this kind of system operating, one can easily see how the youngest child who is capable of assuming the duties of running a farm becomes the natural heir. Conflict over succession is minimised because the older children have already taken positions elsewhere. In this case, if the eldest boy leaves at the age of 14, he will have been gone for eleven years at the time of his father's death and nineteen upon the death of his mother.

From all of this it is clear that the Weingarten system would have difficulty in working. For example, in the case where the youngest son was very young when his parents died an elder son would in all likelihood assume succession under a modified system of ultimogeniture. But since ultimogeniture is by contract, upon reaching his majority the youngest son could sue for possession. Then the system is very likely to create conflict. I will suggest further on that there might be an explanation as to why the cloister rigidified the system despite the problems inherent in it, but I think it is safe to say that the cloister adopted ultimogeniture itself because it tended to be the rule in practice, and that ultimogeniture works if the elder children tend to leave the farm at a fairly early age.

In closing this section it would be useful to construct from the foregoing information a model showing lines of dependence between related day-labourers and tenant farmers. Let us look at the problem from the point of view of a day-labourer (ego) whose father is a farmer. His closest kin who are landholders would be the natural ones for him to call upon for help and contacts regarding work, aid in time of need, obtaining a wife, getting a loan or a place to live. From the point of view of ego, the closest kin from which he can expect help are his father and youngest brother, his mother's youngest brother and his youngest son, his father's sister's husband and his youngest son, his sister's husband, his wife's father and youngest brother. A good deal depends here on the position of the household as a social unit. If it predominates, the ties between kin not living under the same roof are not apt to be so important. In particular, ties between siblings will diminish. From the point of view of ego, his family of origin is important for his early nurturing. His father plays the key role in placing him in another household when he first leaves the domestic unit. After that, ties are likely to become less important, unless, once independent, he looks for employment from his father and brother. After his marriage his affines become important in this respect. Which kin are important depends largely upon where he resides, although in this area of dispersed settlement the network is likely to be geographically quite wide. The place of residence may also be chosen because of prior kinship ties.

Apart from relations with members of the family of origin, which may well be weak so as to prevent possible conflict over succession, the closest consanguineous kin who owns property is ego's mother's brother. Early in ego's life this is perhaps the most important kinship relation. Later, his wife's father and her younger brother may become dominant. Incidentally, there is a close relationship between the mother's brother and the sister's son wherever unigeniture prevails in Western Europe. This is the key relationship in the medieval epic, for example, and it is for the same reason as here.

The picture that emerges is one of a series of patron–client relationships based partly on residence and partly on kinship. As long as the number of day-labourers is not too great, most sons not succeeding to land are dependent upon landholders for wives. Obtaining a wife establishes a connection by which one man offers his labour and loyalty while the other dispenses work and help in time of need. Even when the number of day-labourers grows the most advantageous marriage from this point of view is with the daughter of a landholder. If conflict should develop in these relationships, it could be most explosive.

Leibeigenschaft *and rights in land*

In dealing with the problems posed for land tenure by the status of personal bondage known as *Leibeigenschaft*, we can take for a case study the one of Weingarten and its disputes with the regional court (*Landvogtei*) in Swabia. The situation was created by the extreme fragmentation of political authority, this area being the classical land of petty territorial states (cf. Bader, 1950). Here lords exercised control over subjects by three different means: through (1) the ownership of land, (2) the administration of justice, or (3) the exercise of authority over the person as bondsman (*Leibeigener*). Very often the lord having rights over a peasant was different in each case. The peasants could be in the legal jurisdiction of one lord, hold land from another and be the bondsman of a third. Naturally, such a situation was often cause for dispute among the lords themselves. Serious conflict arose when a lord attempted to extend his power by claiming greater rights for one of these relationships. For example, a lord (*Leibherr*) could claim the right to tax his subjects as his *Leibeigene* in a territory where the lord with legal jurisdiction claimed the same privilege on the basis of his exercise of a civil function.

One of the regular points of conflict involved the control of resources through the ownership of land and the control of people through the extension of the number of subjects under bondage. The problem arose from the fact that the status of bondage descended matrilineally. Thus, if a peasant holding land from Lord A married a bondswoman belonging to Lord B, the children claiming rights to succession to the property would be *Leibeigene* of Lord B. By custom of the region, the *Leibherr* had certain rights to the adjudication of property disputes, which meant that Lord B would now have important rights in the control of the people holding property from Lord A and in the control of the latter's land.

The lords of the region often worked out a *modus vivendi* to deal with the problem by exchanging *Leibeigene* (WHSA, B523, doc. 2672). Nonetheless disputes often arose, depending on how ambitious any particular lord might be. Many of them specified in the lease contracts that any marriage outside their *Leibeigenschaft* would lead to forfeit of a farm. Those subjects who did not hold land from a lord could usually purchase their freedom, formally putting themselves in bondage to another lord; normally a woman became the bondswoman of her husband's lord. There are, for example, hundreds of documents of manumission from the cloister of Weissenau preserved in the archives (cf. WHSA, B523, docs. 2678–82).

The status of *Leibeigenschaft* was detested by the peasants. Although the annual economic charges were not great, it involved a heriot amounting to one third of a legacy. This became harder to take at a time when heirs were coming into increasing conflict over succession. To provide for the non-succeeding sons would lessen the conflict. A further problem involves the havoc it created for normal lines of inheritance. For example, if a daughter married outside the *Leibeigenschaft* of her lord, she would lose her rights to inherit property belonging to his bondsmen. This would be all right if the expected heir succeeded to the farm. But if he died, she or her children might be in a position to claim succession. Some lords had reciprocal agreements, allowing their *Leibeigene* to inherit movable property, and even landed property, so long as they sold the latter to a *Leibeigener* of the lord who owned the land (cf. WHSA, B470, Büschel 4).

The conflict between the cloister of Weingarten and the *Landvogtei* was based on the relationships we have just outlined. To understand how it developed we should put the dispute into its political context. The *Landvogtei* was established by the Emperor Rudolph of Habsburg after the break-up of the Duchy of Swabia in order to administer imperial rights in the area. Centred in Ravensburg and the town of Altdorf just outside the walls of the cloister of Weingarten, the *Landvogtei* did not form a closed territory. Rather it exercised jurisdiction over an extended area north of the Lake of Constance. The office and its rights were held as a mortgage (*Pfand*) from the Empire. Throughout the fifteenth century, various local lords held the mortgage. Under this system, the most that the contiguous territories had to fear was the pressure of greater financial exactions.

In the middle of the fifteenth century, however, the house of Habsburg began its great imperial policies. One of its objects was to link up its Austrian territories with those along the Rhine: in the Breisgau and Alsace. In fact, the Habsburgs were out to re-create the old Swabian duchy in order to have a strong southern base for their operations (cf. Bader, 1950). To this end, one of their policies was to suppress the imperial rights of the rich Swabian cloisters and make them properties of the house of Habsburg. As a result they redeemed the *Landvogtei* and took over the mortgage themselves. However, being unable to afford the expense, they leased it on a second mortgage (*Afterpfandschaft*) to their own men. These officers of the Habsburgs began to bring pressure to bear, especially on the imperial abbey of the area.

The attack on Weingarten took several forms. The *Landvogt* used first of all his jurisdiction rights as holder of high justice in the area and claimed the right to appoint the cloister officials dealing with low justice. He harassed cloister officials and supported its subjects in their independence. One point of conflict that occurred over and over again was that the *Landvogt* supported the claims to tenancy of cloister farms by people that the cloister claimed had no such rights. A hint as to what was involved here was the accompanying dispute over whether the *Landvogt* had the right to be present at marriages and the apportionment of legacies (WHSA, B517, Missivband 41, 40–46). Perhaps we can clarify the situation by referring to the models we have developed above.

Under the form of contract by which farms were leased by the cloister prior to 1485, all of the children shared in the inheritance of property. As I have pointed out, some sort of modified ultimogeniture probably worked in practice. With a rise in population, however, children either delayed leaving the domestic group or began to put forward claims to succession. With all of them sharing in the inheritance, probably in actuality only one succeeded to the property, the rest perhaps receiving their share in cash or movable goods. Opportunity arose, however, for the *Landvogt* to intrude himself in the case of a disputed succession. The best method would have been to encourage one son to marry a bondswoman of another lord and protect his right of succession. In the next generation Weingarten would lose a considerable amount of control over the tenants, with the *Landvogt* the mediator in any dispute. The change to formal ultimogeniture was then really a move on the part of the cloister to end disputes over succession. Knowledge of this context helps to explain why such a rigid system, very difficult to work in practice, was adopted.

Even after the new contracts were put into use, the disputes continued along the same lines, but the new system made it harder for the *Landvogt*. The contracts specified that the tenancy was forfeit if any of the parties to it married bondsmen of other lords. The *Landvogt* could still protect those who did, but it would be harder for him to change a contracted succession. For one thing, a contract dispute would be settled in Weingarten's own court, while land-tenure of *Leibeigene* would involve the *Leibherr*. Once the dispute became a contract dispute, the right to succession fell under the jurisdiction of Weingarten alone. In the new situation the attack could best come by forcing or encouraging the younger son to marry outside the *Leibeigenschaft*. Alternatively, the *Landvogt* could encourage all other sons to marry outside so that in the event that the younger son died before succeeding to the property, he could support one of them in the succession.

The right to succession was thus guaranteed by contract only for the second generation. None the less *de facto* succession in the same family was the rule in the area. A farm tenant would naturally expect one of his sons to succeed him. Even though, as in the two models above, the contracts have been violated and the farms formally forfeit, the right of a family to continue in succession coupled with the support of the *Landvogt* would have presented the cloister with a severe threat. How the cloister dealt with the situation can only be surmised, but there is some evidence on which we can base a tentative conclusion. There is a complete register dating from the year 1531 of the farms belonging to the cloister, giving the names of the present and previous tenant (WHSA, H235, 29–33). In slightly more than 50 per cent of the cases the surname changes. There are several possible reasons for this, but it is highly improbable that failure of male succession could account for such a high turnover. At the lapse of the contracts the cloister must have given the farms to someone other than the direct male heir.

A solution for the cloister would lie in following the female line in succession upon the establishment of a new contract. This would ensure that the next generation would be bondsmen of the cloister with succession to the property remaining in the kin group. In fact it would create a conflict within the kin group with one party at least supporting the cloister. The solution has several advantages. The sons of the third generation are likely to be of similar age. The cloister can pick any son in the third generation of any daughter in the second, since all will be by definition *Leibeigene* of the cloister. It does not even matter if the husband in the second generation is a bondsman of the cloister so long as the wife has not purchased her freedom. Furthermore, the outside marriage of the defined heir in any contract can be tolerated since his heirs are not guaranteed succession.

In the Twelve Articles, the peasants demanded an end to *Leibeigenschaft*. One can see here perhaps another reason for their opposition to the system. As we have pointed out the stated ends of the rebellion were for local affairs to be controlled by the *Gemeinde*, which meant, in effect, by the tenant farmers. If we examine again our model based on probable lines of patronage, we can see that the most important patron–client relation was precisely the one that would be disrupted by the solution suggested above for the cloister of Weingarten (Figure 14.2).

The first possible conflict over succession is between ego and his brother, with ego's brother supported by their father. Under such conditions, as we pointed out, ego would first (especially prior to his marriage) be dependent on his mother's youngest brother (Case A), his closest property-owning consanguineous kin outside of his nuclear family of origin. However, in the event that the cloister followed succes-

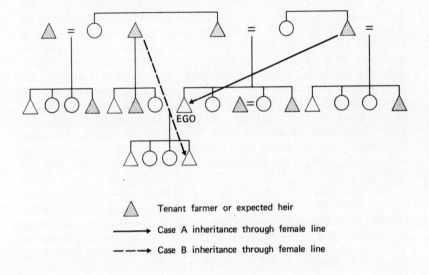

△   Tenant farmer or expected heir

⟶   Case A inheritance through female line

--➤   Case B inheritance through female line

Figure 14.2

sion through the female line, he would be the likely heir rather than his cousin. Thus conflict intrudes where lines of dependence are potentially strongest. In Case B the cloister is following the same solution. This time ego's son succeeds through the maternal line. Thus where ego would normally find important help and support from his wife's father, he is now in the position of supporting his son over succession. From the point of view of tenant farmers, their normal control over people, in this case kin who are day-labourers subject to their patronage, is disrupted.

Conclusions

I have tried up to now to present a tentative framework for research into the nature of rural society just before the Peasant War. I think it also offers a good approach for investigating the nature of rural society anywhere in Europe in this period. Building models allows the historian to discover how the system operates and what its structural principles are. He can locate the points of potential recurring conflict and show what tensions are generated when the structure itself undergoes change. As a method it allows him to fit different types of data into a coherent picture. For example, more lease contracts over a wider area and longer time span could show the variations and extent of the system we have seen here. Many criminal proceedings and civil actions will show where conflict is built in. Genealogies constructed from parish records should reveal the workings of the alliance system and furnish data on the demographic structure of the family and its domestic cycle.

With the suggestions we have offered so far we can give a tentative picture of the patterns of kinship and land tenure in the society under consideration, and show how conflict operated. We have seen that rural society in Upper Swabia faced the prospect of increasingly restricted resources. In the period of less pressure, ultimogeniture was the normal pattern of inheritance, but as siblings faced increasing difficulty in obtaining positions elsewhere, conflict developed over succession. This must be seen in the background when examining the articulated complaints of the Peasant War. The long-term solution, however, was probably similar to that found in Ireland in the nineteenth century, where a pattern of deferred marriage and celibacy developed (cf. Arensberg, 1940: 153ff.). The Cameralist writers of the eighteenth century point this out as a feature of the system in Upper Swabia and argue that it put a severe limit on the development of the population.

An immediate fact is apparent when one examines the potential lines of dependence in the society: the tenant farmers controlled resources, employment and women. As a result, day-labourers were dependent on them. The son of a tenant farmer probably worked for his kin and married one of their daughters or was dependent upon them for contacts and information. If marriages were arranged for sons by their parents, we can look upon the subsequent alliance as one primarily between tenant farmers. One provides an under-populated farm with a satellite work force. Farmer A offers Farmer B a son-in-law tied to his patronage. Similarly, the son of a day-labourer might marry the daughter of a tenant farmer or the daughter of another day-labourer tied into the patronage system of a tenant farmer.

One of the controlling factors in the situation was locality. Day-labourers were scattered among dispersed settlements composed by and large of small farms. Thus dependence was immediate and direct. Large farmers would probably have had a wider network, as is evidenced by the fact that it was they who led the rebellion. In northern Upper Swabia, the settlement pattern displayed larger villages and greater numbers of day-labourers. As a result, kinship ties between farmers and labourers were less important and the conflict was clearer. In the south the conflict followed two main lines. First, there was simply rivalry between siblings for succession, and secondly, day-labourers who were kin became a threat to succession in the disputes over *Leibeigenschaft*. Still, we can by no means imagine that conflict always existed, for the succession was not always disputed and normal patronage along kinship lines often worked out in practice.

Finally, we should take note of the issue as we have seen it develop from the point of view of the lords. Weingarten, in fact, pursued a very successful course. It was able to protect its property holdings by and large through the manipulation of succession. Further, in its control of people it was also successful. It encouraged its bondswomen to marry outside the *Leibeigenschaft*, not forcing them to buy themselves free (WHSA, H14/15, 266, fo. 62ff.). By the normal process of inheritance, it maximised the points of friction with other lords, winning a good deal in the long-protracted processes of arbitration. Weissenau, on the other hand, sought to minimise problems of this nature by requiring all of its bondswomen to buy themselves free upon contracting such a marriage. The success of Weingarten can be measured by the fact that, in the eighteenth century, it formed a closed independent state, while Weissenau was essentially just a property of the house of Habsburg.

References

(Works in English of especial relevance are asterisked*.)

Abbreviations:
MEW   =   *Marx-Engels-Werke*
VSWG   =   *Vierteljahrschrift für Sozial-und Wirtschaftsgeschichte*
ZfA   =   *Zeitschrift für Agrargeschichte und Agrarsoziologie*
ZfG   =   *Zeitschrift für Geschichtswissenschaft*

Abel, W., 1955, *Die Wüstungen des ausgehenden Mittelalters*, second edition, Stuttgart.
Abel, W., 1966, *Agrarkrisen und Agrarkonjunktur*, second edition, Hamburg.
Abel, W., 1967, *Geschichte der deutschen Landwirtschaft*, Stuttgart.
Allen, P. S., and Allen, H. M. (eds.), 1926, *Opus Epistolarum Des. Erasmi Roterodami*, VI: *1525-7*, Oxford.
Angermeier, H., 1966, 'Die Vorstellungen des "gemeinen Mannes"', VSWG, 53.
Arensberg, C., and Kimball, S. T., 1940, *Family and Community in Ireland*, Cambridge, Mass.
Bader, K. S., 1950, *Der deutsche Südwesten*, Stuttgart.
Bader, K. S., 1957, 1962, *Studien zur Rechtsgeschichte des mittelalterlichen Dorfes*, 2 vols., Weimar and Cologne.
Baillet, L., 1967, 'La Guerre des paysans: un cas de conscience dans la famille de Ribeaupierre', *Bulletin philologique et historique*.
*Bak, Janos (ed.), 1976, *The German Peasant War*, London (reprint of *Journal of Peasant Studies*, October 1975).
Barack, K. A. (ed.), 1869, 'Zimmersche Chronik', *Bibliothek des litterarischen Vereins in Stuttgart*, Tübingen.
Barth, F. (ed.), 1970, *Ethnic Groups and Boundaries. The Social Organisation of Cultural Differences*, Bergen and Oslo.
Barth, M., 1959, *Der Rebbau im Elsass und die Absatzgebiete seiner Weine*, Strasbourg.
Barton, P. F. (ed.), 1975, *Sozialrevolution und Reformation. Aufsätze zur Vorreformation und zu den 'Bauernkriegen' in Südmitteleuropa*, Vienna.
Bauer, C., 1956, 'Jakob Villinger, Grosschatzmeister Kaiser Maximilians', *Syntagma Friburgense. Festschrift H. Aubin*, Lindau.
Baumann, F. L. (ed.), 1876, *Quellen zur Geschichte des Bauernkrieges in Oberschwaben*, Tübingen.
*Bax, E. B., 1899, *The Peasant War in Germany 1525-6*, London.
Bemmann, R., 1915, *Mühlhausen im späten Mittelalter*, Mühlhausen.
Bensing, M., 1966, *Thomas Müntzer und der Thüringer Aufstand*, Berlin.
Bensing, M., and Hoyer, S., 1970, *Der deutsche Bauernkrieg 1524-6*, second edition, Berlin.

References 191

Bergsten, T., 1961, *Balthasar Hubmaier. Seine Stellung zur Reformation und zum Täufertum 1521–8*, Kassel.

Bezold, F. von, 1878, 'Die "armen Leute" und die deutsche Literatur des späten Mittelalters', *Historische Zeitschrift*, 41.

Blaschke, K. H., 1956, 'Soziale Gliederung und Entwicklung der sächsischen Landbevölkerung', ZfA, 4.

Blickle, P., 1967, 'Leibeigenschaft als Instrument der Territorialpolitik im Allgäu', *Festschrift G. Franz*.

Blickle, P., 1972, 'Bauer und Staat in Oberschwaben', *Zeitschrift für Württembergische Landesgeschichte*, 31.

Blickle, P., 1973, *Landschaften im Alten Reich*, Munich.

Blickle, P., 1974, 'Die spätmittelalterliche Leibeigenschaft in Oberschwaben', ZfA, 22.

Blickle, P., 1975, *Die Revolution von 1525*, Munich.

Boelcke, W., 1957, *Bauer und Gutsherr in der Oberlausitz*, Bautzen.

Bog, I., 1958, 'Geistliche Herrschaft und Bauer in Bayern und die spätmittelalterliche Agrarkrise', VSWG, 45.

Bog, I., 1968, 'Wachstumsprobleme der oberdeutschen Wirtschaft', *Wirtschaftliche und soziale Probleme* (ed. F. Lütge).

Böhm, L. (ed.), 1893, 'S. Ranft, Kitzingen und der Bauernkrieg', *Archiv des historischen Vereins für Unterfranken*, 36.

Brackert, H., 1975, *Bauernkrieg und Literatur*, Frankfurt am Main.

Brady, T. A., 1973, 'Jakob Sturm of Strasbourg and the Lutherans at the Diet of Augsburg 1530', *Church History*, 42.

Brandt, O. H. (ed.), 1925, *Der grosse Bauernkrieg. Zeitgenössische Berichte, Aussagen und Aktenstücke*, Jena.

Braun, R., 1960, *Industrialisierung und Volksleben (Zürcher Oberland vor 1800)*, Erlenbach.

*Buck, L. P., 1971, *The Containment of Civil Insurrection: Nuremberg and the Peasants' Revolt 1524–5*, Michigan.

*Buck, L. P., 1973, 'Opposition to Tithes in the Peasants' Revolt: A Case Study of Nuremberg in 1524', *Sixteenth Century Journal*, 4.

*Buck, L. P., 1976, 'Civil Insurrection in a Reformation City: The Versicherungsbrief of Windsheim, March 1525', *Archiv für Reformationsgeschichte*, 67.

Bücking, J., 1968, *Kultur und Gesellschaft in Tirol um 1600*, Lübeck.

Bücking, J., 1970, 'Das Geschlecht der Stürtzel von Buchheim', *Zeitschrift für Geschichte des Oberrheins*, 118.

Bücking, J., 1971, 'Reformation und katholische Reform in Tirol', *Der Schlern*, 45.

Bücking, J., 1973, 'Der "Oberrheinische Revolutionär" heisst Conrad Stürtzel, seines Zeichens königlicher Hofkanzler', *Archiv für Kulturgeschichte*, 56.

Buszello, H., 1969, *Der deutsche Bauernkrieg als politische Bewegung*, Berlin.

Cambridge Economic History of Europe, 2, 1952.

*Carsten, F. L., 1954, *The Origins of Prussia*, London.

Claus, H. (ed.), 1975, *Der deutsche Bauernkrieg in Druckschriften der Jahre 1524–6*, Verzeichnis der Flugschriften und Dichtungen, Gotha.

Clemen, O., 1908, *Flugschriften aus den ersten Jahren der Reformation*, volume two, Leipzig.

*Cohn, H. J., 1965, *The Government of the Rhine Palatinate in the Fifteenth Century*, Oxford.

Colditz Town Council, 1965, *700 Jahre Stadt Colditz.*

Cornelius, C. A., 1862, 'Studien zur Geschichte des Bauernkrieges', *Abhandlungen der königlich bayrischen Akademie der Wissenschaften*, 3 Kl. Bd. IX, I, Munich.

Cronthal, M., 1887, *Die Stadt Würzburg im Bauernkrieg* (ed. M. Wieland).

Czok, K., 1975, 'Vorstädte: Sozialökonomischer Bestandteil der Stadt (zu ihrer Entwicklung im 15. Jh.)', *Sammelband des Zentralinstituts für Wirtschaftsgeschichte der Akademie der Wissenschaften der DDR*, Berlin.

Czok, K., 1975a, 'Bauernkriegsereignisse im Leipziger Land', *Jahrbuch für Regionalgeschichte*, 5.

Czok, K., 1975b, 'Zum Widerhall des deutschen Bauernkrieges in Leipzig 1524–5', *Der Bauer im Klassenkampf*, Berlin.

Czok, K., and Steinmetz, M., 1975c, *Das Leipziger Land im Bauernkrieg*, Leipzig.

*Davies, C. S. L., 1973, 'Peasant Revolt in France and England: a comparison', *Agricultural History Review*, 21.

Denzinger, I., 1848, 'Weisung des Bischofs Conrad von Thüngen', *Archiv des historischen Vereins für Unterfranken*, 9.

Deutsche Reichstagsakten unter Karl V, 1963, vol. 1 (1519), second edition.

Dietz, B., 1925–6, *Der Bauernkrieg im Obermaintal*, Lichtenfels.

Dobel, F., 1877, *Christoph Schappeler, der erste Reformator von Memmingen 1513–25*, second edition, Augsburg.

Droeger, G., 1966, 'Die finanziellen Grundlagen des Territorialstaates', VSWG, 53.

Duggett, M., 1975, 'Marx on Peasants', *Journal of Peasant Studies*, 2.

Dülmen, R. van, 1976, *Reformation als Revolution*, Munich.

Eitner, T., 1903, 'Erfurt und die Bauernaufstände im 16. Jh.', *Mitteilungen des Vereins für Geschichte zu Erfurt*, 24.

Elkar, R. S., 1976, 'Forschungen in der DDR zur Geschichte der "deutschen frühbürgerlichen Revolution" (Literaturbericht)', *Blätter für deutsche Landesgeschichte*, 112.

Elliott, J. H., 1969, 'Revolution and Continuity in Early Modern Europe', *Past and Present*, No. 42.

Endres, R., 1963, *Die Nürnberg–Nördlinger Wirtschaftsbeziehungen*.

Endres, R., 1967, 'Zur Geschichte des fränkischen Reichskreises', *Würzburger Diözesangeschichtsblätter*, 29.

Endres, R., 1968, 'Zur wirtschaftlichen und sozialen Lage in Franken', *Jahrbuch für fränkische Landesforschung*, 28.

Endres, R., 1971, 'Probleme des Bauernkriegs im Hochstift Bamberg', *Jahrbuch für fränkische Landesforschung*, 31.

Endres, R., 1974, 'Der Bauernkrieg in Franken', *Festschrift G. Wunder. Württembergisch Franken*, 58, Schwäbisch Hall.

*Engels, Friedrich, 1926, *The Peasant War in Germany*, London.

*Engels, Friedrich, 1956, *The Peasant War in Germany*, Moscow.

Engels, Friedrich, 1964, 'Der deutsche Bauernkrieg', MEW, 7, Berlin.

*Engels, Friedrich, 1967, *The German Revolutions; the Peasant War in Germany* (ed. L. Krieger), Chicago.

Engels, Friedrich, 1970, *Der deutsche Bauernkrieg*, ninth edition, Berlin.

Englert-Faye, C., 1940, *Vom Mythos zur Idee der Schweiz,* Zürich.

Feige, W., 1965, 'Die Sozialstruktur der spätmittelalterlichen deutschen Stadt im Spiegel der historischen Statistik', Bd 1, Leipzig University thesis.

Fevre, D., Lavergne, J., Riep, J. P., 1976, 'Anthropologie des paysans massacrés en 1525', *Der deutsche Bauernkrieg und Thomas Müntzer* (ed. M. Steinmetz), Leipzig.

Foschepoth, J., 1976, *Reformation und Bauernkrieg im Geschichtsbild der DDR,* Berlin.

Franz, G., 1933, *Der Deutsche Bauernkrieg,* first edition, Munich and Berlin.

Franz, G. (ed.), 1935, *Der Deutsche Bauernkrieg, Aktenband,* Munich and Berlin.

Franz, G., 1939, 'Die Entstehung der Zwölf Artikel', *Archiv für Reformationsgeschichte,* 36.

Franz, G., and Fuchs, W. P. (eds.), 1942, *Akten zur Geschichte des Bauernkrieges in Mitteldeutschland,* volume two, Jena (reprint, Aalen, 1964).

Franz, G., 1956, *Der Deutsche Bauernkrieg,* fourth edition, Darmstadt.

Franz, G., 1961, 'Christoph Schappeler', *Religion in Geschichte und Gegenwart,* 5.

Franz, G. (ed.), 1963, *Quellen zur Geschichte des Bauernkrieges,* München.

Franz, G., 1969, *Der Deutsche Bauernkrieg,* ninth edition, Darmstadt.

Franz, G., 1970, 'Die soziale Schichtung des Dorfes', *Geschichte des deutschen Bauernstandes.*

Franz, G., 1972, *Der Deutsche Bauernkrieg,* ninth edition (reprint), Darmstadt.

Franz, G., 1975, *Der Deutsche Bauernkrieg,* tenth edition, Darmstadt.

Franz, H., 1924, Studien über den militärischen Charakter des Bauernkrieges in Oberschwaben und im Allgäu, Giessen University thesis.

Fries, L., 1883, *Die Geschichte des Bauern-Krieges in Ostfranken* (eds. A. Schäffler and T. Henner), volume two.

*Friesen, A., 1965, 'Thomas Müntzer in Marxist Thought', *Church History,* 34.

*Friesen, A., 1974, *Reformation and Utopia. The Marxist Interpretation of the Reformation,* Wiesbaden.

Furet, F., 1965, 1970, *Livres et société en France du 18ᵐᵉ siècle,* two volumes, Paris.

Gautier, E., and Henry, L., 1958, *La Population de Crulai,* Paris.

Gerlach, H., 1969, *Der englische Bauernaufstand von 1381 und der deutsche Bauernkrieg. Ein Vergleich,* Meisenheim.

Gess, F. (ed.), 1905, 1917, *Akten und Briefe zur Kirchenpolitik Herzog Georgs von Sachsen,* 2 vols., Leipzig.

Goody, J. (ed.), 1962, *The Development Cycle in Domestic Groups* (introduction, Meyer Fortes), Cambridge.

Götze, A., 1901, 'Die Artikel der Bauern 1525', *Historische Vierteljahrschrift,* 4.

Götze, A., 1902, 'Die Zwölf Artikel der Bauern 1525. Kritisch herausgegeben', *Historische Vierteljahrschrift,* 5.

Götze, A., and Schmitt, L. E., 1953, *Aus dem sozialen und politischen Kampf. Flugschriften aus der Reformationszeit,* 20, Halle.

*Gritsch, E. W., 1967, Reformer without a Church: The Life and Thought of Thomas Müntzer 1488–1525, Philadelphia.

Gross, Michael, of Trockau, 1855, in Anzeiger für Kunde der deutschen Vorzeit, 3.

Hansjakob, H., 1867, Die Salpeterer, eine politisch-religiöse Sekte aus dem südöstlichen Schwarzwald, Waldshut.

Hartmann, A. (ed.), 1947, Die Amerbachkorrespondenz, Die Briefe aus den Jahren 1525–30, Basel.

Hasel, K., 1967, 'Die Entwicklung von Waldeigentum und Waldnutzung als Ursache für den Bauernkrieg', Allgemeine Forst- und Jagdzeitung, 138.

Haupt, H., 1888, 'Hussitische Propaganda in Deutschland', Historisches Taschenbuch, VI/7.

Heimpel, H., 1964, 'Fischerei und Bauernkrieg', Festschrift P. Schramm, vol. 1.

Heitz, G., 1961, Ländliche Leinenproduktion in Sachsen 1470–1555, Berlin.

Hesselbarth, H., 1953, 'Eine Flugschrift aus dem Grossen Deutschen Bauernkrieg', ZfG, 4.

Heumann, G., 1976, La Guerre des paysans d'Alsace et de Lorraine 1525, Paris.

*Heymann, F. G., 1970, 'The Hussite Revolution and the German Peasants' War', Medievalia et Humanistica, new series, 1.

*Hillerbrand, H. J., 1972, 'The German Reformation and the Peasants' War', The Social History of the Reformation (eds. L. P. Buck and J. W. Zophy), Columbus.

*Hilton, R., 1974, 'Medieval Peasants – Any Lessons?', Journal of Peasant Studies, 1.

Hinrichs, C., 1952, Luther und Müntzer, ihre Auseinandersetzung über Obrigkeit und Widerstandsrecht, Berlin.

*Hobsbawm, E. J., 1959, Primitive Rebels, New York.

Hoffmann, A., 1952, Wirtschaftsgeschichte des Landes Oberösterreich, vol. 1, Salzburg.

Höfler, C. (ed.), 1849, Ritter Ludwigs von Eyb Denkwürdigkeiten.

Hollaender, A., 1968, 'Gabriel Salamanca . . . und die Tiroler Empörung', Grannea, III.

*Hollaender, A., 1957, 'Articles of Almayne. An English Version of German Peasants' Gravamina 1525', Studies Presented to H. Jenkinson (ed. J. C. Davies), Oxford.

Honigman, J. J. (ed.), 1973, Handbook of Social and Cultural Anthropology, Chicago.

Hoyer, E., 1952–3, Fürstbischof Konrad III von Thüngen als Richter', Würzburger Diözesangeschichtsblätter, 14–15.

Hoyer, S., 1970, 'Martin Reinhart und der erste Druck hussitischer Artikel in Deutschland', ZfG, 18.

Hoyer, S., 1975, Das Militärwesen im deutschen Bauernkrieg 1524–6, Berlin.

Hoyer, S., and Rüdiger, B. (eds.), 1975, An die Versammlung gemeiner Bauerschaft, Leipzig.

Hubatsch, W., 1960, Albrecht von Brandenburg-Ansbach, Deutschordensmeister und Herzog in Preussen 1490–1568, Cologne.

Hubmaier, Balthasar, 1962, *Schriften* (eds. G. Westin and T. Bergsten), Gütersloh.

Humm, A., 1971, *Villages et hameaux disparus en Basse-Alsace*, Strasbourg.

Jäger, C., 1892, 'Markgraf Casimir und der Bauernkrieg in den südlichen Grenzämtern', *Mitteilungen des Vereins für Geschichte Nürnbergs*, 9.

Jörg, J. E., 1851, *Deutschland in der Revolutionsperiode 1522–6*.

Kaczerowsky, K. (ed.), 1970, *Flugschriften des Bauernkrieges*, Hamburg.

Kelter, E., 1953, 'Das deutsche Wirtschaftsleben des 14. und 15. Jhs.', *Jahrbuch für Nationalökonomie und Statistik*.

Kessler, Johannes, 1866, *Sabbata* (ed. E. Götzinger), St Gallen.

Kiener, F., 1904, 'Zur Vorgeschichte des Bauernkriegs am Oberrhein', *Zeitschrift für Geschichte des Oberrheins*.

Kiessling, R., 1971, *Bürgerliche Gesellschaft und Kirche in Augsburg im Spätmittelalter*, Augsburg.

Kinter, P. L., 1971, 'Memmingens "Ausgetretene". Eine vergessene Nachwirkung des Bauernkrieges 1525–7', *Memminger Geschichtsblätter*.

Köhler, W. (ed.), 1914, *Zwinglis Briefwechsel, 2, 1523–6*, Leipzig.

Kötschke, R., 1953, *Ländliche Siedlung und Agrarwesen in Sachsen*, Remagen.

Kreutzer, J., 1909, *Zwinglis Lehre von der Obrigkeit*, Stuttgart.

Kunze, A., 1958, *Der Frühkapitalismus in Chemnitz*, Karl-Marx-Stadt.

Kunze, A., and Aubin, G., 1940, *Leinenerzeugung und Leinenabsatz im östlichen Mitteldeutschland zur Zeit der Zunftkämpfe*, Stuttgart.

Kurze, D., 1966, *Pfarrerwahlen im Mittelalter*, Cologne and Graz.

Kurze, D., 1974, 'Märkische Waldenser und Böhmische Brüder', *Festschrift W. Schlesinger*, vol. 2, Cologne.

Lamprecht, K., 1921, *Deutsche Geschichte*, fifth edition, vol. 5, part 1.

*Langbein, J. H., 1974, *Prosecuting Crime in the Renaissance, England, Germany, France*, Cambridge, Mass.

Langhans, S., 1962, *Chroniken der deutschen Städte, 27, Magdeburg, 2* (reprint), Göttingen.

Laube, A. (*et al.*), 1974, *Illustrierte Geschichte der deutschen frühbürgerlichen Revolution*, Berlin.

Le Roy Ladurie, E., 1974, 'Über die Bauernaufstände in Frankreich 1548–1648', *Festschrift W. Abel*, vol. 1, Hanover.

Lösche, D., 1960, 'Achtmänner, Ewiger Rat und Ewiger Bund Gottes', *Jahrbuch für Wirtschaftsgeschichte*, 1, Berlin.

Lötscher, V., 1943, 'Der deutsche Bauernkrieg in der Darstellung und im Urteil der zeitgenössischen Schweizer', *Basler Beiträge zur Geschichtswissenschaft*, 11.

Lotzer, Sebastian, 1902, *Schriften* (ed. A. Goetze), Leipzig.

Lütge, F., 1963, 'Luthers Eingreifen in den Bauerkrieg', and 'Das 14./15. Jahrhundert', both in *Studien zur Sozial- und Wirtschaftsgeschichte*, Stuttgart.

Luther, Martin, *Werke* (Weimar edition), 11, 18.

*Luther, Martin, 1962–71, *Works, 44–7: Christian in Society, 1–4*, Philadelphia.

Macek, J., 1960, 'Das revolutionäre Programm des deutschen Bauernkrieges, *Historica*, 2.

Macek, J., 1965, *Der Tiroler Bauernkrieg und Michael Gaismair*, Berlin.

Marx, Karl, 1961, *Das Kapital* (MEW, 23), Berlin.

196   *The German Peasant War of 1525 – New Viewpoints*

Marx-Engels-Werke, 1969, third edition, Berlin.

Maschke, E., 1973, 'Die Unterschichten der mittelalterlichen Städte Deutschlands', *Die Stadt des Mittelalters*, 3, Darmstadt.

Maschke, E., and Sydow, J., 1969, *Stadterweiterung und Vorstadt*, Stuttgart.

Merx, O., 1907, 'Beiträge zur Geschichte der religiösen und sozialen Bewegung in den Stiftern Mainz, Würzburg und Bamberg 1524–6', *Archiv des historischen Vereins für Unterfranken*, 49.

Meyer, M., 1972, 'Zur Haltung des Adels im Bauernkrieg', *Jahrbuch für Regionalgeschichte.*

Mittenzwei, I., 1968, *Der Joachimsthaler Aufstand 1525*, Berlin.

Moeller, Bernd, 1962, *Reichsstadt und Reformation*, Gütersloh.

Moeller, Bernd, 1972a, 'Kleriker als Bürger', *Festschrift H. Heimpel*, vol. 2, Göttingen.

Moeller, Bernd, 1972b, *Pfarrer als Bürger*, Göttinger Universitätsreden, 56.

Mone, F. J. (ed.), 1854, *Quellensammlung der badischen Landesgeschichte*, Karlsruhe.

*Moore, Barrington, 1966, *Social Origins of Dictatorship and Democracy. Lord and Peasant in the Making of the Modern World*, London.

Motteck, H., 1957, *Wirtschaftsgeschichte Deutschlands*, vol. 1, Berlin.

Müller, K. O., 1939, 'Zur wirtschaftlichen Lage des Schwäbischen Adels', *Zeitschrift für Württembergische Landesgeschichte*, 3.

Müller, N., 1911, *Die Wittenberger Bewegung 1521–2*, Leipzig.

Müller-Streisand, R., 1964, *Luthers Weg von der Reformation zur Restauration*, Halle.

Naujoks, E., 1958, *Obrigkeitsgedanke, Zunftverfassung und Reformation*, Stuttgart.

Nef, J. U., 1941, 'Silver Production in Central Europe 1450–1618', *Journal Political Economy*, 49.

Neubauer, T., 1914, 'Zur Geschichte der mittelalterlichen Stadt Erfurt', *Mitteilungen des Vereins für Geschichte Erfurts.*

Neuss, E., 1958, *Entstehung und Entwicklung der Klasse der besitzlosen Lohnarbeiter in Halle*, Berlin.

Nipperdey, T., 1973, 'Die anthropologische Dimension der Geschichtswissenschaft', *Geschichte Heute* (ed. G. Schulz), Göttingen.

Oberman, H. A., 1973, 'Thomas Müntzer: van verontrusting tot verzet', *Kerken Theologie*, 24.

Ott, H., 1970, *Studien zur spätmittelalterlichen Agrarverfassung im Oberrheingebiet*, Stuttgart.

Pfeiffer, G., 1971, 'Sozialrevolutionäre, spiritualistische und schulreformerische Bestrebungen', *Nürnberg. Geschichte einer europäischen Stadt.*

Pfeiffer, G., 1972, 'Wasser und Wald', *Jahrbuch für fränkische Landesforschung*, 32.

Pferschy, G., 1963, 'Die steirischen Bauernaufstände', *Zeitschrift des Historischen Vereins für Steiermark*, 7.

Pfleger, L., 1923, 'Der elsässische Bauer am Ausgang des Mittelalters', *Elsassland.*

Pitz, E., 1965, 'Die Wirtschaftskrise des Spätmittelalters', VSWG, 52.

*Pollard, A. F., 1903, 'Social Revolution and Catholic Reaction in Germany', *Cambridge Modern History*, vol. 2, ch. 6.

Prochno, J., 1933, 'Beiträge zur Wirtschaftsstatistik Leipzigs 1470–1570', *Schriften des Vereins für die Geschichte Leipzigs*, 16.

Radlkofer, M., 1887, *Johann Eberlin von Günzburg und sein Vetter Hans Jakob Wehe von Leipheim*, Nördlingen.

Ranke, Leopold von, 1925, *Deutsche Geschichte im Zeitalter der Reformation* (ed. P. Joachimson), vol. 2, Munich.

Rapp, F., 1967, 'L'aristocratie paysanne du Kochersberg', *Bulletin philologique et historique*.

Rapp, F., 1974, *Réformes et Reformation à Strasbourg*, Paris.

*Rebel, H., 1975, 'Peasant Credit, Marketing and Rebellion in Southeast Central Europe during the Early Seventeenth Century', *Peasant Studies Newsletter*, 4.

Rohling, E., 1864, 'Die Reichsstadt Memmingen in der Zeit der evangelischen Volksbewegungen', Munich University thesis.

Rosenberg, Hans, 1969, 'Deutsche Agrargeschichte in alter und neuer Sicht', *Probleme der deutschen Sozialgeschichte*, Frankfurt am Main.

Rosenkranz, A. (ed.) 1927, *Der Bundschuh*, vol. 2, Heidelberg.

Rössler, H. (ed.), 1965, *Deutscher Adel 1430–1555*, Darmstadt.

Rublack, H. C., 1976, 'Die Stadt Würzburg im Bauernkrieg', *Archiv für Reformationsgeschichte*.

*Rupp, Gordon, 1969, *Patterns of Reformation*, London.

Saalfeld, D., 1971, 'Die Wandlungen der Preis- und Lohnstruktur', *Beiträge zu Wirtschaftswachstum* (ed. W. Fischer), Berlin.

*Sabean, D., 1969, 'The Social Background to the Peasants' War of 1525 in Southern Upper Swabia', Wisconsin University thesis.

Sabean, D., 1972, *Landbesitz und Gesellschaft*, Stuttgart.

*Sabean, D., 1976, 'The Communal Basis of Pre-1800 Uprisings in Western Europe', *Comparative Politics*.

Scheible, H., 1974, 'Reform, Reformation, Revolution', *Archiv für Reformationsgeschichte*, 65.

Schmid, Heinrich, 1959, *Zwinglis Lehre von der göttlichen und menschlichen Gerechtigkeit*, Zürich.

Schnyder, W., 1925–6, 'Die Bevölkerung von Stadt und Landschaft Zürich vom 14, bis zum 17. Jh.', *Schweizer Studien zur Geschichtswissenschaft*, 14.

Schornbaum, K., 1952, 'Zur Lebensgeschichte des Bauern von Wöhrd', *Mitteilungen des Vereins für Geschichte Nürnbergs*, 43.

Schreiber, H., 1866, *Der deutsche Bauernkrieg, gleichzeitige Urkunden*, vol. 3, Freiburg.

Schulz, Helga, 1972, 'Bäuerliche Klassenkämpfe zwischen frühbürgerlicher Revolution und Dreissigjährigem Krieg', ZfG, 20.

Schulze, Wilhelm R., 1957, 'Neuere Forschungen über Balthasar Hubmaier in Waldshut', *Allemanisches Jahrbuch*.

Schulze, Winfried, 1973, 'Reformation oder frühbürgerliche Revolution? – Überlegungen', *Jahrbuch für die Geschichte Mittel- und Ostdeutschlands*, 22.

Schulze, Winfried, 1975, 'Die veränderte Bedeutung sozialer Konflikte im 16. und 17. Jahrhundert', *Der Deutsche Bauernkrieg 1524–6* (ed. H. U. Wehler), Göttingen.

*Scott, James C., 1976, *The Moral Economy of the Peasant, Rebellion and Subsistence in Southeast Asia*, Yale.

*Scott, Tom, 1973, 'Relations between Freiburg in Breisgau and the Surrounding Countryside 1450–1520', Cambridge University thesis.

*Scribner, Bob, 1977, 'Is There a Social History of the Reformation?', *Social History*, No. 4.

*Sessions, K. C. (ed.), 1968, *Reformation and Authority*, Boston.

*Sessions, K. C., 1972, 'The War over Luther and the Peasants', *Sixteenth Century Journal*, 3.

Smelser, N. J., 1971, *Theory of Collective Behaviour*, Toronto.

Smirin, M. M., 1955, *Deutschland vor der Reformation*, Berlin.

Smirin, M. M., 1956, *Die Volksreformation des Thomas Müntzer*, second edition (first edition, 1952), Berlin.

Smirin, M. M., 1956a, 'Eine anonyme politische Flugschrift', *Festschrift A. Meusel*, Berlin.

*Stayer, J. M., 1969, 'Müntzer's Theology and Revolution in Recent non-Marxist Interpretation', *Mennonite Quarterly Review*, 43.

Steinmetz, M., 1961, 'Thesen', *Die frühbürgerliche Revolution in Deutschland* (ed. G. Brendler), Berlin.

Steinmetz, M., 1961, 'Probleme', *Die frühbürgerliche Revolution in Deutschland* (ed. G. Brendler), Berlin.

Steinmetz, M., 1965, *Deutschland von 1476 bis 1648*, Berlin.

Steinmetz, M., 1967, 'Die Entstehung der marxistischen Auffassung von Reformation und Bauernkrieg als frühbürgerliche Revolution', ZfG, 15.

Steinmetz, M., 1971, *Das Müntzerbild von Martin Luther bei Friedrich Engels*, Berlin.

Stern, A., 1926, 'Der Zusammenhang politischer Ideen in der Schweiz und in Oberdeutschland', *Abhandlungen und Aktenstücke zur Geschichte der Schweiz*, Aarau.

Stern, A., 1929, 'Über zeitgenössische Quellen und Darstellungen der Geschichte des grossen deutschen Bauernkrieges', *Sitzungsberichte, Preussische Akademie der Wissenschaften*, Phil-hist Klasse.

Stern, S., 1959, *Josel von Rosheim*, Stuttgart.

Stolze, W., 1926, *Bauernkrieg und Reformation*, Leipzig.

Stone, L., 1972, *The Causes of the English Revolution*, New York.

*Strauss, G. (ed.), 1971, *Manifestations of Discontent in Germany on the Eve of the Reformation*, Bloomington.

Thomas, U., 1976, *Bibliographie zum deutschen Bauernkrieg*, Stuttgart.

Thompson, E. P., 1963, *The Making of the English Working Class*, London.

*Thompson, E. P., 1971, 'The Moral Economy of the English Crowd in the Eighteenth Century, *Past and Present*, No. 50.

Tischler, M., 1963, *Die Leibeigenschaft im Hochstift Würzburg*.

Töpfer, B., 1963, 'Fragen der hussitischen revolutionären Bewegung', ZfG, 11.

Uhle, P. (ed.), 1922, *Quellenbuch zur Geschichte von Chemnitz im Mittelalter*, Chemnitz.

Vahle, H., 1972, 'Der deutsche Bauernkrieg als politische Bewegung im Urteil der Geschichtsschreibung', *Geschichte in Wissenschaft und Unterricht*.

Vetter, A., 1910, 'Bevölkerungsverhältnisse der ehemals freien Reichsstadt Mühlhausen', Leipzig University thesis.

Vocht, Henry de (ed.), 1928, *Literae ad Franciscum Craneveldium 1522–8*, Louvain.

Vogler, G., 1975, 'Der deutsche Bauernkrieg und die Verhandlungen des Reichstags zu Speyer 1526', ZfG, 23.

Vogt, W., 1879–85, 'Die Correspondenz des schwäbischen Bundeshauptmannes Ulrich Artzt von Augsburg aud den Jahren 1524–7', *Zeitschrift des historischen Vereins für Schwaben und Neuburg*, 6–10.

Waas, A., 1964, *Die Bauern im Kampf um Gerechtigkeit 1300–1525*, Munich.

Walder, E., 1954, 'Der politische Gehalt der Zwölf Artikel', *Schweizer Beiträge zur allgemeinen Geschichte*, 12.

Wappler, P., 1908, *Thomas Müntzer in Zwickau und die 'Zwickauer Propheten'*, Zwickau.

Weber, Max, 1956, *Wirtschaft und Gesellschaft*, fourth edition, Tübingen.

Wehler, H. U., 1970, 'Theorieprobleme der modernen deutschen Wirtschaftsgeschichte', *Festschrift H. Rosenberg* (ed. G. Ritter), Berlin.

Wehler, H. U. (ed.), 1975, *Der deutsche Bauernkrieg (Geschichte und Gesellschaft*, Sonderheft 1), Göttingen.

Wendorf, H., 1928, 'Zwinglis Stellung zum Staate', *Festschrift Brandenburg*, Leipzig.

Wiegelmann, G., 1972, 'Volkskundliche Studien zum Wandel der Speisen und Mahlzeiten', *Der Wandel der Nahrungsgewohnheiten unter dem Einfluss der Industrialisierung* (eds. H. Teuteberg and G. Wiegelmann), Göttingen.

Wiegerstein, E., 1856–7, 'Diarium (1525) des Bürgers von Reichenweiher', *Alsatia*, 6.

*Williams, G. H., 1962, *The Radical Reformation*, Philadelphia, ch. 4.

Wittmer, C., and Meyer, C. (eds.), 1948–61, *Le Livre de bourgeoisie de la ville de Strasbourg 1440–1530*, 3 vols.

Wohlfeil, R., 1972, *Reformation oder frühbürgerliche Revolution?*, Munich.

Wolf, E., 1966, *Peasants*, Englewood Cliffs.

Wolf, E., 1967, 'Types of Latin American Peasantry: a Preliminary Discussion', *Tribal and Peasant Economies* (ed. G. Datton), New York.

*Wolf, E., 1971, *Peasant Wars of the Twentieth Century*, London.

Wolf, E., 1973, 'Aspects of Group Relations in a Complex Society: Mexico 1956', *Peasants and Peasant Societies* (ed. T. Shanin), second edition, London.

Wollbrett, A. (ed.), 1975, *La Guerre des Paysans 1525* (Études alsatiques suppt. 93), Saverne.

Wunder, Heide, 1968, *Siedlungs- und Bevölkerungsgeschichte der Komturei Christburg (13.–16. Jh.)*, Wiesbaden.

Wunder, Heide, 1975, 'Der samländische Bauernaufstand von 1525', *Der Bauernkrieg 1524–6* (ed. R. Wohlfeil), Munich.

Wustmann, G. (ed.), 1889, *Quellen zur Geschichte Leipzigs*, vol. 1, Leipzig.

*Zins, H., 1959, 'Aspects of the Peasant Rising in East Prussia in 1525', *Slavonic and East European Review*, 38.

Zschäbitz, G., 1964, 'Über den Charakter und die historischen Aufgaben von Reformation und Bauernkrieg', ZfG, 12.

Zweifel, T., 1878, 'Rothenburg an der Tauber im Bauernkrieg', *Quellen zur Geschichte des Bauernkriegs aus Rothenburg* (ed. F. L. Baumann), Stuttgart.

Zwingli, Huldrych, 1908, 'Usslegen und grund der schlussreden oder articklen', *Werke, 2, Corpus Reformatorum 89*, Leipzig.

Index